Asian Sport Celebrity

What does the 'Asian' mean in Asian sport celebrity? With a collection of nine essays on Asian sport celebrities variously associated with Australia, Belgium, China, Japan, New Zealand, North Korea, the Philippines, South Korea, Taiwan and the United States, this book offers a comprehensive understanding of the multi-faceted construction of what it means to be Asian from the perspectives of race, ethnicity, and regionality. Sport celebrity, as a modern invention, is disseminated from the West to the rest of the globe including Asia, and so are its functions of symbolizing particular values, desires, and personalities idolized and idealized within their respective societies. While Asian athletes were historically depicted as weak, fragile, and biologically 'unsuited' to modern sport, the emergence of more than a few world-class Asian athletes in the twenty-first century demands an in-depth inquiry into the relationship between sport celebrity and the representation of Asia.

This book is therefore essential for those interested in a range of socio-cultural issues—including globalization, transnationalism, migration, modernity, (post-)coloniality, gender politics, spectacle, citizenship, Orientalism, and nationalism—within and beyond Asia.

The essays in these anthologies were originally published as a special issue of *The International Journal of the History of Sport*.

Koji Kobayashi is Associate Professor in the Center for Glocal Strategy at Otaru University of Commerce, Japan, and Adjunct Senior Lecturer at Lincoln University, New Zealand. His research interests include globalization, cultural production, practice of representation, and identity politics as they relate to sport and recreation.

Younghan Cho is Professor of Korean Studies at the Graduate School of International and Area Studies at Hankuk University of Foreign Studies, Seoul, South Korea. He has published widely on global sports, fans and celebrity; the Korean Wave and East Asian pop culture; and nationalism and modernity in Korea and East Asian society.

Sport in the Global Society: Historical Perspectives

Series Editors: Mark Dyreson, Thierry Terret and Rob Hess

Titles in the Series:

Sport in the Americas
Local, Regional, National, and International Perspectives
Edited by Mark Dyreson

Sport and Protest
Global Perspectives
Edited by Cathal Kilcline

A Half Century of Super Bowls
National and Global Perspectives on America's Grandest Spectacle
Edited by Mark Dyreson and Peter Hopsicker

Sport in Socialist Yugoslavia
Edited by Dario Brentin and Dejan Zec

The Olympic Movement and the Middle East and North African Region
Edited by Mahfoud Amara

Sport Development and Olympic Studies
Past, Present, and Future
Edited by Stephan Wassong, Michael Heine and Rob Hess

Match Fixing and Sport
Historical Perspectives
Edited by Mike Huggins and Rob Hess

New Dimensions of Sport in Modern Europe
Perspectives from the 'Long Twentieth Century'
Edited by Heather L. Dichter, Robert J. Lake and Mark Dyreson

Asian Sport Celebrity
Edited by Koji Kobayashi and Younghan Cho

For more information about this series, please visit: https://www.routledge.com/Sport-in-the-Global-Society—Historical-perspectives/book-series/SGSH

Asian Sport Celebrity

Edited by
Koji Kobayashi and Younghan Cho

LONDON AND NEW YORK

First published 2021
by Routledge
2 Park Square, Milton Park, Abingdon, Oxon, OX14 4RN

and by Routledge
52 Vanderbilt Avenue, New York, NY 10017

Routledge is an imprint of the Taylor & Francis Group, an informa business

© 2021 Taylor & Francis

Chapter 1 © 2019 Brent McDonald and Jorge Knijnik. Originally published as Open Access.

With the exception of Chapter 1, no part of this book may be reprinted or reproduced or utilised in any form or by any electronic, mechanical, or other means, now known or hereafter invented, including photocopying and recording, or in any information storage or retrieval system, without permission in writing from the publishers. For details on the rights for Chapter 1, please see the chapter's Open Access footnote.

Trademark notice: Product or corporate names may be trademarks or registered trademarks, and are used only for identification and explanation without intent to infringe.

British Library Cataloguing-in-Publication Data
A catalogue record for this book is available from the British Library

ISBN13: 978-0-367-69531-6

Typeset in Minion Pro
by codeMantra

Publisher's Note
The publisher accepts responsibility for any inconsistencies that may have arisen during the conversion of this book from journal articles to book chapters, namely the inclusion of journal terminology.

Disclaimer
Every effort has been made to contact copyright holders for their permission to reprint material in this book. The publishers would be grateful to hear from any copyright holder who is not here acknowledged and will undertake to rectify any errors or omissions in future editions of this book.

Contents

Citation Information   vii
Notes on Contributors   ix
Series Editors' Foreword   x

Introduction: Asian Sport Celebrity: The Nexus of Race, Ethnicity, and Regionality   1
Koji Kobayashi and Younghan Cho

1 'Ono, oh Yes!': An A-League *Tensai* (Genius) Made in Japan   16
Brent McDonald and Jorge Knijnik

2 Globalization, Migration, Citizenship, and Sport Celebrity: Locating Lydia Ko between and beyond New Zealand and South Korea   33
Ik Young Chang, Steve Jackson and Minhyeok Tak

3 Reading Tiffany Chin: The Birth of the Oriental Female Skater on White Ice   50
Jae Chul Seo, Robert Turick and Daehwan Kim

4 Disrupting the Nation-ness in Postcolonial East Asia: Discourses of Jong Tae-Se as a *Zainichi* Korean Sport Celebrity   71
Younghan Cho and Koji Kobayashi

5 The Absent Savior? Nationalism, Migration, and Football in Taiwan   88
Tzu-hsuan Chen and Ying Chiang

6 The Heroic White Man and the Fragile Asian Girl: Racialized and Gendered Orientalism in Olympic Figure Skating   104
Chuyun Oh

7 Reading Yani Tseng: Articulating Golf, Taiwanese Nationalism, and Gender Politics in Twenty-First-Century Taiwan   121
Daniel Yu-Kuei Sun

8   China's Sports Heroes: Nationalism, Patriotism, and Gold Medal   138
    Lu Zhouxiang and Fan Hong

9   Sports Celebrities and the Spectacularization of Modernity at the Far
    Eastern Championship Games, 1913–1934   154
    Lou Antolihao

    Index   169

Citation Information

The chapters in this book were originally published in *The International Journal of the History of Sport*, volume 36, issue 7–8 (2019). When citing this material, please use the original page numbering for each article, as follows:

Introduction
Asian Sport Celebrity: The Nexus of Race, Ethnicity, and Regionality
Koji Kobayashi and Younghan Cho
The International Journal of the History of Sport, volume 36, issue 7–8 (2019) pp. 611–625

Chapter 1
'Ono, oh Yes!': An A-League *Tensai (Genius) Made in Japan*
Brent McDonald and Jorge Knijnik
The International Journal of the History of Sport, volume 36, issue 7–8 (2019) pp. 626–642

Chapter 2
Globalization, Migration, Citizenship, and Sport Celebrity: Locating Lydia Ko between and beyond New Zealand and South Korea
Ik Young Chang, Steve Jackson and Minhyeok Tak
The International Journal of the History of Sport, volume 36, issue 7–8 (2019) pp. 643–659

Chapter 3
Reading Tiffany Chin: The Birth of the Oriental Female Skater on White Ice
Jae Chul Seo, Robert Turick and Daehwan Kim
The International Journal of the History of Sport, volume 36, issue 7–8 (2019) pp. 660–680

Chapter 4
Disrupting the Nation-ness in Postcolonial East Asia: Discourses of Jong Tae-Se as a Zainichi *Korean Sport Celebrity*
Younghan Cho and Koji Kobayashi
The International Journal of the History of Sport, volume 36, issue 7–8 (2019) pp. 681–697

Chapter 5
The Absent Savior? Nationalism, Migration, and Football in Taiwan
Tzu-hsuan Chen and Ying Chiang
The International Journal of the History of Sport, volume 36, issue 7–8 (2019) pp. 698–713

Chapter 6
The Heroic White Man and the Fragile Asian Girl: Racialized and Gendered Orientalism in Olympic Figure Skating
Chuyun Oh
The International Journal of the History of Sport, volume 36, issue 7–8 (2019) pp. 714–730

Chapter 7
Reading Yani Tseng: Articulating Golf, Taiwanese Nationalism, and Gender Politics in Twenty-First-Century Taiwan
Daniel Yu-Kuei Sun
The International Journal of the History of Sport, volume 36, issue 7–8 (2019) pp. 731–747

Chapter 8
China's Sports Heroes: Nationalism, Patriotism, and Gold Medal
Lu Zhouxiang and Fan Hong
The International Journal of the History of Sport, volume 36, issue 7–8 (2019) pp. 748–763

Chapter 9
Sports Celebrities and the Spectacularization of Modernity at the Far Eastern Championship Games, 1913–1934
Lou Antolihao
The International Journal of the History of Sport, volume 36, issue 7–8 (2019) pp. 764–778

For any permission-related enquiries please visit:
http://www.tandfonline.com/page/help/permissions

Contributors

Lou Antolihao Department of Sociology, National University of Singapore, Singapore.

Ik Young Chang Department of Community Sport, Korea National Sport University, Seoul, South Korea.

Tzu-hsuan Chen Graduate Institute of Physical Education, National Taiwan Sport University, Taoyuan City, Taiwan.

Ying Chiang Department of Leisure and Recreation Management, Chihlee University of Technology, New Taipei City, Taiwan.

Younghan Cho Department of Korean Studies, Graduate School of International and Area Studies, Hankuk University of Foreign Studies, Seoul, South Korea.

Fan Hong The University of Bangor, UK.

Steve Jackson School of Physical Education, Sport and Exercise Sciences, University of Otago, Dunedin, New Zealand.

Daehwan Kim Institute of Sport Science, Seoul National University of Education, South Korea.

Jorge Knijnik Western Sydney University, Australia.

Koji Kobayashi Otaru University of Commerce, Japan, and Lincoln University, New Zealand.

Brent McDonald Institute for Health and Sport, Victoria University, Melbourne, Australia.

Chuyun Oh The School of Music and Dance, San Diego State University, USA.

Jae Chul Seo Department of Physical Education, Seoul National University, South Korea.

Daniel Yu-Kuei Sun Department of Kinesiology, Towson University, USA.

Minhyeok Tak Sport and Exercise Science, Loughborough University, UK.

Robert Turick School of Kinesiology, Ball State University, Muncie, USA.

Lu Zhouxiang School of Modern Languages, Literatures and Cultures, National University of Ireland, Ireland.

Series Editors' Foreword

Sport in the Global Society: Historical Perspectives explores the role of sport in cultures both around the world and across the timeframes of human history. In the world we currently inhabit, sport spans the globe. It captivates vast audiences. It defines, alters, and reinforces identities for individuals, communities, nations, empires, and the world. Sport organizes memories and perceptions, arouses passions and tensions and reveals harmonies and cleavages. It builds and blurs social boundaries—animating discourses about class, gender, race, and ethnicity. Sport opens new vistas on the history of human cultures, intersecting with politics and economics, ideologies, and theologies. It reveals aesthetic tastes and energizes consumer markets.

Our challenge is to explain how sport has developed into a global phenomenon. The series continues the tradition established by the original incarnation of *Sport in the Global Society* (and in 2010 divided into *Historical Perspectives* and *Contemporary Perspectives*) by promoting the academic study of one of the most significant and dynamic forces in shaping the historical landscapes of human cultures.

In the twenty-first century, a critical mass of scholars recognize the importance of sport in their analyses of human experiences. *Sport in the Global Society: Historical Perspectives* provides an international outlet for the leading investigators on these subjects. Building on previous work and excavating new terrain, our series remains a consistent and coherent response to the attention the academic community demands for the serious study of sport.

Mark Dyreson
Thierry Terret
Rob Hess

INTRODUCTION

Asian Sport Celebrity: The Nexus of Race, Ethnicity, and Regionality

Koji Kobayashi and Younghan Cho

Drawing on P. David Marshall's understanding of the celebrity,[1] David Andrews and Steve Jackson delineated sport celebrities as 'significant public entities responsible for structuring meaning, crystallizing ideologies, and offering contextually grounded maps for private individuals as they navigate contemporary conditions of existence'.[2] This interpretation alludes to an important role for sport celebrities in linking the public projection of particular values, desires, and personalities and the private experience in association with, or consumption of, such values, desires, and personalities in everyday life. Like classic celebrity figures in cinema and films, the sport celebrity is constructed through the historical development of mass media including newspapers, radio, television and, now more pervasively, the internet. While the sport celebrity has become a popular topic in sport studies,[3] there has been little attention devoted to an understanding of the commonality and difference in how Asian athletes may embrace, embody, reproduce, or re-code the notion of sport celebrity. With the emergence of more than a few world-class Asian athletes in the twenty-first century, this phenomenon demands scholarly attention. As such, *Asian Sport Celebrity* provides the first collection of its kind to take an in-depth and holistic look at a range of socio-cultural issues related to the Asian sport celebrity including globalization, transnationalism, migration, post/coloniality, gender politics, spectacle, citizenship, and nationalism.

Three considerations illustrate the importance of studying the Asian sport celebrity. First, there are variegated and diverse stories of globalization. As products of Western modernization, the institutions of sport and celebrity were both disseminated from the West to Asia. In the same vain, sport celebrities have been produced and represented as part of the transformation of Asian societies in an accelerated and non-linear fashion through globalization. However, the ways in which the sport celebrity is embraced and (re-)articulated by the Asian contexts, experiences and interpretations have been underexplored. Second, Asian sport celebrities have become more and more salient across national, regional, and global levels due to their increasing visibility via the media as well as the recent rise of sport mega-events in Asia. The latter has been reinforced by several governments in Asia seeking to host and use sport mega-events as a platform to showcase their cultural economic power and celebrate their own sport stars as symbols of national success and identity. For instance, the recent and future mega-events hosted in Asia include the 2002 FIFA World Cup in Korea and Japan, 2008 Beijing summer Olympics and Paralympics, 2018 PyeongChang winter Olympics and Paralympics, 2020 Tokyo summer Olympics and Paralympics, 2022 FIFA World Cup in Qatar[4] and 2022 Beijing-Zhangjiakou winter Olympics and Paralympics. Third, there is a scholarly interest and sensibility in rectifying the relative paucity of academic writing on Asian athletes who are historically excluded or marginalized in the English-speaking world. Indeed, within a historical context of globalization and civilization, Asian athletes have been typically underrepresented and often depicted as weak, fragile, and biologically 'unsuited' to modern sports.[5] With this in mind, the following is a collection of interdisciplinary and cross-regional dialogues on the past, the present, and the potential of the Asian sport celebrity.

By using the term *Asian* sport celebrity, this collection of essays aims to critically analyse representations of 'Asian' as constructed through the nexus of regionality, race, and ethnicity. In other words, Asian is a multi-faceted construct, connoting multiple collective configurations based on geography (the region or continent which borders Africa and Europe to the west and the Pacific Ocean to the east); race (the group of people sharing assumed phenotypical characteristics associated with populations in/from the Asian region); and ethnicity (the group of people who self-identify as Asian based on shared history, identity and values). While these configurations are not mutually exclusive, and in most cases overlapping through discursive formations, *Asian Sport Celebrity* not only interrogates the nuanced differences but also reveals interrelationships among them, which constitute the semantic multiplicity and theoretical complexity. As Stuart Hall located black popular culture as 'a sight of strategic contestation', Asian popular culture, and sport celebrity in particular, can be approached in a similar manner to enable 'the surfacing, inside the mixed and contradictory modes even of some mainstream popular culture, of elements of a discourse that is different—other forms of life, other traditions of representation'.[6] It is in this sense that Asian-ness is contested in its meaning, politically mobilized in a variety of contexts and semantically complicated by the geo-political contestations between the regionality and the nationality, the nuanced differences between race and ethnicity, and the struggles over the power and cultural identity of Asian people, and athletes in particular.

Sport, Celebrity, Globalization, and Asia

Previous studies of celebrity often started with Daniel Boorstin's definition: '[t]he celebrity is a person who is well-known for his [sic] well-knownness'.[7] The invention of mass media technologies, television in particular, was central to the development of celebrityhood as it generated the public space for the consumption of familiar personalities and figures.[8] The rise of celebrityhood was often traced back to cinema stars in the early twentieth century when the images and stories of the stars were produced (or manufactured to a great extent) and consumed via the print media and newsreels.[9] This early star production system out of Hollywood served as 'a forum for the general public to develop more intimate, visually informed, relationships with an array of public personalities'.[10] Consequently, celebrities came to signify particular values, styles or identities that were admired or fondly associated by their fans and the public more generally.

As Andrews and Jackson contend, the celebrity is 'a *potentially* potent "representative subjectivity" (source of cultural identification) pertaining to the "collective configurations" (social class, gender, sexuality, race, ethnicity, age, nationality) through which individuals fashion their very existence'.[11] In other words, particular social values, practices and institutions 'are principally represented to, and understood within, the popular imagination through the actions of celebrated individuals'.[12] Nevertheless, as Graeme Turner explains, media representations of celebrity should not be regarded only as a reflection of societal values and norms but also as a collective battleground through which such values and norms are constantly re-affirmed or contested.[13] For instance, celebrity persona, which is often manufactured and constructed by the media, can be 'frequently derailed by the unscripted, unpredictable, and often scandalous, exploits of celebrities *in process*'.[14] Similarly, David Rowe asserts that the relationships among celebrity, sport, and media are 'always everywhere in process, influencing and being influenced by each other in a perpetual dance of assertion and counter-assertion'.[15] To put it simply, there is no guarantee that celebrity persona, as a cultural product, is consumed and decoded as intended by the producers of the signs.[16]

In comparison to film stars and television personalities who were the main focus of the early studies on celebrities,[17] sport celebrities can be distinguished by their excellence of athletic performances (in contrast to skillful acts and arts), their associations with national or local sensibilities and identities (in contrast to isolated individuals) and their authenticity in being 'real individuals participating in unpredictable contests' (in contrast to fictive roles played by film actors).[18] Andrews and Jackson also note that sport celebrities are frequently subject to 'idiosyncratic instabilities' that may arise from failures on the field of play or off-the-field scandals (as in the case of O.J. Simpson).[19] Also, sport celebrities are relatively more prone to the commodification of bodies through advertising and marketing of transnational corporations due to the centrality of their bodies as performative instruments and their perceived transcendence of spatial, linguistic, cultural and racial boundaries.[20]

Studies of the sport celebrity are a relatively new field. For many, this may come as a surprise given that the significance of sport celebrities in terms of the public individuals known for physical supremacy has been unmistakable within popular culture since the nineteenth century. What is new about today's environment is 'the scale and scope with which variously celebrated individuals infuse and inform every facet of everyday existence'.[21] Perhaps then, it may be less surprising that studies of the global sport celebrity were necessitated by the ever-expansive popularity of Michael Jordan in the 1990s. The earlier socio-cultural analyses of Jordan were prompted by Andrews[22] and his collaborative work with other scholars in the field.[23] For Andrews, Jordan was the most emblematic icon of American, neoliberal and consumer cultures as well as a 'floating racial signifier' that was (re-)articulated by the cultural politics at a particular time.[24] Since then, scholars in sport studies have extended the socio-cultural enquiry into a range of sport celebrities such as Ben Johnson,[25] David Beckham,[26] Tiger Woods,[27] and Serena Williams.[28] There have also been influential scholarly books published with a focus on sport celebrity or stardom.[29] Yet, Asian athletes have been rarely given the spotlight.[30] While they have been historically underrepresented in Western sports and the global media, the lack of attention needs to be rectified due to the emergence of Asian sport celebrities and scholarly sensibility to improve the understanding of a marginalised 'Other' in sport.

The central question that needs to be addressed here then is: 'How do studies of the Asian sport celebrity enhance our understanding of the relationships among sport, globalization and Asia?' In order to answer this, it is important to highlight *globality*, *glocality* and *inter-regional dynamics* of the Asian sport celebrity. First, the Asian sport celebrity provides understanding of *globality* or *universality* in the politico-economic and social-cultural integration of Asia into a global society through the multi-faceted historic passages of imperialism/colonialism, the Cold War, and globalization. As countries in Asia embraced modernization as a Western invention, sports were also introduced and diffused across the region along with the establishment of modern institutions, education systems, and collective – and often ethnocentric – identities.[31] As Zhouxiang Lu and Fan Hong and Lou Antolihao illustrate in their contributions, Asian nation-states strategically used sport events such as the Far Eastern Championship Games and the Olympics as a means to construct national unity and pride as well as to catch up with the West for industrial and military developments. By representing their nations and winning in these international sport events, many athletes and teams came to gain the status of national celebrity and signify the national success on an international stage.[32] More recently, more than few Asian sport stars have emerged as *global celebrities* such as Virat Kohli, Manny Pacquiao, Park Ji-Sung, Li Na, and Jeremy Lin.[33] Like their Western counterparts,[34] they have been increasingly subject to the re-configurations of nationality through the discourses of flexible citizenship, mixed-race, and multiculturalism, which are rapidly becoming more common across many Asian cities and countries through globalization.[35]

Second, the Asian sport celebrity represents *glocality* through which the *universality* of sport and the *particularity* of political regimes and national cultures are negotiated and (re-)articulated at the nexus of the global and the local. In this context, Asian sport celebrities exemplify the process of glocalization, or indigenization, of sport as a global practice as they simultaneously embody and signify their associated national or local culture, identity, and values.[36] As sport has become a crucial component of globalization through its mediatization, commercialization, and commodification, today's elite athletes are increasingly embedded into, and governed by, a 'new international division of cultural labour'.[37] On one hand, the unequal relationship between the West and the East has been evident in that many Asian athletes with high mobility and celebrity status opt to migrate to the West, and the USA or Europe in particular, for higher levels of competitions and salaries. On the other hand, Asian sport celebrities are often mobilized as a vehicle of national success and ethnic representation in international cultural exchanges. For example, global sport celebrities such as Suzuki Ichiro[38] and Yao Ming are regarded as national heroes and symbols of national triumphs by Japan and China respectively on a global scale.[39] In certain sports such as cricket and baseball, Asian nations are emerging as dominant groups in what has been called the era of 'post-Westernization'.[40] Furthermore, the recent rise of sport mega-events hosted in Asia and the accelerated migration of European and American sport celebrities to the Chinese or Japanese sport leagues hint at a possible disruption to the Western-dominated global hierarchy of sport.

Third, the Asian sport celebrity facilitates *inter-regional dynamics* due to its intensified inter-Asian tensions and mobility. As Asian sport celebrities are located within a particular cultural, political, religious, and historical context that has been constructed over centuries, they are often heavily affected and implicated by regional rivalries, political tensions, historic memories, and postcolonial desires in Asia. For instance, a salient stream of anti-Japan sentiments and expressions through many international sport events between Japan and its former colonies represents a 'symptom of unsettled historic trauma of the Japanese empire and its legacy',[41] in postcolonial East Asia.[42] In this collection, Younghan Cho and Koji Kobayashi illustrate how these tensions among North Korea, South Korea and Japan play out in the case of Jong Tae-se who expressed his multiple sources of national belongingness. Daniel Yu-Kuei Sun demonstrates that the Taiwan-Korea rivalry was an important factor in Tseng Yani's rise to fame as she outperformed Michelle Wie. Likewise, Tzu-hsuan Chen and Ying Chiang emphasize Taiwan's high regard for Xavier Chen as the savior of Taiwanese football in contrast to Jeremy Lin who remained ambiguous about his ethnic identification as Chinese or Taiwanese. While rivalries and tensions are often sensationalized in the media, it is also important to attend to inter-regional connections, solidarity and friendship through Asian sport celebrities. For instance, future research may benefit from examining the cases of transnational friendship between Sun Yang and Park Tae-hwan during the 2008 Beijing summer Olympics or between Lee Sang-hwa and Kodaira Nao during the 2018 PyeongChang winter Olympics. Another area, where more research is needed, is an increasing trend of inter-Asian mobility of athletes and sport celebrities and its impact on the changing connections and relations among Asian societies, cities and countries.

The Multi-Faceted Construction of 'Asian' as Regionality, Race, and Ethnicity

'Asian' is a contested term comprising of multiple collective configurations. To start with, as opposed to Asia that only carries the denotation of a geographic continent/region, 'Asian' can evoke multiple meanings with respect to regionality, race, and ethnicity. By using *Asian* sport celebrity, the anthology highlights the intersectionality of these three configurations and interrogate how different meanings are generated and mobilized in a variety of contexts, which are clearly illustrated by the contributions in this collection.

First, *Asian as a regionality* is used to refer to a geographical area with deliberate inattention, or only an inference, to its constructs of historical, political, and cultural identity. For example, many sport organisations that have 'Asian' in their names primarily use the term to demarcate their regional boundaries (e.g., the Asian Games, Asian Athletics Association, and Asian Football Confederation). In this sense, Asian as a regionality is a relatively politically neutral and a most commonly preferred descriptor to represent the people from the geographic location of their origin. Nevertheless, as a geographical location it is not entirely immune from its articulation with historical, political, and cultural meanings, and the geographical proximity does not necessarily guarantee the unity, or conflicts, within the geographical boundaries. A case in point is the issue of inclusion and exclusion of participating nation-states in regional events such as the Asian Games where the boundaries of Asia have been constantly negotiated and re-defined. For instance, the People's Republic of China (PRC) did not take part in the Asian Games from 1954 to 1970 due to the existence of 'two Chinas'.[43] The Republic of China, or Taiwan, was expelled from the Asian Games in 1974 and was re-admitted in 1990 as Chinese Taipei. Likewise, Israel was expelled from the Asian Games in 1981 due to the Arab-Israeli conflict. Another compelling example of the boundary blurring is occurring between Asia and Oceania. Prompted by Football Federation Australia moving from the Oceania Football Confederation to the Asian Football Confederation in 2006, Australian sport organisations have been increasingly re-structured into Asian regional bodies, events and pathways to qualify for global mega-events such as the Olympics and the FIFA World Cup.[44] As Brent McDonald and Jorge Knijnik demonstrate in *Asian Sport Celebrity*, as the most celebrated Asian player in the A-League Ono Shinji was inevitably mobilized by, and incorporated within, this cultural politics and discourse of 'Australia within Asia'. While a regionality may seem more stable than the other two configurations, Asia as a region is nonetheless constantly challenged and re-defined for its boundaries.

Second, *Asian as a race* can be used to refer to 'a population of people who are believed to be naturally or biologically distinct from' non-Asian populations.[45] This classification of people has been constructed on the basis of phenotypical characteristics or physical appearance/traits. In terms of studies on sport and race, much attention has been devoted to the racial construction of 'blackness' through representations of, for instance, Michael Jordan,[46] Dennis Rodman,[47] Venus Williams,[48] and Ian Wright.[49] In contrast, Asian athletes have received far less attention. Unlike the black athlete who is often articulated with physical prowess and superiority, the Asian athlete as a product of the discursive formation has been historically demarcated as weak, fragile, and biologically 'unsuited' to modern sports.[50] For example, Jae Chul Seo, Robert Turick and Daehwan Kim in this collection suggest that Pierre de Coubertin's Olympism was closely associated with the ideas of colonial modernity and social Darwinism through which the Asian race was deemed inherently inferior and potentially civilized only under paternalistic guidance of white Europeans. Nevertheless, with the recent rise of Asian athletes attaining the status of global stardom 'against the odds', there has been an emerging strand of scholarly works that interrogate the racialization of Asian sport celebrities. Among those stars are Jeremy Lin,[51] Yao Ming,[52] Nomo Hideo,[53] Sachin Tendulkar,[54] Imran Khan,[55] Li Na,[56] and Kim Yuna. In this collection, Lu and Hong's contribution notes the rise of Chinese athletes to global fame including Liu Xiang who became the first Asian track and field athlete to win a gold medal in the Olympics and

Li Na who became the first Asian tennis player to win a Grand Slam singles event. In particular, Jeremy Lin is a salient example of how his global fame was constructed in relation to his Asian race and the ways in which his athletic performance 'challenged the narrative that Asian American men are unable to excel in a physical sport like basketball'.[57] In a similar vein, Seo, Turick and Kim's contribution identifies the emergence of Tiffany Chin in the 1980s as the birth of gendered and racialized representation of Asian-American figure skaters as 'the Oriental girl'. Likewise, Chuyun Oh's contribution offers a more recent case and examines the ways in which Kim Yuna, a Korean Olympic gold medal winning figure skater, was both gendered and racialized as the 'fragile Asian girl' in stark contrast to the ways in which her coach was constructed as the 'heroic white man' through the narratives of the North American media.

Finally, while race and ethnicity are not mutually exclusive and thus interrelated,[58] *Asian as an ethnicity* can be heuristically used to refer to 'a category of people regarded as socially distinct' from non-Asian populations 'because they share a way of life, a collective history and a sense of themselves as a people'.[59] This classification is therefore constructed on the basis of the commonality and unity through similarly self-identified social practices and cultural values. However, this definition then may pose a question as to what extent Asian populations share a way of life, a collective history, and a sense of unity given the Asian region cuts across a variety of nations and cultures. Nevertheless, Asian as an ethnicity is most commonly understood as an ethnic minority in non-Asian nation-states. For instance, the previous literature in sport studies revealed common challenges and the multiplicities of identities for 'British Asians'[60] and 'Asian Americans'.[61] Beyond the understanding of Asians as an ethnic minority defined by the boundaries of nation-states, Asian as an ethnicity also alludes to the possibility of what Arif Dirlik calls 'transnational ethnicity'. Hence, it is worthwhile to re-visit Dirlik's discussion on transnational ethnicity and its (g)localization:

> Over the last few years, the question of ethnicity has emerged as a primary intellectual concern, mainly because of ethnic conflicts around the world, but also because of the emergence of transnational ethnicities that have brought to the fore questions suppressed by an earlier assumption of some kind of equation between ethnicity and the nation. One fundamental question pertains to the nature of ethnicity itself: the very phenomenon of diaspora, while it gives rise to a quest for a transnational ethnic identity, also defies any easy definition of such an identity because it of necessity implies the localization of identity in a variety of diasporic sites.[62]

As such, a diasporic, transnational ethnic identity traverses the boundaries of the nation-states, giving both global and regional significance to an idea of Asian-ness and simultaneously producing the sites through which such an idea of Asian-ness is constructed and negotiated across the East and the West as well as the global and the local. In this sense, the recent studies on transnationalism and sport celebrity are illustrative of how the transnational ethnic identification and relationships are more tenable to be imagined through Asian sport celebrities' transcendence of national borders.[63] For example, in *Asian Sport Celebrity*, Ik Young Chang, Steve Jackson and Minhyeok Tak contrast Lydia Ko and Michelle Wie in terms of how their Korean-ness, or transnational Korean ethnicity, was embodied by themselves and represented by the multiple national media.[64] Cho and Kobayashi infer the possibility of an inter-

Asian conscience emerging through Jong Tae-se's multiple identities of North Korea, South Korea and Japan while Oh suggests the possible emergence of a pan-Asian ethnicity through Kim Yuna's identification with the preceding and succeeding American figure skaters of Asian descent.

However, the construction of ethnicity or 'transnational ethnicity' may not necessarily result in countering or eradicating the forces of racialization and Orientalization. As Grant Jarvie argued, '[w]hile ethnicity itself is a social construct which allows us to identify different social, cultural and sporting identities, it is not synonymous with racism and should not obscure the way in which racism permeates sporting experiences'.[65] Furthermore, the understanding of Asian through lenses of regionality, race, and ethnicity should not detract from considering other forms of collective identity. As Hall insisted, '[d]ominant ethnicities are always underpinned by a particular sexual economy, a particular figured masculinity, a particular class identity'.[66] In this sense, different collective configurations of what Asian means are informed and shaped by the intersectionality of multiple differences or representative subjectivities.[67] For example, Sun's contribution in this compendium points out entrenched hegemonic ideas about the gender hierarchy and roles in Taiwan, and Asian societies more generally, and the ways in which the gender politics in sport, as in the case of Tseng Yani, may stir controversies and challenge established social norms.

Contributions to *Asian Sport Celebrity*

Asian Sport Celebrity comprises a collection of nine essays on Asian sport celebrities who are geographically, politically, ethnically, or culturally associated with a range of nations including Australia, Belgium, China, Japan, New Zealand, North Korea, Philippine, South Korea, Taiwan, and the USA. While the multi-national and multicultural nature of Asia is certainly captured by the essays in this anthology, it must be acknowledged that the coverage is more or less centred on the context of East Asia. As discussed earlier, Asia as a region encompasses areas and nations bordering Africa and Europe to the west and the Pacific Ocean to the east, and such geographic boundaries are also demarcated by many major international sport associations including the International Olympic Committee. This limitation needs to be addressed by future research which can then examine the efficacy and relevance of what is proposed in *Asian Sport Celebrity*.

The first essay by Brent McDonald and Jorge Knijnik presents a discussion of Ono Shinji as a marquee Japanese/Asian football player and his meteoric rise to fame during the 2012/2013 season of the A-League in Australia. By locating Ono within the context of the cultural and identity politics of Australia, McDonald and Knijnik reveal how his success story was mobilized to re-define Australia's relationship *with* Asia and simultaneously its position *within* Asia. With the increased prevalence of multicultural narratives in Western societies, Australian Prime Minister Paul Keating's acknowledgement of, and strategic response to, the 'Asian Century' became more crystalized and materialized through the celebration of Ono and his team, Western Sydney Wanderers. Nevertheless, McDonald and Knijnik also question the extent to which the success of an Asian footballer and fans' celebration of multiculturalism were leveraged and nurtured beyond the case of Ono. In other words, there seems to be an enduring distance between the rhetoric of multiculturalism in 'Australia within Asia' and the actual absence of Asian presence and impacts after Ono in football, and wider Australian society more generally.

Another country which has seen increased engagement with Asian migrants in the Pacific is New Zealand. In the second essay, Ik Young Chang, Steve Jackson and Minhyeok Tak present analysis of Lydia Ko, a Korean-born New Zealand golfer, through lenses of globalization, migration, citizenship and national identity. In doing so, Ko is located within the context of New Zealand's immigration policy, which was developed in response to multicultural narratives and a discourse of Asianization. By deploying the classifications of golfers with Korean roots based on their birthplace, education, and nationality, Chang, Jackson, and Tak contend that Ko herself and the Korean media never emphasized or capitalized on her Korean-ness in the way it was adopted, performed and promoted by the preceding world-class golfers of Korean descent such as Christina Kim and Michelle Wie. In contrast to Kim and Wie, Ko distanced herself from explicit association with Korea and instead repeatedly proclaimed being a Kiwi while obtaining New Zealand citizenship and representing New Zealand in the Olympics. As such, Chang, Jackson, and Tak assert that the de-emphasis of her Korean-ness was reinforced by the Korean media that denounced the opportunistic use of Korean-ness, the New Zealand media that promoted the national vision of being young, female, and ethnically diverse and Lydia Ko herself who was proud to be a Kiwi.

Moving to the context of the USA, the third contribution by Jae Chul Seo, Robert Turick and Daehwan Kim locates Tiffany Chin as the first Asian-American female figure skater to be represented and characterized in a racialized and gendered manner. By framing figure skating as a site for the reproduction of 'whiteness' or the privilege enjoyed by the white race, Seo, Turick and Kim demonstrate how the media representations of Chin were articulated with an Oriental style and an exotic beauty of a 'China Doll' in contrast to the extant dominant aesthetic norms embodied by the 'white American princess skaters' such as Peggy Fleming and Dorothy Hamill. Moreover, they assert that the media narratives of Chin's skating style, personal character, youthfulness, and her family relations were all intertwined with the emerging discourses of multiculturalism and American Orientalism in the 1980s. Such representations of Chin as a docile girl, a super-human like training machine, and the model minority were established as rhetorical patterns of representing Asian-American figure skaters of later generations including Kristi Yamaguchi and Michelle Kwan.

In the fourth contribution, Younghan Cho and Koji Kobayashi examine a Japanese-born Korean male footballer, Jong Tae-se, who transcended the national borders as well as the West-East division. However, unlike Lydia Ko, Jong was explicit in expressing his Korean-ness even though he was neither born nor raised in Korea. As a rare case of a postcolonial subject, Jong Tae-se is a footballer with complex cultural and ethnic backgrounds being a third-generation *zainichi* (residing in Japan) Korean resident in Japan, a citizen in South Korea, and a national football representative of North Korea. In this account, Cho and Kobayashi provide analysis of media discourses and self-narratives surrounding his backgrounds, national identities, and motives through lenses of inflexible citizenship, Japanese imperialism, and Cold War ideology. In doing so, Jong's case is located and highlighted to exemplify the arbitrariness of nation-ness and the reproduction of unresolved geopolitical and historical issues between Korea and Japan, and within East Asia more generally. In turn, Cho and Kobayashi suggest the importance of studying the subjectivity of *zainichi* Koreans such as Jong as a means to de-colonize or destabilize a range of postcolonial and post-war ideological forces that shape the cultural politics of contemporary East Asia.

Following the theme of football, the fifth essay by Tzu-hsuan Chen and Ying Chiang examines another ethnically diverse player, Xavier Chen, who was born and raised in Belgium before being naturalized as Taiwanese in order to play for Taiwan. In particular, Chen and Chiang point out the oddity in the case of Xavier Chen as he was able to receive the status of a 'savior' and 'noble prince' of football with little linguistic and cultural capital as a Taiwanese. This oddity is explained by several reasons. First, unlike Jeremy Lin who holds U.S. citizenship and avoids questions about his ethnic identification with China or Taiwan, Xavier Chen made it clear that he wanted to represent and play for Taiwan to honour his Taiwanese father and grandfather. Second, being colonized by Spain, the Netherlands, and Japan since the seventeenth century and represented mostly as Chinese Taipei in many international sport events, Taiwan is desperate for both success in elite sport and athletes that provide a window to proclaim and project its own national identity on a global stage. Chen and Chiang therefore conclude that his Taiwanese roots made it possible for Xavier Chen to become the 'absent' savior of Taiwanese football because he never left Belgium as his home.

In the sixth contribution, Chuyun Oh focuses on Kim Yuna and provides analysis of North American media coverage of her gold-medal-winning performance at the 2010 Vancouver winter Olympics. Like Seo, Turick and Kim who approached Tiffany Chin through the lens of Orientalism, Oh's essay reveals the ways in which the pattern of signifying 'the Oriental girl' is similarly deployed by the North American media to describe and narrate Kim's performance and relationship with her coach. By locating Kim within the genealogy of the racialization of Asian-American figure skaters such as Kristi Yamaguchi and Michelle Kwan, Oh argues that Kim was constantly linked to the legendary Asian-American skaters with her ethnic Korean-ness being largely underplayed. More specifically, Oh pays attention to the construction of the fetishized relationship between Kim as 'the fragile Asian girl' and her coach Brian Orser as 'the heroic white man' in the James-Bond-themed short programme. In doing so, Oh contends that the historical Orientalist gaze towards the Asian American legends continues to be operationalized and exemplified through the consumption of Kim as the sexualized and racialized 'Other'. Yet, Oh also proposes the possibility of the pan-Asian identity, as a form of transnational ethnicity, emerging from learning and friendship between Asian and Asian-American figure skaters.

In keeping with the theme of gender politics, Daniel Yu-Kuei Sun presents an analysis of Tseng Yani, a Taiwanese golfer whose gender, sexuality and physical prowess are scrutinized by the Taiwanese media. According to Sun, Tseng brought a renewed significance to the study of Taiwanese sport celebrities due to her gender in contrast to such celebrated male counterparts as Wang Chien-Ming in baseball and Xavier Chen as discussed by Chen and Chiang earlier. By deploying critical discourse analysis of major newspaper coverage in Taiwan, Sun demonstrates that Tseng is undeniably embedded into, and mobilized by, the politics of Taiwanese nationalism. For instance, Sun reasons that Tseng's rise to fame was initially fueled by her rivalry with Michelle Wie who was represented as a proxy of Korea – Taiwan's significant 'Other'. Moreover, Tseng is often described by the media as 'gender neutral' or 'completely like a male golfer' and even questioned over her gender due to her superior physical ability to hit almost 300 yard drives and her 'manly' appearance. Sun contends that it is evident in the case of Tseng that the traditional notion of Taiwanese femininity and gender roles is being challenged yet still maintains a strong hold in reinforcing the ideologies that discourage women from pursuing sport achievements in Taiwan.

The eighth contribution by Zhouxiang Lu and Fan Hong illuminates the historical context of sport heroes and nationalism in China. By tracing the modern history of China's involvement and engagement with sport, Lu and Hong explore the importance of the international events such as the Far Eastern Championship Games and the Olympics. These events were mobilized by the Chinese government as a platform to celebrate athletes' achievements, and gold medals in particular, as evidence of a national success, strength, and unity. While such a focus on elite sport success was disrupted by the Cultural Revolution which resulted in shaming and humiliating of former elite sport stars, the People's Republic of China has since the 1980s re-focused on 'gold medal fever'. Yet, Lu and Hong also point out the case of Liu Xiang who failed to meet the high public expectations at the 2008 and 2012 Olympics as evidence of how national heroes can be denounced for not upholding the national values and characters. Li Na was another divisive figure who stirred a national controversy with her comment on her motive to play tennis for herself rather than for the country, which, according to Lu and Hong, illustrates ongoing tensions among individualism, liberalism, and nationalism in China.

Finally, in keeping with historical analysis, Lou Antolihao examines the emergence of early Asian sport celebrities at the Far Eastern Championship Games (FECG) from 1913 to 1934. By locating the FECG as a pinnacle platform for the birth of modern sport celebrities in Asia, Antolihao elucidates the ways in which celebrities were produced with heroic narratives that intertwined personal stories with political rhetoric through the spectacularization of modernity. Moreover, in comparison to today's sport celebrities who are prone to intensive commercialization and commodification, early Asian sport stars functioned primarily to fulfil their duties and loyalty to their own nations through acts of heroism and serve as vehicles of collective achievements and modern nationalism across the region. By highlighting key individual achievements from a series of the FECG, Antolihao emphasizes the importance of the central roles played by the officials from China, Japan, and the Philippines in mobilizing and organizing the major sport events where the first wave of modern sport celebrities emerged in Asia. Antolihao illuminates the context of early modernization of Asian societies through which sport celebrities symbolized each Asian nation's embrace and indigenization of the Western-originated modern institutions, practices, and values. On the last note, we as editors hope that *Asian Sport Celebrity* will contribute to the development of understandings about the interpenetration and interdependence between Asia and the West and encourage more transnational dialogues and collaborations among communities of Asian studies and sport studies.

Notes

1. P. David Marshall, *Celebrity and Power: Fame in Contemporary Culture* (Minneapolis: University of Minnesota Press, 1997).
2. David L. Andrews, and Steven J. Jackson, eds., *Sport Stars: The Cultural Politics of Sporting Celebrity* (London: Routledge, 2001), 2.
3. Ibid.; Barry Smart, *The Sport Star: Modern Sport and the Cultural Economy of Sporting Celebrity* (London: Sage Publications, 2005); Lawrence A. Wenner, ed. *Fallen Sports Heroes, Media, and Celebrity Culture* (New York: Peter Lang, 2013); Garry Whannel, *Media Sport Stars: Masculinities and Moralities* (London: Routledge, 2005).
4. Qatar is included here in accordance with the understanding of Asia as a region defined by international sport organizations such as the International Olympic Committee which groups such nation-states as Qatar, Lebanon, Saudi Arabia and Jordan into a zone of West Asia under the governance of the Olympic Council of Asia.
5. Jonathan Long, Ben Carrington, and Karl Spracklen, '"Asians Cannot Wear Turbans in the Scrum": Explorations of Racist Discourse within Professional Rugby League.' *Leisure Studies* 16, no. 4 (1997): 249–59.
6. Stuart Hall, 'What Is This 'Black' in Black Popular Culture?' in *Stuart Hall: Critical Dialogues in Cultural Studies*, ed. David Morley and Kuan-Hsing Chen (London: Routledge, 1996): 473.
7. Daniel Boorstin, *The Image* (New York: Anthenuem, 1962), 58.
8. Graeme Turner, *Understanding Celebrity* (London: Sage Publications, 2004).
9. Chris Rojek, *Celebrity* (London: Reaktion Books, 2001).
10. Andrews and Jackson, *Sport Stars*, 3.
11. Ibid., 5, emphasis in original.
12. Ibid., 4.
13. Turner, *Understanding Celebrity*.
14. Andrews and Jackson, *Sport Stars*, 5, emphasis in original.
15. David Rowe, *Sport, Culture and the Media: The Unruly Trinity*, 2nd ed. (Buckingham: Open University Press, 2004), 7.
16. Andrews and Jackson, *Sport Stars*.
17. See Joshua Gamson, *Claims to Fame: Celebrity in Contemporary America* (Berkeley: University of California Press, 1994).
18. Andrews and Jackson, *Sport Stars*, 8.
19. Ibid.
20. Steven. J. Jackson and David L. Andrews, eds., *Sport, Culture and Advertising: Identities, Commodities and the Politics of Representation.* (London: Routledge, 2005).
21. Andrews and Jackson, *Sport Stars*, 3.
22. David L. Andrews, 'The Fact(s) of Michael Jordan's Blackness: Excavating a Floating Racial Signifier', *Sociology of Sport Journal* 13, no. 2 (1996): 125–158.
23. David L. Andrews, ed. *Michael Jordan, Inc.: Corporate Sport, Media Culture, and Late Modern America.* (Albany: SUNY Press, 2001); David L. Andrews, Ben Carrington, Steven J. Jackson, and Zbigniew Mazur, 'Jordanscapes: A Preliminary Analysis of the Global Popular', *Sociology of Sport Journal* 13, no. 4 (1996): 428–57.
24. Andrews, 'The Fact(s) of Michael Jordan's Blackness'.

25. Steven J. Jackson, 'A Twist of Race: Ben Johnson and the Canadian Crisis of Racial and National Identity', *Sociology of Sport Journal* 15, no. 1 (1998): 21–40.
26. Ellis Cashmore and Andrew Parker, 'One David Beckham? Celebrity, Masculinity, and the Soccerati', *Sociology of Sport Journal* 20, no. 3 (2003): 214–31.
27. C.L. Cole and David L. Andrews, 'America's New Son: Tiger Woods and America's Multiculturalism,' in *Sport Stars* (see note 2), 70–86.
28. Jaime Schultz, 'Reading the Catsuit: Serena Williams and the Production of Blackness at the 2002 U.S. Open', *Journal of Sport and Social Issues* 29, no. 3 (2005): 338–57.
29. Andrews and Jackson, *Sport Stars*; Smart, *The Sport Star*; Whannel, *Media Sport Stars*.
30. Notable exceptions include those mentioned in a later section and Dennis J. Frost, *Seeing Stars: Sports Celebrity, Identity, and Body Culture in Modern Japan* (Cambridge: Harvard University Press, 2010).
31. Younghan Cho and Charles Leary, 'Introduction: Modern Sports in Asia: Cultural Perspective', *Sport in Society* 15, no. 10 (2012): 1323–8.
32. Younghan Cho, 'Unfolding Sporting Nationalism in South Korean Media Representation of the 1968, 1984 and 2000 Olympics', *Media, Culture & Society* 31 no. 3 (2009): 347–64; Guoqi Xu, *Olympic Dreams: China and Sports 1895-2008.* (Cambridge: Harvard University Press. 2008), 12–54.
33. In this essay, where appropriate, we use the name order with a family name first followed by a given name to be consistent with the convention in certain Asian countries (e.g., China, Japan and Korea) except the names of authors. All names of authors are ordered with given names first to avoid a confusion in references/citations.
34. Andrew D. Grainger, Joshua I. Newman and David L. Andrews, 'Global Adidas: Sport, Celebrity and the Marketing of Difference,' in *Global Sport Sponsorship*, ed. John M. Amis and T. Bettina Cornwell (Oxford: Berg, 2005), 89–105.
35. Ji-Hyun Ahn, *Mixed-Race Politics and Neoliberal Multiculturalism in South Korean Media* (Cham, Switzerland: Palgrave Macmillan, 2018), 75–101.
36. Younghan Cho, Charles Leary and Steven J. Jackson, eds. Glocalization and Sports in Asia. Special Issue. *Sociology of Sport Journal* 29, no. 4 (2012): 421–32; Richard Giulianotti and Roland Robertson, 'Glocalization and Sport in Asia: Diverse Perspectives and Future Possibilities', *Sociology of Sport Journal* 29, no. 4 (2012): 433–54; Koji Kobayashi. 'Globalization, Corporate Nationalism and Japanese Cultural Intermediaries: Representation of *Bukatsu* through Nike Advertising at the Global–Local Nexus', *International Review for the Sociology of Sport* 47, no. 6 (2012): 724–42.
37. Toby Miller, Geoffrey Lawrence, Jim McKay and David Rowe, *Globalization and Sport: Playing the World* (London: Sage Publications, 2001).
38. Yuka Nakamura, 'The Samurai Sword Cuts Both Ways: A Transnational Analysis of Japanese and US Media Representation of Ichiro', *International Review for the Sociology of Sport* 40, no. 4 (2005): 467–80.
39. Chih-ming Wang, 'Capitalizing the Big Man: Yao Ming, Asian America, and the China Global', *Inter-Asia Cultural Studies* 5, no. 2 (2004): 263–78.
40. Younghan Cho, 'Toward the Post-Westernization of Baseball? The National-Regional-Global Nexus of Korean Major League Baseball Fans during the 2006 World Baseball Classic', *International Review for the Sociology of Sport* 51, no. 6 (2016): 752–69; Chris Rumford, 'More Than a Game: Globalization and the Post-Westernization of World Cricket', *Global Networks: A Journal of Transnational Affairs* 7, no. 2 (2007): 202–14.
41. Leo T.S. Ching, *Anti-Japan: The Politics of Sentiments in Postcolonial East Asia* (Durham, NC: Duke University Press, 2019), 2–3.
42. Victor D. Cha, *Beyond the Final Score: The Politics of Sport in Asia* (New York: Columbia University Press, 2009).
43. Peter Horton, 'Guangzhou: The Asian Games and the Chinese "Gold-Fest" – Geopolitical Issues for Australia', *International Journal of the History of Sport* 30, no. 10 (2013): 1165–75.

44. Ibid.; Koji Kobayashi, 'Corporate Nationalism and Glocalization of Nike Advertising in "Asia": Production and Representation Practices of Cultural Intermediaries', *Sociology of Sport Journal* 29, no. 1 (2012): 42–61.
45. Jay Coakley, Chris Hallinan, Steve Jackson, and Peter Mewett, *Sports in Society: Issues and Controversies in Australia and New Zealand* (North Ryde: McGraw-Hill Australia, 2009), 286, emphasis removed.
46. Andrews, 'The Fact(s) of Michael Jordan's Blackness'.
47. Mélisse Lefrance and Geneviéve Rail, 'Excursions into Otherness: Understanding Dennis Rodman and the Limits of Subversive Agency', in *Sport Stars* (see note 2), 36–50.
48. Nancy E Spencer, 'From "Child's Play" to "Party Crasher": Venus Williams, Racism and Professional Women's Tennis', in *Sport Stars* (see note 2), 87–101.
49. Ben Carrington, 'Postmodern Blackness and the Celebrity Sports Star: Ian Wright, 'Race' and English Identity', in *Sport Stars* (see note 2), 102–23.
50. Long, Carrington and Spracklen, '"Asians Cannot Wear Turbans in the Scrum"'.
51. Ying Chiang and Tzu-hsuan Chen, 'Adopting the Diasporic Son: Jeremy Lin and Taiwan Sport Nationalism', *International Review for the Sociology of Sport* 50, no. 6 (2015): 705–21; David J. Leonard, 'A Fantasy in the Garden, a Fantasy America Wants to Believe: Jeremy Lin, the NBA and Race Culture', in *Race in American Sports: Essays*, ed. James L. Conyers (Jefferson, NC: McFarland & Company, Inc., 2014), 144–65.
52. Haozhou Pu, 'Mediating the Giants: Yao Ming, NBA and the Cultural Politics of Sino-American Relations', *Asia Pacific Journal of Sport and Social Science* 5, no. 2 (2016): 87–107.
53. Hirai Hajime, 'Hideo Nomo: Pioneer or Defector?' in *Sport Stars* (see note 2), 187–200.
54. Abilash Nalapat and Andrew Parker, 'Sport, Celebrity and Popular Culture: Sachin Tendulkar, Cricket and Indian Nationalisms', *International Review for the Sociology of Sport* 40, no. 4 (2005): 433–46.
55. Peter Corrigan, 'Imran Khan: The Road from Cricket to Politics', in *Sport Stars* (see note 2), 231–42.
56. Haozhou Pu, Joshua I. Newman, and Michael D. Giardina, 'Flying Solo: Globalization, Neoliberal Individualism, and the Contested Celebrity of Li Na', *Communication & Sport* 7, no. 1 (2019): 23–45.
57. Michael K Park, 'Race, Hegemonic Masculinity, and the "Linpossible!": An Analysis of Media Representations of Jeremy Lin', *Communication & Sport* 3, no. 4 (2015): 369.
58. Daryl Adair and David Rowe, 'Beyond Boundaries? "Race", Ethnicity and Identity in Sport', *International Review for the Sociology of Sport* 45, no. 3 (2010): 251–7.
59. Coakley, Hallinan, Jackson and Mewett, *Sports in Society*, 286, emphasis removed.
60. Daniel Burdsey, *British Asians and Football: Culture, Identity, Exclusion* (London: Routledge, 2006).
61. C. Richard King, ed., *Asian American Athletes in Sport and Society* (New York: Routledge, 2014).
62. Arif Dirlik, 'Critical Reflections on "Chinese Capitalism" as Paradigm', *Identities* 3, no. 3 (1997): 311.
63. Rachael Miyung Joo, *Transnational Sport: Gender, Media, and Global Korea* (Durham: Duke University Press, 2012); Jinsook Kim, 'Why We Cheer for Viktor Ahn: Changing Characteristics of Sporting Nationalism and Citizenship in South Korea in the Era of Neoliberal Globalization', *Communication & Sport* 7, no. 4 (2019): 488–509; Pu, Newman and Giardina, 'Flying Solo'.
64. For a discussion of global Korean-ness through Michelle Wie, see Joo, *Transnational Sport*.
65. Grant Jarvie, 'Introduction: Sport, Racism and Ethnicity', in *Sport, Racism And Ethnicity*, ed. Grant Jarvie. (London: Taylor & Francis, 1991), 4.
66. Hall, 'What Is This "Black" in Black Popular Culture?', 477.
67. Koji Kobayashi, Steven J. Jackson, and Michael P. Sam. 'Multiple Dimensions of Mediation within Transnational Advertising Production: Cultural Intermediaries as

Shapers of Emerging Cultural Capital' *Consumption Markets & Culture* 21, no. 2 (2018): 129–46.

Acknowledgement

We would like to thank the Special Projects Editor Greg Ryan for his timely and effective communication and tireless assistance for editorial matters, which contributed substantially to the quality and coherence of this collection.

Disclosure Statement

No potential conflict of interest was reported by the authors.

Funding

This study was supported by the Hankuk University of Foreign Studies Research Fund.

OPEN ACCESS

'Ono, oh Yes!': An A-League *Tensai* (Genius) Made in Japan

Brent McDonald and Jorge Knijnik

ABSTRACT
In 2005, Football Federation Australia (FFA) launched its latest attempt to create a professional men's soccer football league in Australia, the A-League. The new competition aimed to distance itself from the old National Soccer League, which was based around ethnically affiliated clubs and in doing so appeal to a bigger, more mainstream, market. The formation of the A-League also coincided with Australia's alignment with the Asian Football Confederation for World Cup qualification and related championship play. Ambitious thinkers within FFA envisaged soccer football providing a vehicle to facilitate economic, cultural and political linkages into Asia in what has been termed the 'Asian Century'. However, while teams boosted their rosters with international players, there was a noticeable lack of players from Asia. In this paper we focus on Japanese international Shinji Ono, a marquee signing for the Western Sydney Wanderers (WSW) in 2012, who arguably became the first 'Asian' sporting celebrity in Australia. Hs impact on the A-League is considered both for fans of the WSW and in the marketing of the league more generally. Affectionately known as *tensai* (genius), Ono embodied characteristics that marked him as uniquely Japanese and captured the imagination of Australian football fans as few other players have.

Farewell to a Legend

April 4, 2014. It was a nice Saturday evening in Parramatta, one of the fourteen cities that constitute the Western Sydney region in New South Wales, Australia. Considered by many as the 'heartland of football in Australia'[1], the Western Sydney area is one of the largest multicultural settlements not only in this Southern Hemisphere country, but also in the world.[2] Of the many different and diverse cultural traditions that migrants have brought to Australia in the past hundred years, there was a common trait that remained strongly rooted in the region: the passion

---

This is an Open Access article distributed under the terms of the Creative Commons Attribution-NonCommercial-NoDerivatives License (http://creativecommons.org/licenses/by-nc-nd/4.0/), which permits non-commercial re-use, distribution, and reproduction in any medium, provided the original work is properly cited, and is not altered, transformed, or built upon in any way.

for the game of football.[3] Hence, since the inception of the region's professional club, the Western Sydney Wanderers FC (hereafter Wanderers or WSW) in the 2012/2013 A-League season, it was no surprise to see Parramatta stadium packed with Western Sydney fans to support a football team which thousands had craved for so long.

However, on that autumn night, in addition to supporting their beloved WSW in their last game of the 2013/2014 regular season of the A-League (before the final rounds) against the Brisbane Roar FC, there was another massive reason for the Westie fans to fill the stadium: they wanted to bid farewell to their favourite Japanese *tensai*, the playmaker who had arrived in Western Sydney just a few days before their inaugural A-League game and led the club to their immediate success: Shinji Ono[4], the star Asian[5] player who headed the club to the League's Premiership in their foundation season.

This research examines Shinji Ono as an Asian sporting celebrity in Australia. Ono, as a celebrity athlete, has the potential to provide insight into 'contemporary debates about identity politics' in Australia.[6] As such he acts as a cultural product that is represented and consumed across a range of markets and spaces including the Wanderers fans, the A-League, the Australian media, and the broader public. Ono is not the first 'Asian' sporting celebrity, indeed cricket teams from India, or tennis players such as Li Na from China have been very popular and garnered enormous support from the Australian public. However, unlike these touring international stars, Ono is unique as his position as a marquee signing in the 2012/2013 season anchors him to a 'contextually sensitive' domestic locale (Western Sydney) and national discussion (Australia in Asia).[7]

This research draws on a content analysis of mainstream and social media that references Shinji Ono and the WSW both during Ono's time at the club, and after his retirement. Official documents from the club, FFA and government reports both in relation to Ono but also to the variety of ambitions that each organization held, were also examined. Finally, the ethnographic experiences of the second author, who was in attendance at the Wanderers' games during its first two seasons, are utilized. These experiences were captured in field notes and include various conversations and statements from other fans and the club's officials.

The article begins by concisely tracking the progression of football from a marginalized 'ethnic' game to becoming the 'sleeping giant'[8] on the Australian sport landscape. Placing football in context we therefore consider its position in the broader cultural and political discussions regarding multiculturalism and national identity. In particular the focus is on how the formation of the A-League and Football Federation Australia's realignment with the Asian Football Confederation (AFC) fit within Australia's geopolitical and cultural relationship with Asia. Following this is discussion of the formation and rise of the newest A-League team in 2012, the WSW, in relation to its multicultural and geographical context. Next, the FFA and the A-League 2012 marquee signing strategy are considered, by briefly explaining its aims but then focusing on Ono's history with the WSW. It is important to understand how Ono's profile, as a player, but also as a Japanese man, fits the multicultural narrative brought by the Wanderers to the region. Evidence is provided of the impact that Ono has left on the club, on its fans, and in the local community. The conclusion questions why, looking at Ono's meteoric success in the League and the clubs, FFA have not had a more strategic approach for the signing of Japanese and other Asian marquee players, which would definitely support Australian engagement in the Asian region.

Sleeping Giants

The long history of football in Australia has been one of marginalization. For most of the twentieth century the game struggled to gain broader acceptance outside of those communities who held it dear as it played second fiddle to the rugby codes in New South Wales and Queensland and Australian Rules football in the southern states of Victoria, South Australia and Western Australia. The exact reasons for its failure to grab the imagination of sports fans are a basis for conjecture, though historian Roy Hay lists a range of factors including resistance from colonial and Australian elites, animosity from other codes especially in relation to playing spaces, geographical distance, financial mismanagement and corruption, difficulty in presenting a unified direction for the game, lack of free-to-air television coverage, and until recently a failure to accommodate (both as spectators and players) women.[9] A feature of football clubs in Australia, and particularly due to post World War Two migration, was that many were formed around an ethnic identity derived from the country or region where these migrants originated. As such football has been trapped in a battle of identity politics, which was not helped by a mainstream media that was often hostile to the game and chose to highlight (and exaggerate) ethnic tensions between clubs that drew particularly on conflicts in home countries.[10]

Despite the identity politics affecting professional football in Australia, through the efforts of the aforementioned clubs and grassroots organizations, the game itself is a sleeping giant, as evidenced when it became the number one participation sport in 2003.[11] The issue of how to translate the enormous participatory support into mainstream commercial success was taken in hand by Football Australia (replaced by Football Federation Australia, FFA, in 2004) with the most radical revamp of the sport. Informed by an independent review in 2003,[12] and basing itself on the success of the J-League in Japan and to a lesser extent the K-League in Korea and Major League Soccer in the USA,[13] the Hyundai A-League was launched in 2005. The A-League made an explicit departure from the previous National Soccer League, creating an eight team league with clubs being based around city or regional identity and mainly playing out of generic 'mega-stadiums'.[14] 'Soccer' was replaced with 'football', the league shifted from the traditional autumn-winter season to a spring-summer programme to avoid direct market competition with the Australian Football League (AFL) and rugby league, and introduced a salary cap for all clubs with the addition of the 'marquee' player category, which was not governed by the salary cap restrictions.[15] Within only two seasons the A-League would be heralded a success based on the unprecedented popularity of the product that saw it rise to a level similar to the rugby codes, and comparable to leagues in Korea, Scotland and Argentina.[16]

The creation of the A-League was not only focused on appealing to a domestic market. A broader realignment of football occurred at the same time with FFA successfully moving from FIFA's Oceania zone to be rezoned as part of Asia. The move to the Asian Confederation was significant on many levels. FFA recognized that the future commercial success of football relied on the ability of the national teams the Socceroos (men) and Matildas (women) to regularly qualify for the World Cup finals and other international tournaments. Compared to Oceania's half-place for the WC finals, the Asian zone was afforded four direct qualifying places and the home and away qualifying process promised to provide the national teams with more game time, greater media exposure, and a more secure route to the finals.[17]

The alignment to Asia was about more than FIFA World Cup qualification. As Carniel observes the shift from Oceania to Asia indicated a 'broader context and significance' that represented 'Australia's shifting identity on the global stage' as well as its own self-identity within the nation.[18] A 2005 report commissioned by the Lowy Institute for International Policy (Frank Lowy was then the chairman of FFA) suggested that football provided a common point of communication with Asian countries from which to build significant relationships.[19] Indeed, 'given the centrality of sport in the Australian psyche, the development of a sporting relationship with regional neighbours could transform local perceptions and preconceptions of what individual Asian societies are really like'.[20] FFA saw some role for football to contribute to former Prime Minister Paul Keating's commitment to the 'Asianization of Australian life',[21] conceived at least in part to maximize the opportunities of the 'Asian Century'.[22]

Australia has had what can be described as an ambivalent relationship with Asia dating back to the nineteenth century.[23] From 1901 until 1973 Australia operated racist exclusionary practices in relation to migration known as the White Australia Policy. This policy was driven by a desire to maintain 'racial homogeneity' and a fear of 'Asian invasion'.[24] These 'fears' reappear throughout the twentieth century including during the Second World War and more recently through the successful rise, and anti-immigration platform, of Pauline Hanson's One Nation Party.[25] Nevertheless Australia's geographical and economic interests have undeniably been shaped through an imagination focused on Asia. China and Japan are Australia's first and second largest trading partners respectively and Japan has shifted from enemy, and subsequent source of resentment following the Second World War, to a strategic regional ally.[26] Further, at a cultural level, Japanese 'soft power' and other cultural exports (for example manga, anime, sushi, etc.), have been integrated into Australian culture.[27]

The repositioning of Australia to Asia is central to the following analysis of Shinji Ono. Is Australia 'part of Asia'[28] or is this an awkward fit? As He observes, Australia is not 'perceived as an Asian country, but a white country, belonging to an English speaking world' and also Australians in general 'do not think that Australia should be, or is, a part of Asia'.[29] FFA's contention that 'Australia is more than simply involved in Asia through competition; it is also representative of Asia in competition'[30] is countered by the very real potential that football 'may reinforce stereotypes, given the role sporting rivalries often play as a manifestation of national animosities'.[31] An analysis of the numbers of foreign players in the A-League since 2005 shows clearly that there have been very few players from 'Asia' relative to the preferred football markets of Europe and South America. It was into this context that the A-League expanded in 2012 with the introduction of WSW.

A Brief History of the Wanderers: The Initial Years

In late September 2009, then FFA CEO Ben Buckley was hoping to announce a second Sydney-based team in the A-League[32] – the first was the founding A-League club Sydney FC. He looked then to the most logical alternative for the national competition to have a team in Western Sydney, a region with two million inhabitants, 120,000 registered football players and, most importantly, a rich football history.[33] Many ethnic clubs of the aforementioned 'old soccer'[34] era were based in the Western Sydney region. Clubs such as the Italian Marconi Stallions FC, or the Greek Sydney Olympic (also known in the past as Pan-Helenic) and the Croatian Sydney United (known in the past as Sydney Croatia), just to mention a few 'soccer powerhouses' among many other ethnic-community based clubs,[35] would certainly provide the fan-base that the FFA was hoping for in an expanded A-League in the Greater Western Sydney region. Despite the competition of other football codes, particularly rugby league,[36] the Western Sydney area has always been considered the Australian birthplace for the 'round ball code', hence the strategic view of the FFA to place a new team there.

Buckley and FFA chairman, the billionaire real estate mogul Frank Lowy, tried to work with several investors to place their bid submissions for that club, including a bid linked to Lucas Neill, then the Socceroos captain. For different reasons, though, all of these bids were unsuccessful.[37] However, this failed FFA attempt to constitute what would be the 'Western Sydney Rovers' did not pass unnoticed by Western Sydney residents and football followers. A group of 20 or so of Rovers' supporters attended an exhibition match where the (Western) Sydney Rovers played Sydney FC in Parramatta stadium. They were hoping the new Western Sydney team would be born in the following year. Despite the failure, this effort laid the seeds for the next step. The supporters were already there, waiting for a team to be born and represent their beloved Western Sydney region.[38]

Hence, the region was ecstatic when in April 2012 Buckley and then Prime Minister Julia Gillard announced that Western Sydney would have a team for the forthcoming 2012/2013 A-League season. The announcement, made from the Football New South Wales headquarters, included a commitment for a $5,000,000 grant from the Federal Government to support the club's inception.[39] FFA worked with key local stakeholders to promote several community forums (or fan forums) across different Western Sydney cities, in order to gather the pulse of what the *Westies* wanted from their new team. The forums came up with the team colours (red and black) and the team's name (Wanderers). Most importantly, though, the Western Sydney communities discussed the club's core values: forum attendees were not concerned with immediate wins, but they wanted a club who would represent their region well and make them proud of Western Sydney.[40]

Western Sydney's culturally diverse populations endure every day hardships. Situated far away from the costly real estate nearby the shoreline of Eastern and Northern Sydney and the billionaire sights of the Sydney Harbour, they face growing rates of criminality, lower paid job choices and deficiency of public facilities.[41] Their adversities also include mainstream media and hegemonic Anglo prejudice towards their communities of immigrants.[42] In spite of, or perhaps motivated from, these sufferings, they want to be proud of their home. The creation of the WSW had an instantaneous impact on the community's feelings. For many and particularly for the second generation of migrants who did not live the 'golden era of old soccer', it brought their honour back.[43]

The team made a major impact on-field, attracting national media attention by winning their debut competition – the 2012-2013 A-League Premiership – within a few months of their creation.[44] The club also created a strong international media buzz by winning the 2014 Asian Champions League (ACL) against all prospects. They built their way to the top of the Asian football realm by beating traditional clubs such as the Chinese powerhouse Guangzhou Evergrande in the ACL quarterfinals and the Saudi Arabian billionaire club Al-Hilal in the continental tournament final.

In addition to their immediate on-field success, the Wanderers also brought to the country a major off-field novelty: their voluble support group, the Red & Black Block (RBB). This group of *ultras* supporters, with their colourful *tifos*, flags and banners, their non-stop dancing and chanting in the stands, have been proudly displaying their love for the Wanderers and for Western Sydney since the club's foundation.[45] The RBB definitely transformed the Wanderers' games atmosphere into a carnivalesque one, and added more public and media attention to the club and the region – though not always in a positive manner.[46]

International Marquees and Shinji Ono

The 2012-2013 A-League season was remarkable. The League received a strong spur with the birth of the new club in the football heartland. The commencement of the Wanderers – and the excitement of a Sydney Derby - combined with the arrival of global marquee star players, increased the thrill around the competition. There was a surge in the number of fans engaging with the League and its media coverage.[47] With the support of FFA, football stars such as the Italian World Cup winner and Juventus legend, Alessandro Del Piero (for Sydney FC), the English striker Emile Heskey (for the Newcastle Jets) and finally the Japanese playmaker Shinji Ono (Wanderers) landed on Australian shores in mid or late 2012, bringing local, national and international attention to the League. The momentum could not have been better for Australian football.

Ono was announced as the Wanderer's international marquee player[48] on September 28, 2012, just a week prior to the season's kick-off. Tony Popovic, a former Socceroo player and also a boy who grew up and learnt all his football in the Western Sydney suburbs, had been announced in May as the club's inaugural head coach. He worked tirelessly but with no rush to sign the right players for the team. He did not seem interested in super stars' names such as the German midfielder and 2002 World Cup runner-up Michael Ballack.[49] He was looking everywhere to find the right men who 'embodied the west, who would fit the Wanderers spirit'.[50] From all accounts, Shinji Ono personified this spirit. According to Lyall Gorman, the first CEO appointed for the Wanderers, despite his stardom status, Ono was the humblest person, who was capable to spend hours talking to fans or to carry the water bottles for the fitness coaches after training sessions.[51]

Ono was a player of a global standard, having played in big European leagues and also for the Japan national team in three World Cups. However, the impact of his signing was somehow overshadowed in the media by the other two marquees who arrived in the League earlier that year. Del Piero's signing for Sydney FC was the talk of the city.[52]

Shinji Ono – a Brief Profile

Born in 1979, in Numazu, Shizuoka Prefecture, Shinji Ono started to show his footballing talent for this country early in his life. He was only 18 when selected for the Japanese team in the 1998 FIFA World Cup hosted in France. One year later, he led Japan to second place in the Under-20s World Championship.

Shinji Ono was part of the 'Japanese golden generation' of footballers who captivated the country in the early and mid-2000s. Alongside Naohiro Takahara and Shunsuke Nakamura, Ono played a central role in the unforgettable Japanese squad that won the 2000 Asian Cup hosted by Lebanon. He was also part of the team that played the 2002 FIFA World Cup, co-hosted by Japan and South Korea. In that time, he was already playing in a high-level European league, for the Dutch side Feyenoord Rotterdam, making him one of just a handful of Japanese players who in the early 2000s were plying their trade abroad.[53] It was with Feyenoord that Ono achieved a milestone in his career, by winning the 2001-2002 UEFA Cup,[54] beating the German powerhouse Dortmund in the final. In 2002, Ono was presented with the Asian Football Confederation 'footballer of the year' award, defeating the other two nominees: his countryman Junichi Inamoto and the South-Korean Ahn Jung-hwan.[55] After leaving Feyenoord, he went back to Japan where he played for Urawa Red Diamonds until 2010, when he once again starred in Europe, for the German side VfL Bochum. Then he moved back to Japan to join the Shimizu S-Pulse until making the move to Australia to play for the Wanderers in 2012.[56]

Ono: the Perfect Fit for the Wanderers Tale

Two ideological pillars underpinned the Wanderers narrative throughout its first competitive seasons. On the one hand, there is a discourse about the Western Sydney people being humble, hard workers who are the strength that holds society together. This narrative is perfectly echoed in the lyrics of two of the active supporters' chants. The first is 'More glorious than death', a chant the RBB and the whole stadium sing *a cappella* as the team walks out of the tunnel to the pitch:

> For all the time we've been
>
> They speak about the west
>
> We know the lives we lead
>
> The hearts upon our chest

and for West Sydney we

Will stand atop the crest

And sing for you again

More glorious than death

Considered by many as the unofficial anthem of the club, this chant's words ('we know the lives we lead, the hearts upon our chest') are evidence that the *Westies*' narrative is filled with awareness of the difficult lives that the hard workers from Western Sydney live, with long working hours and little cash or relaxation time.[57] At the same time, they took their responsibility with the team as a priority task of their lives, a mission that is 'more glorious than death'.

The second chant that holds a similar narrative is 'Matador' ('The Killer'). Here the RBB claims that:

We are the RBB, listen to our call

Together we are the blood of this city

Suits will come and go

But the BLOC will never fall

Its lyrics express that fans regard themselves as the burdened employees who preserve the running of the society.[58] The 'suits', the rich people on the top, might not be loyal to the team and the region, but they, the real and hardworking fans will always stay there through thick and thin.

Coach Tony Popovic was the one who inculcated this narrative within the group of players he signed. Initially criticized for being a manager who just signed 'rejects' from other clubs he believed that these players had something to prove to the football world. They were to be humble hard workers that would leave everything on the training track and the playing fields. Then, when the possibility of bringing Ono to the club arose, the *tensai* actually personified the 'modest but resilient footballer' narrative that was being built across the club and beyond.[59]

Every single anecdotal account portrays Ono as the supreme professional and humble player. From the club's CEO to the most modest volunteer, they all repeat the same story about Ono. A junior coach told us an episode that exemplifies his humility:

It was a hot humid summer week and we had two training sessions scheduled for that day. Ono arrived very early with a package and a smirk on his face, and left something on the fridge. After the sessions, as everyone was rushing to leave, he asked his teammates and staff to go to the office, and went out to find the cleaning lady who also washed their uniforms. Somehow he had found out that it was her birthday, and brought a cake for her. It was just glorious seeing her face. He tried unsuccessfully to teach the whole team to sing the Japanese version of Happy Birthday. Ono knew how to be nice with everyone.[60]

The second ideological pillar supporting the Wanderers tale is the multicultural narrative. In the heart of the most culturally diverse region in the country; being the ambassadors of the region's footballing culture in the top Australian league, the Wanderers community embraced the multicultural discourse and the team reflected this diversity.[61] The Wanderers multicultural narrative is also reflected in the supporters' chants. In one of the most appreciated of the RBB chants ('This city we own') the whole stadium comes together to sing their appreciation of the multicultural community formed by the Wanderers' supporters:

These colours unite us all,

All the places we're from

In this city we own

We call Western Sydney home

As fans talked about this chant in their online forum, a supporter summarized the feelings of the online thread members, asserting that this sentiment of unity was 'the Wanderers' gift to Western Sydney'.[62]

With his popularity in Japan, once again Ono proved to be the perfect match for the Wanderers' tale. As the Wanderers' campaign in their first A-League season gained volume and visibility, more and more fans from the multiple locations and diverse Western Sydney communities were filling up not only the Parramatta stadium but also travelling to away games to cheer on the team. The growing presence of Japanese communities in the stands was particularly noticed. They were not loud and noisy as their South American or Southern and Eastern European counterparts, but it was pleasing to watch Japanese families with children, adults and elderly members around and within stadia. Japanese men and women of all ages were dressed up in Wanderer's jerseys marked on the back with their favourite player's number and name: 21, Ono.[63]

Beyond the field, Ono was a remarkable ambassador of the Japanese culture within Western Sydney, helping to disseminate the interest for Japanese topics in an already diverse community. In 2013 he was nominated as the first ever cultural ambassador of the 17th Japanese Film Festival in Australia. Ono was happy to share his experiences about Japanese sport and culture with the audiences, and proud to facilitate cross-cultural connections between Japan and all Australian communities. Festival Director Masafumi Konomi stated that Ono was the best ambassador for the festival as 'through sport he crosses cultural bridges, bringing fans from all walks of life and from all different countries together'.[64]

The Tensai Shakes the Australian Fields – and its Football Nets

More than 10,000 fans attended the first official competitive match for the Wanderers in the Parramatta stadium. The numbers were good considering the novelty and the rain on that early October night. Shinji Ono, who was still finding his best fitness form, was on the bench and entered the field at the 60th minute of play, but could not break the Central Coast Mariners' defensive efforts. Despite the lack of goals on both sides, the fans did admire their marquee player and cheered Ono on every touch he gave on the ball. Spectators sensed that his skills were of another level when compared to the average Australian player.

As the first match finished, Ono approached the RBB and spent nearly half an hour taking pictures and talking to the fans.[65] A close and special relationship had been born; the RBB loved Ono, and he reciprocated these feelings as much as he could. Ono talked and cheered with the group *cappos* (leaders). When the main RBB leader had to leave the country during the second season to go back to Croatia, Ono was one of the players to hand him a special gift prepared by the club: an official Wanderers jersey with the word CAPPO engraved on the back.[66]

It took four matches for the Wanderers to finally find the back of the net for the first time in the competition.[67] It did not take that long though for the RBB to create a dedicated *Ono chant*. This was unusual as most of the group's songs had been about the club, their region or themselves.[68] In the history of the group, there was only one other player who deserved a whole chant, the goalkeeper Ante Covic.[69] Ono, though, was the first to have his dedicated chant: it's a simple one, but the whole stadium joined as the RBB started clapping their hands and sang: 'Ono, Ono Ono, Ono Ono, Ono SHINJI! Ono!'.[70]

As the team's official set piece taker (corners, free kicks and penalty shots) Ono was involved in the Wanderers' first goal ever.[71] While taking a corner, he decided that, instead of making a big cross into the box, he would play a short corner to Youssouf Hersi, who then crossed to Mark Bridge to score away from home against the then defending champions, the Brisbane Roar. That goal ignited the Wanderers' campaign. After a defeat against the Mariners in January, the team went on a ten-game winning streak.[72] They topped the A-League's table with four rounds of the season remaining. Ono continued to be the brain of the team. With his magical touches and positioning, he pushed the team forward. He assisted several of his teammates' goals. He also scored eight goals for the club in this first season, including in the final rounds.[73] However, everyone involved in the game – journalists, fans, coaches, administrators, occasional viewers – would notice that when passing or scoring, his skills were uncommon. These passes and goals could only come from a *Tensai*. Television commentators were stunned after each of his goals, and could not say any other words but 'Ono... oh, yes!!!' after he demonstrated his magnificent ball control as he prepared to score another superb goal.[74]

Banners and flags carrying Ono pictures and Japanese characters quickly filled the stands.[75] Fans could not stop praising Ono on their social media channels. 'We love our marquee man!'; 'he is part of our family!'[76] Video tributes on YouTube appeared incessantly. As the end of 2013 approached and it was time for him to discuss a possible contract extension with the Wanderers, Ono went to the media to declare that he did 'want to stay as long as possible because I love this club, I love these supporters, I love these teammates'.[77]

Reality, though, was not so simple. Despite his key role in leading the club to obtain its first silverware in its first season; in spite of his leadership during the 2013-

2014 A-League campaign and also in the group phase and initial knock-out rounds of the 2014 Asian Champions League, a decision was made by the club to not extend Ono's contract. Different and contradictory versions for this result were never clarified. Some say that he wanted to re-join his wife and two young children who remained in Japan; others say that the club and Ono did not agree in the contract extension period, as he wanted a two-year contract extension and the club offered just one-year.[78] The fact is that in January 2014 the club announced that Ono would depart at the end of the A-League season. Fans' disappointment was enormous.

The Wanderers finished in second place at the end of the regular 2013-2014 A-League season. Their last game for that season, as described above, was then the perfect celebratory occasion to not only cheer the team and send positive vibes as they progressed into the finals, it was also the moment to farewell their favourite family member, their inaugural international marquee and genius Shinji Ono. The club prepared a nice send-off. Ono masks were distributed to the fans at the stadium gates. On the 21st minute of play, as a reference to Ono's jersey number, fireworks were let off on the stadium surroundings and the public clapped and sang his special song once again, waving their masks in the air.

The RBB also prepared a special goodbye to Ono. His face was pictured in the middle of their enormous white and red *tifo* (ultras banner) with the Japanese flag as its background; on the sides two other smaller banners with thank you (*arigatou*) written in Japanese characters. Throughout the whole game, the group also modified a few of their chants in order to include his name. For example, in the first half, in lieu of executing their famous call and response chant[79] 'Who do we sing for?' and different sectors of the stadium replying 'We sing for the Wanderers!', the RBB started the call by saying 'Shinji!' for the rest of the stadium to scream 'Ono!'. When the whole stadium was singing 'Ole Ole Ole Western Sydney Ole ole'", they replaced the region's name by coming up with 'Ole Ole Ole Shinji Ono, ole ole'.[80]

Fans and journalists could see that Ono was having a superb performance during that game. He was doing his best to justify all the affection that fans demonstrated towards him. Despite his efforts, and in spite of having created a few goal scoring chances, Ono unfortunately could not find the back of the net on that night. That did not undermine his farewell. As Tony Popovic took him out of the game just a few minutes prior to the final whistle, the whole stadium stood up and gave him a big ovation, singing for the last time his unique chant led by the active supporters' band. He was about to go but his legacy would stay forever within the fans' heart and in the club's history.

Marketing for the A-League
Shinji Ono appeared for the WSW on only fifty-one occasions. Whilst he was undoubtedly a fan favourite, what, if any, was his broader impact on the community and on the position of football in the Australian sports market? Just prior to his departure in 2014, the Lord Mayor of Parramatta presented Ono with a medal of honour and stated:

> You have been a true role model to our youth. My little boy has converted from rugby league to football because of you. You have been an ambassador to our city, you have

united not only Parramatta, but the whole Western region. You have raised the profile of football in this region. When we look back at what you have done, you'll always be remembered as our hero, you'll be remembered for the great things that you've done on the field and off the field and always remember you have a home back in Parramatta.[81]

During his time as a marquee player, Ono's image was utilized extensively by Foxsports (the pay television provider of the A-League) and continued to be after his departure. Indeed, Ono's photo was on the side bar of the Foxsports subscription page until the end of 2018 when his image was replaced by another Japanese marquee player, Keisuke Honda. The significance of this is that the A-League has hosted many marquee players since 2014, however Ono's symbolic capital would appear to have held its currency in comparison to these other players. As one commentator on the game put it: 'There's no doubt that Ono and Del Piero will leave a legacy and in ten and twenty years' time we'll be saying. Remember when those two legends of the game played in the A-League.'[82] It could be that Ono's celebrity for WSW had as much to do with the narrative of the fledgling club and his contribution to their incredible first season and that his continued presence in some media settings is an attempt to keep the buzz of those days in the league alive. In the ultra-competitive Australian sport market, WSW, and its marquee player Ono, had been a 'far bigger success story than the AFL's Greater Western Sydney, despite the tens of millions the AFL has spent on establishing a foothold' in Western Sydney.[83]

Perhaps it was Ono's 'Japaneseness' that endeared him to fans and created a point of difference to the other, European and South American, imports. Ono might have been so marketable because he satisfied the broader audience's imagination of characteristics that are 'uniquely Japanese'. Commenting on Ono's departure from WSW, Spillane wrote: 'Shinji Ono didn't win over fans by being physically imposing or handsome, by getting belted and bravely playing on, or by being cocky and aggro or saying outrageous things. He was polite, technically outstanding, and, ok, I'll say it: Asian.'[84] If one examines Australian media representation of Japan's national men's team, the Blue Samurai, one is likely to find similar descriptions regarding collective technical brilliance, hard work and humility, apparently 'Japanese' cultural tropes.

The other plus side of having Shinji Ono playing in the A-League is that it generated considerable media interest from the Japanese press. The primary author was based in Kyoto during 2013 and notes that the daily papers would update the progress of most Japanese players in overseas competitions. As Ono had a very successful season with WSW his fortunes put the A-League at least on the radar of the Japanese football public.

Ono therefore presents a somewhat paradoxical character in relation to Australian football. His undoubted celebrity and popularity whilst at WSW suggests a football audience happy to embrace players from the Asian (or at least East Asian) region. Ono, as a representative from the Asian region, provides a potential link for Australians of Asian heritage to find a place in sport fandom that has previously been absent, especially in mainstream sport. Further, Australia hosted a very successful Asian Cup in 2015, with stadiums packed full of supporters from numerous Asian diaspora. However, the number of Asian imports remains almost non-existent. For example at the beginning of the 2018-19 A-League season, of the 43 internationals only one, Melbourne Victory marquee Keisuke Honda, is from the FIFA Asian confederation.[85] Surely the success of Ono is a blueprint for further recruitment from Asia, and yet, to date, this has not happened.

Shinji Ono's Legacy?

Shinji Ono was a quality asset for the WSW since his arrival in Australia. After his departure, the club is yet to find another international marquee whose profile on and off the field would have a similar effect as Ono had. Ono impacted the A-League by leading the Wanderers to their first (and only) Premiership title as well to two Championship finals, but without winning the ultimate Champion's title. In addition, he helped the club in winning the ACL title at their first attempt. As his contract expired, he did not reach the final stages of the Asian top clubs competition with the Wanderers, but his Asian and international experience gave the younger players the confidence they needed to move along and be successful in the final rounds of the tournament. Ono was also a people's favourite, always willing to spend his time with fans and the humblest of the club's staff members. He embodied and personified the Wanderers' tale of humility and hard work. Furthermore, he added a strong Asian component to the club's and the Western Sydney multicultural narrative.

In footballing terms, Ono's influence can still be seen as he inspired other Japanese players to consider an A-League adventure. In 2013, as Ono was revitalizing his career in the Australian league, other Japanese 'golden generation' stars such as Naohiro Takahara also thought about a move to the A-League.[86] More recently, in 2016, Ono's advice was instrumental to convince his countryman Jumpei Kusukami to come to the Wanderers from the J-League. Both talked on the phone and Ono had highly praised the fans, the club and the league, and that had a final weight in Kusukami's decision to play overseas for the first time in his career.[87] However there has only been one Asian marquee player since Ono. The arrival of Honda might be the catalyst to finally build on the enormous success of his forerunner Ono and for A-league clubs to seek marquee Asian players instead of European or South American ones, but will the imagination of Asian stretch further than a Japanese marquee? The A-League has instituted a new foreign player rule, four plus one. Under this rule, which mirrors that of other Asian Confederations, each team is allowed five foreign players but one must come from an Asian confederation nation.[88] Whether the A-League will come to represent a more 'Asian' profile both in the region and in the players on the pitch remains to be seen, but the evidence of Shinji Ono's impact on and off the field has surely demonstrated that it is a possibility.

Notes

1. WestSydneyFootball. *Football Comes Home: The Early Days of Western Sydney Wanderers FC*, (2013), http://www.westsydneyfootball.com/sitefiles/fch/football_comes_home.pdf., 5
2. Jock Collins, Carol Reid, and Charlotte Fabiansson, *Tapping the Pulse of Youth in Cosmopolitan South-Western and Western Sydney: Report for The Department of*

Immigration and Citizenship (2007) www.immi.gov. au/media/publications/multicultural. Western Sydney is also one of the fastest growing regions in Australia. In 2015, 1 in 11 Australians lived in Western Sydney whose population is characterized by lower levels of employment and tertiary education than the rest of Sydney. Just over 40% of the residents of Western Sydney speak a language other than English at home. Daniel Montoya, Western Sydney: An Economic Profile, *Parliament of NSW Briefing Paper no. 10,* (2015).

3. Christopher J. Hallinan, John E. Hughson, and Michael Burke, 'Supporting The "World Game" in Australia: A Case Study of Fandom at National and Club Level', *Soccer & Society* 8, nos. 2-3 (2007): 283–297.
4. Throughout this paper the Western convention of first name followed by surname is used in regard to Japanese players. This has been done in keeping with their coverage in the Australian media sources used.
5. The concept of 'Asia' is problematic. As a collective descriptor it has the capacity to homogenize enormous geographical, cultural and ethnic diversity. Further, as a concept 'Asia' varies depending on who is deploying it. For example, for FIFA Asia, stretches from Lebanon to Australia whilst in popular discourse in Australia it might be considered the region directly north of the country, including China but stopping at India. Our usage throughout has been in keeping with the meaning of either FIFA, or the A-League or Australian Government.
6. Steve Jackson and David Andrews, 'Olympic Celebrity: Introduction'. *Celebrity Studies,* 3, no.3, (2012): 263-269.
7. David Andrews and Steve Jackson, *Sports Stars: The Cultural Politics of Sporting Celebrity* (New York: Routledge, 2001).
8. Gerard McManus, 'Gallop, a Man in a Hurry', *Management Today,* (April 2013): 12-15
9. Roy Hay, '"Our Wicked Foreign Game": Why has Association Football (Soccer) not become the Main Code of Football in Australia?' *Soccer and Society,* 7, nos. 2-3, (2006): 165-186.
10. David Rowe and C. Gilmore, 'Getting a Ticket to the World Party: Televising Soccer in Australia', in *The Containment of Soccer in Australia: Fencing off the World Game,* ed. Chris Hallinan and John Hughson (New York: Routledge, 2010), 9-26.
11. Hallinan, Hughson, and Burke, 'Supporting the "World Game" in Australia'.
12. David Crawford, *Report of the Independent Soccer Review Committee into the Structure, Governance, and Management of Soccer in Australia,* (Canberra: Australian Sports Commission, 2003).
13. Heath McDonald, Adam Karg, and Daniel Lock, 'Leveraging Fans' Global Football Allegiances to Build Domestic League Support', *Asia Pacific Journal of Marketing and Logistics,* 22, no.1, (2010): 67-89.
14. Hallinan, Hughson, and Burke, 'Supporting the "World Game" in Australia'; Christopher Hallinan and John Hughson, 'The Beautiful Game in Howard's 'Brutopia': Football, Ethnicity and Citizenship in Australia', in Hallinan and Hughson, *The Containment of Soccer in Australia,* 1-8.
15. McDonald, Karg, and Lock, 'Leveraging Fans'.
16. Ian Warren and Roy Hay, 'Fencing Them In: The A-League Policy and the Dilemma of Public Order', in Hallinan and Hughson, *The Containment of Soccer in Australia,* 124-142.
17. Christopher Hallinan and Tom Heenan, 'Australia, Asia and the New Football Opportunity', *Soccer and Society,* 14, no.5 (2013): 751-767. AFP, 'Socceroos Welcome Asia Switch Approval', *ABC News,* June 15 2005, https://www.abc.net.au/news/2005-06-15/socceroos-welcome-asia-switch-approval/1594316 (accessed July 19, 2019).
18. Jessica Carniel, 'Reflections on Race, Regionalism and Geopolitical Trends via Australian Soccer', *The International Journal of the History of Sport,* 29, no.17, (2012): 2405-2420.
19. Anthony Bubalo, *Policy Brief: Football Diplomacy,* (Sydney: Lowy Institute for International Policy, 2005).

20. Ibid., 6-7.
21. Keating was referring to 'East Asia' whereas FIFA's definition of Asia stretches all the way from Japan to Lebanon.
22. Baogang He, 'The Awkwardness of Australian Engagement with Asia: The Dilemmas of Australian Ideas of Regionalism', *Japanese Journal of Political Science*, 12, no.2 (2011), 267-285; Football Federation Australia, *FFA Submission to the Australia in the Asian Century White Paper*, (Sydney: FFA, March 2011).
23. Carol Johnson, Pal Ahluwalia, and Greg McCarthy, 'Australia's Ambivalent Re-Imagining of Asia', *Australian Journal of Political Science*, 45, no.1, (2010): 59-74.
24. David Walker, 'Broken Narratives: Reflections on the History of Australia's Asian Connections, 1880s to present', *Otemon Journal of Australian Studies*, 39, (2013): 61-74.
25. Johnson, Ahluwalia, and McCarthy, 'Australia's Ambivalent Re-Imagining of Asia'; Walker, 'Broken Narratives'.
26. Malcolm Cook and Thomas Wilkins, *The Quiet Achiever: Australia-Japan Security Relations*, (Sydney: Lowy Institute for International Policy, 2011).
27. Carolyn Stevens, 'You Are What You Buy: Postmodern Consumption and Fandom of Japanese Popular Culture', *Japanese Studies*, 30, no.2, (2010): 199-214.
28. Football Federation Australia, *FFA submission*, 23.
29. He, 'The Awkwardness of Australian Engagement with Asia', 278-279.
30. Football Federation Australia, *FFA submission*, 13.
31. Bubalo, '*Policy Brief: Football Diplomacy*', 7.
32. John Stensholt and Shaun Mooney, *A-League: The Inside Story of the Tumultuous First Decade.* (Collingwood: Nero, 2015).
33. Hallinan, Hughson, and Burke, 'Supporting the "World Game" in Australia".
34. Joe Gorman, *The Death and Life of Australian Soccer*' (Brisbane: University of Queensland Press, 2017), 35.
35. Ibid.
36. There are professional rugby league clubs in the area such as the Parramatta Eels and the Penrith Panthers; and in 2008 the AFL established an Australian Rules club in the region, the Giants; but football is still attracting a larger number of participants and fans in the Western Region than the other codes.
37. Stensholt and Mooney, *A-League*.
38. Jorge Knijnik, 'Social Agency and Football Fandom: The Cultural Pedagogies of the Western Sydney Ultras', *Sport in Society*, 21, no.6, (2018): 946-959.
39. Stensholt and Mooney, *A- League*.
40. Fan forums were held at seven locations across Western Sydney: Bankstown, Castle Hill, Parramatta, Campbelltown, Penrith, Rooty Hill, Mount Pritchard, and attended by nearly 1,000 people. (*Football Comes Home*).
41. Kathy Arthurson, 'From Stigma to Demolition: Australian Debates about Housing and Social Exclusion', *Journal of Housing and the Built Environment*, 19, no.1, (2004): 255-270.
42. Bob Bireel and Ernest Healy, 'Metropolis Divided: The Political Dynamic of Spatial Inequality and Migrant Settlement in Sydney', *People and Place* 11, no.2 (2003): 65-87.
43. Gorman, *The Death and Life*.
44. Joe Gorman, 'The Del Piero Effect', *Leopold Method*, (2014): 23-37.
45. Jorge Knijnik, 'Imagining a Multicultural Community in an Everyday Football Carnival: Chants, Identity and Social Resistance on Western Sydney Terraces', *International Review for the Sociology of Sport*, 53, no.4, (2018); 471-489.
46. Michael Visontay, *Welcome to Wanderland: Western Sydney Wanderers and the Pride of the West*, (Richmond: Hardie Grant Books, 2014).
47. Zoran Pajic, '"A' is for Australia": New Football's Billionaires, Consumers and the "Asian Century". How the A-League Defines the New Australia', *Soccer & Society* 14, no.5, (2013): 734-750.

48. At that time, the A-League rules for marquee signings stipulated that each club could have two marquee players (off-salary cap) but only one could be a visa player. This restriction has since been removed and currently clubs can sign two marquee players regardless of their nationality.
49. Stensholt and Mooney, 'A-League.
50. Visontay, *Welcome to Wanderland*, 37.
51. Personal observations of second author at training and after matches. Notes in possession of the second author.
52. Pajic, 'A is for Australia'.
53. Takahashi Yoshio and John Horne, 'Japanese Football Players and the Sport Talent Migration Business', in *Football Goes East: Business, Culture, and the People's Game in China, Japan, and South Korea*, ed. Wolfram Manzenreiter and John Horne, (London; New York: Routledge, 2004), 67-85.
54. Currently UEFA Europa League.
55. Stensholt and Mooney, *A-League*.
56. Worldfootball website, 'Shinji Ono', https://www.worldfootball.net/player_summary/shinji-ono/ (accessed December 17, 2018)
57. Knijnik, 'Imagining a Multicultural Community'.
58. Ibid.
59. Stensholt and Mooney, *A- League*.
60. Personal testimony to the second author, November 2016. Notes in possession of the second author.
61. Kathy Marks, 'How the Westies Won: Wandering through Australia's Heartland', *Griffith Review*, Edition 41: Now we are ten. 1-25.
62. Knijnik, 'Imagining a multicultural community'.
63. Second author field work notes. Notes in possession of the second author.
64. Western Sydney Wanderers Official Website, '17th Japanese Film Festival rolls out the red carpet for Shinji Ono, November 14, 2013, https://www.wswanderersfc.com.au/news/17th-japanese-film-festival-rolls-out-red-carpet-shinji-ono (accessed December 10, 2018).
65. Visontay, *Welcome to Wanderland*.
66. The second author has personally witnessed this fact while on the stands conducting research data collection. Notes in possession of the second author.
67. Visontay, *Welcome to Wanderland*.
68. Knijnik, 'Imagining a multicultural community'
69. Ibid.
70. Second author's personal lived and chanted experience in the stands. Notes in possession of the second author.
71. 'Western Sydney Wanderers First Season Highlights (All Goals)'; posted on YouTube by Daniel Jarosz on June 30, 2013, https://www.youtube.com/watch?v=w4D0LBOoTx4 (accessed June 4, 2019).
72. WestSydneyFootball. *Football Comes Home*.
73. Ibid.
74. 'Shinji Ono? OH YES'. FoxSports Australia footage posted on YouTube by OzSportsVids on October 27, 2013, (accessed June 10, 2019).
75. Second author's personal lived experience in the stands. Notes in possession of the second author.
76. Jorge Knijnik. 'New Culture in the Making: An Ethnographic Pilot Study of the Western Sydney Wanderers Football Club Fandom Culture'. (2014). Western Sydney University, Unpublished research report.
77. Dominic Bossi, 'Shinji Ono Wants to End His Career at Western Sydney Wanderers', *Sydney Morning Herald,* October 27, 2013, https://www.smh.com.au/sport/soccer/shinji-ono-wants-to-end-his-career-at-western-sydney-wanderers-20131027-2w9pc.html (accessed November 10, 2018).

78. Sebastian Hasset, 'Shinji Ono Will Leave, Say Western Sydney Wanderers', *Sydney Morning Herald*, January 16, 2014), https://www.smh.com.au/sport/soccer/shinji-ono-will-leave-say-western-sydney-wanderers-20140116-30w8r.html (accessed November 10, 2018).
79. Meri Kytö, 'We Are the Rebellious Voice of the Terraces, We Are Çarşı': Constructing a Football Supporter Group through Sound', *Soccer & Society* 12, no.1, (2011): 77-93
80. Second author field work notes. Notes in possession of the second author.
81. Lord Mayor of Parramatta, March 19, 2014, https://www.wswanderersfc.com.au/video/shinji-ono-receives-award (accessed February 1 2019).
82. Nathan Cirson, 'What Kind of Legacy Will Ono and Del Poero Leave?', *The Roar*, January 14, 2014, https://www.theroar.com.au/2014/01/15/what-kind-of-legacy-will-ono-and-del-piero-leave/ (accessed September 13, 2018).
83. McManus, 'Gallop, a Man in a Hurry', 14.
84. Deb Spillane, 'Goodbye to that Tensai Guy, Shinji Ono', *The Roar*, April 9, 2014, https://www.theroar.com.au/2014/04/10/goodbye-to-that-tensai-guy/ (accessed October 12, 2018).
85. A-League website, '*Foreign Players*', https://www.a-league.com.au/foreign-players, (accessed February 2, 2019).
86. Sebastian Hasset, 'Shinji Ono Resurgence Sparks Interest in A-League for Japan Star', *Sydney Morning Herald*, November 12, 2013, https://www.smh.com.au/sport/soccer/shinji-onos-resurgence-sparks-interest-in-aleague-for-japan-star-naohiro-takahara-20131211-2z6g6.html (accessed November 22, 2018).
87. Adrian Arciuli, 'Ono Convinced Me to Join the Wanderers', *The World Game*, October 29, 2016, https://theworldgame.sbs.com.au/ono-convinced-me-to-join-wanderers-reveals-kusukami (accessed November 22, 2018).
88. AAP, 'A-League to Adopt Asian Import Quota Rule', *Sydney Morning Herald*, January 16, 2017, https://www.smh.com.au/sport/soccer/aleague-to-adopt-asian-import-quota-rule-20170116-gtsaoo.html (accessed November 22, 2018).

Disclosure Statement

No potential conflict of interest was reported by the author.

ORCID

Brent McDonald http://orcid.org/0000-0002-7455-0940
Jorge Knijnik http://orcid.org/0000-0003-2578-8909

Globalization, Migration, Citizenship, and Sport Celebrity: Locating Lydia Ko between and beyond New Zealand and South Korea

Ik Young Chang, Steve Jackson and Minhyeok Tak

ABSTRACT
The contested terrain surrounding globalization, migration, citizenship, and national identity shape the context in which modern sport celebrity develops in Asia. Focusing on female golf phenomenon Lydia Ko, the analysis locates her celebrity and national identity between her place of birth – Korea – and her place of citizenship – New Zealand. Several intersecting factors influenced Ko's celebrity and identity construction including changes in New Zealand immigration policy, changes in Korean state policy towards overseas nationals, negatively viewed attitudes and behaviours of previous foreign-born celebrities of Korean-descent, and Ko's own public proclamations regarding her national identity.

Globalization has resulted in a wide range of influences, impacts, conflicts, negotiations, and accommodations within and across the cultural, political and economic spectrum. One of the key dimensions of globalization has been the movement of people. While historically humans have always shifted from one place to another, the twenty-first century has witnessed unprecedented numbers of people migrating from their original homelands. The current estimate is that there are about 244 million international migrants in the world, which equates to 3.3 percent of the global population.[1] Crucially, while these figures confirm the quantity of migration, it is important to recognize the fact that these shifts also often involve increasing encounters of different cultures, customs, and values. One consequence of these wide-ranging causes and effects of global migration is increasingly intense and complex debates about the nature and significance of national identity and citizenship. According to the political theorist Peter Nyers:

> In this regard, the challenge for scholarship will be to not only address the institutional and constitutional arrangements of citizenship, but to also examine how citizenship operates as a lived experience. What this often reveals, however, is that for all the

innovations in how we conceive of citizenship, the concept remains deeply embedded with practices that divide humanity according to race, ethnicity, gender and geography.[2]

Without doubt, there is strong evidence of conflict associated with migration particularly in cases involving desperate people seeking refuge in foreign lands in an attempt to escape war, poverty, and religious and cultural persecution. Yet, conflict may also arise where hard-working and highly ambitious migrants seek a new homeland based on lifestyle and better opportunities for their children. While there are popular mantras produced and circulated by nation-states to demonstrate their commitment to diversity, limits remain on the nature and extent to which difference is not only recognized but tolerated and celebrated. Here, the globalization of popular culture may play an influential role in promoting greater cultural awareness of difference and diversity. Whether through popular music, television or movies we have greater exposure to people who are different from ourselves. Notably, one of the key, yet often overlooked, sites for understanding the nature and significance of national identity and citizenship is sport. Not only is sport globally popular and highly visible, but it is also often considered a universal language and there are regularly scheduled events where nations compete against each other, including the Olympics, FIFA World Cup, and others, that bring to the fore aspects of nationalism and identity.

This paper examines sporting celebrity within the context of globalisation, migration, citizenship and national identity. More specifically, it explores female golf phenomenon Lydia Ko and her celebrity and national identity as she is located between her place of birth – Korea – and her place of citizenship – New Zealand. The paper is divided into five main parts including: (a) a brief overview of the significance of sport and celebrity in identity construction; (b) an overview of shifts in New Zealand immigration policies that have influenced greater Asian migration; (c) a discussion of the role of golf in Korean-New Zealanders' lives; (d) an attempt to locate Lydia Ko within a transnational framework; and (e) a brief analysis of how Lydia Ko's public proclamations constructed both her celebrity and national identity. At the outset it is important to acknowledge the contextual specificity of both celebrity and debates around citizenship in order to recognize the idiosyncratic nature of the intersection of people, places and events. As such, the paper begins by offering a brief overview of the social significance of sport as a strategic site for analysing celebrity followed by an overview of the context and shifting interrelationship between New Zealand immigration policy and South Korean migration.

Sport, Celebrity, and Identity

The focus on sport and sport celebrity for understanding wider social processes, politics, and identities is certainly not new but nevertheless requires at least some justification.[3] Steven Jackson and David Andrews offer a comprehensive, though not exhaustive list of some of the key features that make 'sport' such a valuable commodity within the broader cultural circuit of production, representation, and consumption in contemporary society.[4] They note that sport is highly desirable because it: (a) attracts large and passionately devoted audiences; (b) is cheaper to produce, relative to other types of media programming; (c) is human drama at its finest, providing a stimulus and an acceptable arena for the expression of the full range of human emotions; (d) displays real people demonstrating the limits of the body in real time; (e) embodies what some consider to be implicit and/or explicit erotic practice[5]; (f) provides us with carefully crafted narratives of heroes and villains[6]; and, (g) is associated with positive images of health and nationhood.[7] Beyond these key points, it is important to note that sport is an ideal conduit of promotional culture because, in myriad ways, it mirrors the idealized version of capitalism; that is, it is based on competition, achievement, efficiency, technology, and meritocracy.[8]

Collectively, these points highlight the cultural value and significance of sport as a cultural commodity. Likewise, these points reveal why sport is such an important site for the production, representation, and consumption of celebrity. Arguably, the sporting and 'celebritized' body is a strategic site for understanding contemporary debates about identity politics (gender, race, sexuality, disability, national), consumer capitalism and migration policy.[9] Here, there is one other unique feature of sport that has important implications with respect to celebrity, identity, and citizenship. Sport, is one of the few, indeed, perhaps the only, professional occupations where nations proactively recruit foreigners to take up citizenship of another country in the pursuit of international sporting status and prestige.[10] As a consequence, a range of characterizations have emerged to describe the process including athletic mercenaries and human sport trafficking. However, amidst these debates, high-profile athletes that shift across national boundaries often emerge as celebrities who provide valuable insights into the increasingly flexible nature of both celebrity and citizenship.[11] To this extent, Lydia Ko, as both everyday citizen and sport celebrity, serves as a strategic site of analysis in relation to her gendered, racial/ethnic, and national identities.

New Zealand Immigration Policies and South Koreans' Inflow to New Zealand

New Zealand is a country characterized by 'Kin-migration'.[12] For example, until the mid-1980s, there was no legal or cultural distinction made between New Zealand-born and British-born people with respect to New Zealand immigration policy. The removal of the unequal opportunity to migrate to New Zealand in 1986, in favour of selection on the basis of personal merit, skilled qualifications and entrepreneurial contribution to New Zealand society, opened the doors to non-traditional sources of immigration from Asia, Africa, and South America and played a significant role in changing the image of New Zealand from a 'mono'- or 'bi'-cultural country to a more 'multi-cultural' society.[13]

The introduction of what was called the 'point system' in 1991, which was designed for the selection of skilled immigrants, resulted in a sharp increase in the number of immigrants, particularly from Asia. Asian immigrants increased from 46,035 in 1986 to 540,000 in 2013, accounting for twelve percent of New Zealand's total population.[14] Within a short period of time, large inflows of Asian immigrants sparked the attention of both New Zealanders and New Zealand media as evident in media responses, political perceptions, and public opinion polls. For example, journalists and politicians expressed their concern that this phenomenon would result in an 'Asianised New Zealand'.[15]

As a result of the combination of the media's curiosity and politicians' focus on the 'immigration problem', some policies, especially for newcomers from non-English-speaking countries, were tightened. However, despite the new regulations, the number of Asian immigrants has continued to increase. Moreover, New Zealanders continued to see the Asian region and Asian immigrants as important to New Zealand's future. According to Andrew Butcher's research on New Zealanders' perceptions of Asians in New Zealand in 2007, 90 percent of New Zealanders indicated that Asia was an important export market in the global marketplace and 77 percent of Kiwis felt that Asia's economic growth would have a positive impact on New Zealand's future. In addition, 76 percent of New Zealanders agreed that Asian immigrants contribute to New Zealand's cultural diversity.[16]

Amongst the rising immigrant inflows from Asian countries, South Koreans began to migrate to New Zealand in increasing numbers. In 1991, 930 South Koreans migrated, with their total number rising from 12,753 in 1996 to 30,171 in 2013, making them the fourth-largest Asian population after the Chinese, Indians, and Filipinos.[17] According to Ik Young Chang, Steven Jackson, and Mike Sam, most of the Koreans in New Zealand were from the middle and upper classes of South Korea and migrated to New Zealand for two main reasons: cleaner, safer, and less crowded and competitive living conditions; and, a better quality education system for their children.[18] In the same vein, a range of other scholars note that many South Korean immigrants consider New Zealand 'a paradise' in terms of its great natural environment, along with a better quality of life and education for their families.[19]

In terms of demographics and geographic concentration, 94 percent of South Korean immigrants living in New Zealand were not born in New Zealand and 87 percent of them have lived in New Zealand for less than ten years.[20] More than 90 percent of South Koreans are living in major cities such as Auckland, Christchurch, Wellington, and Dunedin with about 80 percent of them residing in the North Island.[21] In particular, more than 60 percent of all South Korean immigrants have settled in Auckland, while about 32 percent of the total population of New Zealand is living in this region. The urban concentration of South Korean immigrants residing in New Zealand has contributed to the formation of South Korean communities such as associations of South Korean residents and South Korean churches in major cities. These communities play a significant role in helping new immigrants settle into New Zealand society, developing important relationships with members of the host society and maintaining economic, social, and cultural ties with the home country.[22]

The Role of Golf in Korean New Zealanders' Lives

The growing volume and variety of patterns of global migration have accelerated and broadened its impact on both countries of origin and destination. Such progressive changes of global migration have had a significant effect on the individual lives of both the movers and stayers.²³ In the realm of sport and leisure, sociologists have investigated the relationship between global migration, sport, and identities, noting that sport may play a crucial role in negotiating identities in conjunction with processes of global migration.²⁴ The early research on the adaptation of new migrants focused primarily on the idea that sports play an important role in the acculturation and assimilation of immigrants into mainstream society.²⁵ However, there are other, contrasting and contrary, perspectives about the role of sport and leisure for migrants. For example, some migration studies scholars have challenged the role of sport and leisure as a vehicle of assimilation.²⁶

As previously noted, most Korean immigrants in/to New Zealand are from the well-educated middle class and migrate to New Zealand not to establish themselves financially, but to seek a better or different lifestyle. According to Ik Young Chang's research on South Korean lifestyle migration decision-making and settlement into New Zealand, some informants stated that more opportunities to participate in sport and leisure enabled them to distinguish their lives from those of their friends and family living in both Korea and other overseas migration destinations.²⁷ Notably, although it is certainly not the only pursuit, golf is a great example of a sport and leisure activity that is popular amongst Korean migrants. In his research, Chang noted that Korean New Zealanders highlighted the fact that in New Zealand, they can enjoy golf not only because it is much more accessible, it is also less expensive compared to South Korea where, despite a dramatic increase in the number of amateur golfers, the sport is still recognized as being aligned with wealthier social classes.²⁸ Therefore, many South Koreans migrating to New Zealand also used sport and leisure as a point of distinction and as a useful tool for self-development.

Beyond these functions, within the New Zealand context, golf plays a significant role in serving as a centre and helping develop the local Korean community. In other words, golf provides 'a way of sustaining cultural and emotional continuity despite spatial dislocation',²⁹ and encourages Koreans, as an ethnic minority group, to maintain relationships and aspects of traditional culture following migration. For example, many Koreans in Auckland support South Korean-born New Zealand golfers such as Lydia Ko, by hosting golf festivals for Korean-New Zealanders in conjunction with major tournaments.³⁰ Moreover, the success of local celebrities, like Lydia Ko, in the Ladies Professional Golf Association (LPGA, New Zealand Women's Open, and the Korean Ladies Professional Golf Association (KLPGA), encourages bigger and more organized golf festivals. In this context New Zealand-Korean golfer Lydia Ko is explored as a transnational celebrity including how other overseas-based Koreans' actions influenced how she was perceived, represented and classified within Korea.

Lydia Ko in the Transnational Context

Lydia Ko's family migrated from Seoul, South Korea, to New Zealand in the late 1990s when she was an infant. Originally, the family intended to move to Canada, but eventually changed their mind to look at New Zealand. The choice of New Zealand as a new home was due, in part, to the fact that it has 400 golf courses which are the second highest number per capita in the world after Scotland. Consequently, compared to most countries, golf in New Zealand is relatively inexpensive. Beyond accessibility and cost, New Zealand has increasingly been identified as the best place for Korean golfers to train. Indeed, there are now about 1,000 Koreans playing the game in New Zealand and, as further evidence of Korean influence, almost 70 percent of the qualifying spots for the 2010–2011 New Zealand Open went to Koreans.[31] Extending this point to the international realm, one writer observed, that the surnames on the leader board of a recent US Open read like a Pusan phone book – Bae, Jang, Kim, Lee, Pak, Park, Park, Shin.[32] Beyond the number of Koreans in New Zealand, and particularly those that play golf and other sports, it is worth reiterating a point made earlier about the importance of sport and leisure in the migration decision-making process.

Lydia Ko began playing golf as a five-year-old when her mother took her into the Pupuke Golf Club pro shop owned by Guy Wilson who coached her until December of 2013.[33] She first gained media attention in March 2005 when, as a seven-year-old, she became the youngest competitor in the New Zealand national amateur championships.[34] It was not long before she attained minor celebrity status in New Zealand. Indeed, her meteoric rise in the golf world and within the popular imaginaries of both New Zealand and Korea reads like a fairy tale. Having gained New Zealand citizenship at age 12, two years later, Ko became the youngest person at that point to win a professional golf tournament by winning the 2012 Bing Lee/Samsung Women's NSW Open on the ALPG Tour. At age 15, Ko became the youngest-ever winner of an LPGA Tour event – the 2012 CN Canadian Women's Open, with a score of 275 (thirteen under par). A year later she defended her Canadian championship shooting a 265 (fifteen under par) at the Royal Mayfair Club in Edmonton. Remarkably, Ko was the top-ranked amateur woman in the world for nearly two-and-a-half years before turning professional in late 2013. It is estimated that she had foregone up to $US 1 million in tournament earnings up to that point.[35] In keeping with New Zealand culture, the announcement of her decision to turn professional was handled in both an understated and humorous manner. In October 2013, she joined former New Zealand All Black rugby player Israel Dagg in a four-minute YouTube video. In the video, they play a round of golf with Dagg continually asking Ko when she is going to 'turn pro'. After making her final putt Dagg says 'It must be time now' to which Ko responds 'okay, I'll do it – turn pro'. She played her first professional tournament in November 2013 at the CME Group Titleholders tournament in Florida, tying for 21st place in her pro debut and then went on to hold the world number one ranking from February 2015 to June 2017. Some of her other achievements include (1) recording the lowest-ever closing round score in a women's major championship (the Evian Championship, 2015); and (2) in both 2014 and 2015 she was named in the EspnW Impact25 list of 25 athletes and influencers who have made the greatest impact for women in sports. Clearly, Lydia Ko had reached the pinnacle of the LPGA summit but it is also necessary to understand how she was located and defined with respect to her Korean, New Zealand and female identities particularly in relation to other overseas-based female Korean golf celebrities.

Locating Lydia Ko: 'Korean', 'of Korean Descent' or a 'Foreigner with Black Hair'?

It is important to state from the outset that throughout her career Lydia Ko has consistently identified as a Kiwi while acknowledging her 'Korean' roots. As such in order to understand Lydia Ko's status as a 'Kowi' whose celebrity spans two national identities, it is essential that she, or at least her public persona, is located within a wider transnational context. Thus, the status and success of other Korean golfers and celebrities are discussed and, in particular, how they are perceived, represented and categorized with respect to whether they are Korean citizens and residents, are Korean but live overseas, or are of Korean-descent and are either resident or non-resident. As illustrated, there are a number of factors related to how and why overseas Koreans negotiate, sometimes opportunistically, their national identity, and why there is increasing public scrutiny of their motives and intentions.

South Koreans are no longer surprised by the success of their golfers on the LPGA tour. Over the past three decades since the first victory in 1988 by Ok-hee Ku, a pioneering female Korean golfer, its women have won more than 200 championships. Not only can the nation boast of a long list of LPGA players yielding major titles (Inbee Park, Se Ri Pak, Jiyai Shin, etc.), South Korea has won the most trophies every year since 2015, and produced the most rookies of the year (14 out of 20) since Se Ri Pak's award in 1998. Perhaps due to their success on the world stage, South Korea may be the only country where women's golf is much more popular than men's.[36] Whether these phenomenal achievements are the result of dedicated support from family and strict training regimes,[37] or are a product of the LPGA's well-thought-out plans to expand into new markets combined with the global marketing strategies of transnational corporations such as Samsung,[38] the celebrated success continues to attract young, talented female Koreans into the sport. Thanks to the expansion of specialist television golf channels, South Koreans, whether dedicated golf fans or not, are well aware, if not proud, of the unrivalled success of their female golfers on the LPGA tour. Indeed, Korean golfers have now joined the ranks of K-pop and K-drama stars, with athletes being given an impressive amount of respect on the world stage.[39]

One important point to note is that, when counting the total number of wins or rookies of the year, Korean media does not limit its praise or claim to fame to only Korea resident nationals. As noted Korean migration to so-called advanced, Western countries (e.g. the USA, Canada, Australia, and New Zealand), and the strategic decision to seek training opportunities in countries where golf is more accessible, have expanded the footprint of Korean golf more globally. As a result, the LPGA tour now features a range of 'Koreans' coming from different countries with different backgrounds and identities. Although South Koreans would likely differ with respect to which players they perceive as genuine 'Koreans' there are some common representational categories evident in South Korean media. These include (1) where they were born; (2) where they were raised and educated; and, (3) their current nationality.[40] For example, Se Ri Pak, Inbee Park, and In-gee Chun are called *tojong* (토종, 土種) which means natives because they were born and raised in South Korea and they hold Korean citizenship.[41] However, if a player was born in South Korea and holds Korean citizenship, but was educated overseas, she might be classified as *yuhak-pa* (유학파, 留學派, overseas-educated) and here there are examples such as Grace Park and Amy Yang.[42] Finally, those who were born to Korean parents but hold a different national citizenship (Lydia Ko, Minjee Lee, and Michelle Wie) are categorized as being *hankuk-gye* (한국계, 韓國系, of Korean descent).[43]

As long as they hold Korean citizenship, the first two groups are generally accepted as Koreans no matter where they live. However, Korean-status seems more conditional for the last group. One important condition that the *hankuk-gye* needs to satisfy to be considered Korean seems to be their attitude towards the Korean nation and its culture – whether they maintain, understand or at least respect Korean things (e.g. trying to speak the Korean language, using their Korean name, etc.). Despite their clear Korean heritage but foreign nationality, it is their perceived deference to Korea that determines the degree to which they are accepted as 'Korean'. In other words, although every golfer of Korean descent is entitled to claim to be a Korean, whether the claim is accepted depends upon how they display their *Korean-ness*.[44] For example, Korean-American Christina Kim was branded as a traitor in Korea when she decided to represent the USA in the 2005 Solheim Cup especially given the fact that she painted the American flag on her cheeks.[45] The Korean public felt betrayed particularly because only one year earlier she was granted permission to represent South Korea at the Pinx Cup against Japan after a tearful appeal stating: 'I longed to represent Korea'.[46] Michelle Wie, who had once been celebrated as 'a daughter of Janghung', the place from where her father originated, was redefined as an 'ugly duckling' when it was discovered that she had permanently cancelled her Korean citizenship.[47] Thus, straddling dual national identities is considered opportunistic, and perceived as 'acting like a Korean or an American (or other nationality) as a matter of convenience'.[48]

The suspicions of overseas golfers of Korean descent are part of an emotional and institutional resistance towards a group that has been described as: 'foreigners with black hair' that has been growing since the 2000s. This term was originally invented to describe Koreans disguised as, or hiding behind, foreign investors to evade taxes or/and to manipulate stock prices.[49] In this usage, the term indicated black hair (Koreans) *in nature* and foreigners *in shape*. But having gone through a range of scandals involving overseas Koreans living in South Korea, the term was adapted to capture those who enjoy benefits (e.g. national health insurance) as Koreans, but avoid civic duties (e.g. military service) as foreigners – in other words, Koreans in appearance (black hair) but *de facto* foreigners in nationality.[50]

In the world of 'K-golf',[51] similarly, critical characterizations of 'Americans with black hair' emerged in relation to cases such as Christina Kim and Michelle Wie. Here, the perception was that these two female golfers were considered to have 'hinted at being Korean when strapped for sponsors' but then 'returning to being Americans after falling into disfavour'.[52] Unfortunately, it is within this context that Lydia Ko appeared on South Korea's sporting radar. After the alleged betrayals of previous 'foreigners with black hair' on and off the green, it is no surprise that South Koreans might have been bracing themselves for yet another episode of betrayal. Seong Sik Cho et al.'s analysis of online replies to K-golfers with foreign nationalities shows how Korean fans draw the line between Korean LPGA players and those of Korean descent.[53] Overall, their analysis showed that 40 percent of online comments accepted foreign-born golfers indicating that 'so-called players of Korean descent are of the same blood as us and are daughters of the Korean nation; conversely, 60 percent took a contrary view stating things such as, 'people of Korean descent are foreigners after all, and are not of our country'.[54] As one example of a person challenging the Korean status of foreign-born players, consider the following quotation:

> Here is another journalist who calls Korean descent players Koreans. (Their) parents have all emigrated, and then they are just of Korean descent, not Koreans. I tell you what – no Korean nationality, no Koreans. Hey, pathetic petty journalist, write properly.[55]

Given this context, there was no reason for South Koreans to become excited about yet another world-class female golfer of Korean descent particularly one from a small nation in the South Pacific. Admittedly, if Ko had attended Stanford or a comparable Ivy League University that Koreans respect, or if she had voluntarily and proudly promoted herself as a Korean, she may have gained more attention and acceptance. And, it was not just the Korean public that had reservations. Korean corporations were also increasingly hesitant about sponsoring foreign golfers of Korean descent. For example, one newspaper article with the subject line 'Lydia Ko, what to do with her nationality' points out that it is a gamble to sponsor golfers of Korean descent who could end up competing against Korean players.[56] Indeed, one company official in charge of golf-sponsorship confessed that 'it is a common belief that it would be better for us to sponsor pure foreign players rather than players of Korean descent, due to the negative public sentiment.[57] Consequently, corporate sponsors are more likely to sponsor Korean golfers or non-Korean foreign athletes to avoid any potential backlash from fans and consumers.

Amidst this background, Lydia Ko slowly emerged as an international sport celebrity at least within the world of women's golf. However, while there was some awareness of this rising golfing star in Korea, it was not until she was regularly seen on the LPGA tour alongside Korean golfers that the public took notice. Ultimately, Lydia Ko never really became a sport celebrity within Korea and there may be several reasons for this. Unlike other athletes or celebrities of Korean descent, while she certainly took pride in her Korean heritage she did not seek any favours from, nor did she try to explicitly align herself with Korea. Indeed, she regularly proclaimed herself a 'Kiwi'.[58] For example, at the 2016 Olympics in Rio, Ko represented New Zealand thereby becoming a direct competitor to Korean golfers.[59] Moreover, although she gained admission to Korea University in 2015, the news was not as highly publicized as one might expect. Indeed, what was publicized was the fact that she did not intend to attend classes in person choosing to pursue her professional golf career overseas while completing courses online. This resulted in some rather negative publicity. One golf journalist remarked that: 'it is almost like Korea University plans to award a degree to Lydia Ko regardless of her attendance'.[60] The journalist Hojun Sung regards Ko's case as setting a bad precedent:

> Of course many entertainers and sport stars have gained a degree without attendance… However, those celebrities did not take it for granted… Lydia Ko's entry could set a precedent and make way for so called celebrities to get the signboard of prestigious universities without much academic commitment.[61]

In summary, Lydia Ko, despite her exceptional international golfing success, is less of a celebrity within Korea and in fact may even be viewed negatively. In some respects, aside from her decision to pursue her education at Korea University, she could almost be considered a victim of context linked to both overseas Koreans who are perceived as more Korean and those who have opportunistically exploited the goodwill of the Korean public and system. As noted in the previous section, over the years there have been many overseas female Korean golfers on the LPGA tour with much thicker Korean blood and social capital, in terms of access to media and corporate sponsors compared to Lydia Ko. Consequently, there was little chance or perhaps desire for Ko to identify or capitalize on her Korean-ness. On the one hand, Lydia Ko's global success may have contributed to a popular myth of Korean ethnic superiority in golf. However, as someone of Korean descent as opposed to *tojong*, or even as a 'foreigner with black hair' Ko's public declaration of being a Kiwi tempered any questions of her loyalties, identity, and citizenship.[62] In short, Lydia Ko has, at least to date, never achieved the status of *celebrity* in Korea. It is important to note that this does not mean that her Korean heritage and connections are not acknowledged in South Korea; rather, it suggests that there are just fewer opportunities to amplify her Korean identity.

Lydia Ko's Self-Construction of Celebrity and National Identity

Within Aotearoa/New Zealand there is little doubt that Ko's identity is negotiated and contested but that she is overwhelmingly recognized and even celebrated as a New Zealander. Notably, inasmuch as she was described as a typical Kiwi kid in her early years, there are occasional references to the fact that she was born in Korea or is 'of Korean-descent'. For example, Ko has been described as a 'Kowi', a colloquial term that generally refers to Korean-New Zealanders. Moreover, given that New Zealand is only starting to emerge and view itself as a multicultural nation, high-profile celebrities such as Lydia Ko are often used to highlight a vision of the future: young, female, and more diverse. As Michael Burgess noted in 2011, 'Lydia Ko might not realize it, but she can play a pivotal role in New Zealand society. After emigrating from South Korea in 2003 and gaining New Zealand citizenship in 2009, the 15-year-old has become a poster child for multiculturalism in sport'.[63] Certainly, she has a strong connection with the Korean community in Auckland and, despite the fact that she lives, trains, and competes overseas for much of any given year the New Zealand media maintain a strong interest and provide regular updates on her performances. There are at least two reasons for this interest including (1) a general awareness and celebration of a Kiwi athlete succeeding on the world stage; and (2) particular attention from Sport New Zealand and Golf New Zealand given that Ko is an Olympian. With respect to the latter point Lydia Ko's golfing talent was recognized from a very early age and New Zealand Golf invested thousands of dollars in her training and development. This included sending her overseas to represent New Zealand in prestigious tournaments and events such as the LPGA and KLPGA major championships and Olympics. In Ko's case the investment paid major dividends. However, despite the best efforts of New Zealand Golf, many talented young Korean-born female golfers have, over the years, returned home to South

Korea. Sharon Ahn, who is better known as Shinae Ahn in Korea, is one famous example. She represented New Zealand in international tournaments, but eventually returned home to play under the Korean flag. Expressing the national body's concerns about losing stars like Ko, even though she had taken up New Zealand citizenship in 2009, NZ Golf operations manager Phil Aickinn noted that:

> We would not be thrilled about it. These days we work more closely with individuals and try to assess their commitment but we can't lock them in. Certainly the situation in the past was unfortunate – with a lot of funding put into individuals and then they were gone.[64]

From a New Zealand perspective, the stark reality of this issue emerged in 2014–2015 when, as discussed earlier, Lydia Ko was approached by, and eventually admitted to, Korea University. Prior to this many Kiwis expected Ko to study at an American university, and more specifically, Stanford University, following in the footsteps of her idol, Michelle Wie. However, clues about why she selected a Korean over an American university emerged in a number of interviews. For example, in one, Ko noted the enormous challenge of trying to pursue an academic degree while playing professional golf, something she witnessed in the case of Michelle Wie. Ko realized that a university in the USA would likely require equal commitment to both academics and golf which could impact on her sporting performance. Ultimately, Lydia Ko accepted a place in the Department of Psychology at Korea University for a couple of reasons: (1) she could apply for admission through a special screening process for overseas Korean nationals that does not require completion of the national college entrance exam; and (2) Korea University would allow her to complete the majority of her classes online thus facilitating her ability to pursue her golf career. While this decision was noted in New Zealand media, there was no evidence of critique related to Ko studying by distance like that described earlier within Korea. The challenge of combining university study with a professional golf career is one example of how Lydia Ko negotiated her identity in relation to her educational and career goals.

More recently, there have been a range of controversies associated with Lydia Ko reported in the media, many of which have been framed in relation to her slump in performance. For example, there has been considerable New Zealand media coverage about the fact that she has used a number of different caddies over the past few years. While this is not necessarily unusual in the world of professional golf, the manner in which changes were made certainly attracted attention. For example, in 2018, Ko fired both her coach Gary Gilchrist and her caddie, Peter Godfrey, just prior to the Australian Open, with no warning or explanation. Although she tried to remain positive and upbeat during her slump there were clearly changes afoot. In 2019, Ko took to social media to announce her new 'bad ass' attitude and image. Sharing photos on Instagram, Ko is shown with blonde hair, working out in a gym and there is also an image of her wearing a PXG motor racing helmet – part of her sponsorship from PXG whose new golf drivers use hot rod technology. She explicitly states: 'By the way this is me trying to bring out the badass in me'.[65] In many ways Ko's change in attitude and appearance may simply signal a more mature outlook on life and career as a 21-year old. At the same time, and highlighting the gender dimension of her celebrity identity, her new appearance became the topic of a media controversy. In April 2019, at the ANA Inspiration tournament, American golfing great Juli Inkster was interviewed by former tour pro and now Golf Channel broadcaster, Karen Stupples. During the interview Inkster was asked about Lydia Ko's new look to which she replied: 'looks like she needs to go to the buffet counter a little bit'. In turn, Stupples says: 'We all want to see five more pounds on Lydia'.[66] Perhaps not surprisingly Lydia Ko fans took to social media to share their concerns about what they perceived as 'body shaming'. One respondent stated, 'I think it's awful that [Juli Inkster] is allowed to talk about [Lydia Ko] and her weight live on air. To say that she should hit up a buffet and put on 5 pounds sets the lpga [and] their #driveon message way back'. Another respondent stated: 'No wonder some women have image issues'.[67] Such critiques reveal the pervasive body image surveillance in society, particularly for female celebrities. While it is beyond the scope of this study to advance this issue, analysis of the intersection of Lydia Ko's national, racial and gender identity in relation to contemporary body politics within a transnational framework is certainly worthy of future study.

Although Ko has struggled to maintain a number one ranking over the past two years, it is important to note some of her recent successes. In 2016, she won a silver medal for New Zealand at the Rio Olympics which lead to her winning New Zealand's highest sporting honour: the Halberg Supreme award and she has three times been named sportswoman of the year. Most recently, Lydia Ko became one of the youngest persons to become a Member of the Order of New Zealand (MNZM) in the 2018 New Year's Honours. Commenting after the MNZM announcement Ko stated: 'It is a huge honour for me. I think every moment is special in its own way, and this recognition in particular is very humbling.... I am grateful to be recognized alongside many talented, inspiring New Zealanders, and those who make New Zealand a better country for all of us Kiwis'.[68] Clearly, in this instance Lydia Ko identifies herself as a New Zealander. However, her regular acknowledgement of her Korean descent, combined with her sport celebrity status, renders Ko an enduring subject of media and public discourses that serve to construct and contest her Kiwi and Korean identity within a transnational context.

Globalization, Celebrity, and Citizenship in an Increasingly Asia-Centric World

This study set out to examine Asian sport celebrity within the context of globalization, migration, citizenship and national identity. Focusing on female golf phenomenon Lydia Ko, the analysis located her celebrity and national identity between her place of birth – Korea and her place of citizenship – New Zealand. Analysis reveals that several intersecting factors influenced Ko's celebrity and identity construction including changes in New Zealand immigration policy, changes in Korean state policy towards overseas nationals, negatively viewed attitudes and behaviours of previous foreign-born celebrities of Korean-descent and Ko's self-proclamations regarding her national identity. Notably, negatively perceived behaviours on the part of other foreign-born Korean celebrities directly or indirectly impacted on how Lydia Ko may have been identified by Korean society with respect to her 'Korean-ness'. At the same time, Ko is not a clear case of contested dual national identities, where either two nations claim ownership of an athlete in order to bask in their reflected glory, or where a celebrity athlete attempts to gain favours in another country by strategically promoting their dual national links. Rather, the case of Lydia Ko demonstrates how wider social policies associated with immigration can play an important role in how citizens and quasi-citizens both interact and are defined and represented.

With global migration set to increase dramatically over the next few decades, issues of national identity and citizenship will remain fundamental points of discussion and debate. The issue is especially relevant with respect to the sizeable populations across Asia and the economic, political and military influence of China in particular. For both sport studies and celebrity studies scholars, this will be fertile ground to explore the nature, significance, and uniqueness of transnational spaces and people. In particular, it will be important to interrogate the concept of flexible citizenship with respect to the wider political-economic and sociocultural forces and mechanisms that define, enable and/or constrain statuses such as dual citizenship. As one particular insight into this issue, consider the cultural studies scholar Michael Giardina's observations:

> Concurrent with this repositioning, flexible citizens are more concerned with global market conditions than traditional meanings of citizenship in a particular nation. That is to say, traditional notions of citizenship no longer carry the sort of passionate attachment one expects to be associated with the idea of national citizenship. Instead, transnational celebrities have become more flexible with respect to the formalities of their citizenship: they have separated their citizenship from their culture, where the former is flexible and amorphous and the latter is stable and tied to one's country of origin.[69]

As this exploration of Ko's celebrity demonstrates, sport is a strategic site to explore the veracity and implications of Giardina's reflections. As both the world population and migration levels continue to rise, debates about culture, identity and citizenship will become increasingly important and complex. Indeed, if predictions such as Parag Khanna's *The Future is Asian* are correct, existing discussions about citizenship will need to be reconceptualized as the world shifts from a Euro-centric to an Asia-centric world.[70] We hope this essay provides insights that will inform future studies of the intersection of globalization, migration, citizenship, and sport.

Notes

1. *World Migration Report 2018* (Geneva: Switzerland: International Organization for Migration, 2017).
2. Peter Nyers, 'Introduction: Why Citizenship Studies', *Citizenship Studies* 11, no. 1 (2007): 3.
3. See David L. Andrews and Steven J. Jackson, eds., *Sport Stars: The Politics of Sporting Celebrity* (London: Routledge, 2001); Steven J. Jackson, 'Gretzky, Crisis & Canadian Identity in 1988: Rearticulating the Americanization of Culture Debate', *Sociology of Sport Journal* 11, no. 4 (1994): 428–46; Steven J. Jackson, 'A Twist of Race: Ben Johnson and the Canadian Crisis of Racial and National Identity', *Sociology of Sport Journal* 15 (1998): 21–40; Steven J. Jackson, 'Life in the (Mediated) Faust Lane: Ben Johnson, National

Affect and the 1988 Crisis of Canadian Identity', *International Review for the Sociology of Sport* 33, no. 3 (1998): 227–38; Steven J. Jackson, 'Exorcising the Ghost: Donovan Bailey, Ben Johnson and the Politics of Canadian Identity', *Media, Culture and Society* 26, no. 1 (2004): 121–41; Rachael Miyung Joo, *Transnational Sport: Gender, Media, and Global Korea* (Durham, NC: Duke University Press, 2012); Eunha Koh and Woo Young Lee, 'The Condition of Korean Sport Celebrityhood: Se Ri Pak and Corporate Nationalism', *Journal of Korean Sociology of Sport* 17, no. 1 (2004): 121–37. Haozhou Pu, Joshua I. Newman, and Michael D. Giardina, 'Flying Solo: Globalization, Neoliberal Individualism, and the Contested Celebrity of Li Na' *Communication and Sport* 7, no. 1 (2019): 23–45; Barry Smart, *The Sport Star: Modern Sport and the Cultural Economy of Sporting Celebrity* (London: Sage, 2005); Lawrence Wenner, *Fallen Sport Heroes, Media and Celebrity Culture* (New York: Peter Lang, 2013); Garry Whannel, *Media Sport Stars: Masculinities and Moralities* (London: Routledge, 2002).
4. Steven J. Jackson and David L. Andrews, eds., *Sport, Culture and Advertising: Identities, Commodities and the Politics of Representation* (London: Routledge, 2005).
5. Allen Guttmann, *The Erotic in Sport* (New York: Columbia University Press, 1996).
6. Whannel, *Media Sport Stars*.
7. David Rowe, 'The Global Love-match: Sport and Television', *Media, Culture and Society* 18, no. 4 (1996): 565–82.
8. Jackson and Andrews, *Sport, Culture and Advertising*.
9. Steven J. Jackson and David L. Andrews, 'Olympic Celebrity: Introduction', *Celebrity Studies* 3, no. 3 (2012): 263–9.
10. Steven J. Jackson, 'The Contested Terrain of Sport Diplomacy in a Globalising World', *International Area Studies Review* 16, no. 3 (2013): 275–85; Steven J. Jackson and Stephen Haigh, 'Between and Beyond Politics: Sport and Foreign Policy in a Globalising World', *Sport in Society* 11, no. 4 (2008): 349–58.
11. Aihwa Ong, *Flexible Citizenship: The Cultural Politics of Transnationality* (Durham, NC: Duke University Press, 1999).
12. Douglas Grbic, 'Social and Cultural Meanings of Tolerance: Immigration, Incorporation and Identity in Aotearoa, New Zealand', *Journal of Ethnic and Migration Studies* 36, no. 1 (2010): 126.
13. Malcolm McKinnon, *Immigrants and Citizens: New Zealanders and Asian Immigration in Historical Context* (Wellington: Institute of Policy Studies, Victoria University of Wellington, 1996). Manying Ip, 'Chinese New Zealanders: Old Settlers and new Immigrants', in *Immigration and National Identity in New Zealand: One People, Two Peoples, Many Peoples?* ed. Stuart W. Greif (Palmerston North: Dunmore Press, 1995), 161–99; Andrew Trlin, 'Change and Continuity: New Zealand's Immigration Policy in the late 1980s', in *New Zealand and International Migration: A Digest and Bibliography Number 2*, ed. Andrew Trilin and Paul Spoonley (Palmerston North: Department of Sociology, Massey University, 1992), 1–28.
14. Statistics New Zealand, 'Major Ethnic Groups in New Zealand', https://www.stats.govt.nz/infographics/major-ethnic-groups-in-new-zealand (accessed May 1, 2019).
15. Francis L. Collins, 'Making Asian Students, Making Students Asian: The Racialisation of Export Education in Auckland, New Zealand', *Asia Pacific Viewpoint* 47, no. 2 (2006), 217–34.
16. Andrew Butcher. 'Well, They're Very Good Citizens: New Zealanders' Perceptions of Asia', *Sites: A Journal of Social Anthropology and Cultural Studies. Special Issue: Asia and Aotearoa* 5, no. 2 (2008): 5–30.
17. Statistics New Zealand, 'Major Ethnic Groups in New Zealand', https://www.stats.govt.nz/infographics/major-ethnic-groups-in-new-zealand (accessed May 1, 2019).
18. Ik Young Chang, Steven J. Jackson, and Mike P. Sam, 'Risk Society, Anxiety and Exit: A Case Study of South Korean Migration Decision-making', *Asian and Pacific Migration Journal* 26, no. 3 (2017): 328–51.

19. Suzana Chang, Carolyn Morris, and Richard Vokes, *Korean Migrant Families in Christchurch: Expectations and Experiences* (Wellington: Families Commission, 2006); Inbom Choi, 'Korean Diaspora in the Making: Its Current Status and Impact on the Korean Economy, in *The Korean Diaspora in the World Economy*, ed. Fred C. Bergsten and Inbom Choi (Washington, DC: Institute for International Economics, 2003), 9–30.
20. Chang, Morris, and Vokes, *Korean Migrant Families in Christchurch*.
21. Insoo Han et al., *A History of Koreans in New Zealand* (Auckland, New Zealand: Publishing Committee, 2007).
22. Chang Morris and Vokes, *Korean Migrant Families in Christchurch*.
23. Paul Du Gay, Jessica Evans and Peter Redman, *Identity: A Reader* (London: Sage, 2000).
24. Monika Stodolska, and Konstantinos Alexandris, 'The Role of Recreational Sport in the Adaptation of First Generation Immigrants in the United States', *Journal of Leisure Research* 36, no. 3 (2004): 379–413.
25. Young-Sook Lee and Daniel C. Funk, 'Recreational Sport Participation in Migrants' Acculturation', *Managing Leisure* 16, (2011): 1–16.
26. Monika Stodolska, 'Changes in Leisure Participation Patterns after Immigration', *Leisure Sciences* 22, no.1 (2000): 39–63; Stodolska and Alexandris, 'The Role of Recreational Sport', 379–413. Monika Stodolska and Carla Almeida Santos, 'Transnationalism and Leisure: Mexican Temporary Migrants in the U.S.', *Journal of Leisure Research* 38, no. 2 (2006): 143–67; Monika Stodolska and Jouyeon Yi, 'Impacts of Immigration on Ethnic Identity and Leisure Behaviour of Adolescent Immigrants from Korea, Mexico and Poland', *Journal of Leisure Research* 35, no. 1 (2003): 49–79.
27. Ik Young Chang, 'Exploring the Possibility of Leisure Sports as a Consideration in the Process of Lifestyle Migration Decision Making: A Case of South Korean Immigrants in New Zealand', *Korean Journal of Sociology of Sport* 28, no.1 (2015): 89–107.
28. Ibid.
29. John B. Thompson, *The Media and Modernity: A Social Theory of the Media* (Cambridge: Polity Press, 1995).
30. 'Lydia Ko's Junior Golf Clinic', *Korea Post*, December 2, 2014, https://www.nzkoreapost.com/bbs/board.php?bo_table=news_all&wr_id=13935 (accessed May 2, 2019).
31. Andrew Butcher and George Wieland, 'God and Golf: Koreans in New Zealand', *New Zealand Journal of Asian Studies* 15, no. 2 (2013): 57–77.
32. Michael Burgess, 'Golf: A Question of Loyal-tee', *New Zealand Herald*, March 13, 2011, https://www.nzherald.co.nz/sport/news/article.cfm?c_id=4&objectid=10712032, accessed May 25, 2019.
33. 'Practice Certainly Makes Lydia Perfect, *Dominion Post*, September 1, 2012, http://www.stuff.co.nz/dominion-post/sport/7591195/Practice-certainly-makes-Lydia-perfect (accessed December 31, 2012).
34. Michael Donaldson, *Lydia Ko: Portrait of a Teen Golfing Sensation* (Auckland: Penguin, 2016).
35. 'Golf: Lydia Ko Goes Professional – Finally', *New Zealand Herald*, October 23, 2013, http://www.nzherald.co.nz/sport/news/article.cfm?c_id=4&objectid=11144869 (accessed March 9, 2019).
36. Randall Mell, '"Korean KiWi" Ko Ready to Represent New Zealand in Olympics', *NBC Sports*, February 10, 2016, https://www.golfchannel.com/article/golf-central-blog/proud-korean-kiwi-ko-will-play-olympics-n-zealand (accessed March 30, 2019).
37. Hojun Sung, Young-A Yang, and Kisung Dennis Kwon, 'Female Korean Golfers in the LPGA Tour: Positive and Negative Outcomes, *Asian Journal of Women's Studies* 24 no. 1 (2018): 106–27.
38. Toby Miller, David Rowe, Jim McKay and Geoffrey Lawrence, 'The Over-production of US Sports and the New International Division of Cultural Labor', *International Review for the Sociology of Sport* 38, no. 4 (2003): 427–40; Sun-Yong Kwon and Bang-Chool Kim, 'Globalizing LPGA, the International Division of Sports Labor, and Women's Golf in Korea', *Korean Journal of Sport Science* 17, no. 1, (2006): 95–108.

39. Heather Chen, 'K-Golf: South Korea's Female Golfing Phenomenon', *BBC News*, July 23, 2017, https://www.bbc.com/news/world-asia-40628058 (accessed March 23, 2019).
40. Seong-Sik Cho, Na-Mi Kim, and Wan-Young Lee, 'A Study on the Manifestation of Fans' Pure Blood Identity in the Reports of 'Korean (decent)' LPGA players of Online Newspaper', *Korea Journal of Sports Science* 26, no. 1 (2017): 131–41. Won Me Lee and Hyun Jung, 'The Identity and Appellation of Korean LPGA Athletes in Newspaper', *Korean Journal of Physical Education* 55, no. 1 (2016): 143–52.
41. Hojun Sung, 'PGA, LPGA Korean Players with Foreign Nationalities in Full Blast: Allies or Foes? *Jung-Ang Sunday*, March 2, 2008, https://news.joins.com/article/3059612 (accessed March 25, 2019).
42. Hojun Sung, 'Samsung Supports Yang Hui-Young, Studying Abroad in Australia', *JTBC Golf*, April 19, 2006, http://jtbcgolf.joins.com/news/news_view.asp?ns1=12875&page=&news_type=15&mode=&txt_search=&a12=a2 (accessed March 9, 2019).
43. Yonhap, 'Australian Gyopo Lee Minji Won LA Open Championship', *MK*, April 29, 2019, https://www.mk.co.kr/news/sports/view/2019/04/271379/ (accessed March 19, 2019).
44. Sang-Woo Nam, 'National Identity of 'Wie Sung-Mi' and 'Michelle Wie': Media Discourse on the Rise and Fall of Sports Celebrity', *Korean Journal of Sociology of Sport* 28, no. 2 (2015): 111–35.
45. Jiho Yoo, 'Kim Chorong? No, Christina Kim! American Girl's Bitter Change of Heart', *Jung-Ang Sunday*, December 7, 2008, https://news.joins.com/article/3409554 (accessed March 6, 2019).
46. Ibid
47. Sang-Woo Nam, 'National Identity of 'Wie Sung-Mi' and 'Michelle Wie': Media Discourse on the Rise and Fall of Sports Celebrity'.
48. Iksoo Shin, 'Half Korean, Half American Golfers', *MK*, July 5, 2004, https://www.mk.co.kr/news/home/view/2004/07/245662/ (accessed March 3, 2019).
49. 'Problems with "Foreign Nationality Koreans"', *The Dong-A Ilbo*, October 6, 2015, http://www.donga.com/en/List/article/all/20151006/411575/1/Problems-with-foreign-nationality-Koreans (accessed March 3, 2019).
50. Hyunjung Lee, 'Lax Nationality Act and Healthcare Administration – Foreigners with Black Hair Exploiting Health Insurance', *Seoul Shinmun*, February 19, 2019, https://www.seoul.co.kr/news/newsView.php?id=20190219017018-csidxd82d974cdbe8bc291e98872a8e6ba70 (accessed March 9, 2019).
51. Heather Chen, 'K-Golf: South Korea's Female Golfing Phenomenon', *BBC News*, July 23, 2017, https://www.bbc.com/news/world-asia-40628058 (accessed March 23, 2019).
52. Iksoo Shin, 'Half Korean, Half American Golfers', *MK*, July 5, 2004, https://www.mk.co.kr/news/home/view/2004/07/245662/ (accessed March 3, 2019).
53. Seong-Sik Cho, Na-Mi Kim, and Wan-Young Lee, 'A Study on the Manifestation of Fans' Pure Blood Identity', 131–41.
54. Ibid., 137.
55. Ibid.
56. Hojun Sung, 'Lydia Ko, What to Do with Her Nationality', *JTBC Golf*, November 2, 2013, http://jtbcgolf.joins.com/news/news_view.asp?ns1=23179 (accessed March 14, 2019).
57. Ibid.
58. Ibid
59. Randall Mell, "Korean KiWi' Ko Ready to Represent New Zealand in Olympics', *NBC Sports*, February 10, 2016, https://www.golfchannel.com/article/golf-central-blog/proud-korean-kiwi-ko-will-play-olympics-n-zealand (accessed March 30, 2019).
60. Hojun Sung, 'Korea University Accepting Lydia Ko – Is a Star All That Matters?' *JTBC Golf*, December 1, 2014, http://jtbcgolf.joins.com/news/news_view.asp?ns1=25164 (accessed March 14, 2019).
61. Ibid

62. Eunha Koh and Woo Young Lee, 'The Condition of Korean Sport Celebrityhood: Se Ri Pak and Corporate Nationalism', *Journal of Korean Sociology of Sport* 17, no. 1 (2004): 121–37.
63. Michael Burgess, 'Golf: A Question of Loyal-tee'.
64. Cited, Ibid.
65. Lydia Ko Sharpens up her 'Badass' Image, *Stuff*, January 29, 2019, https://www.stuff.co.nz/sport/golf/110226930/lydia-ko-sharpens-up-her-badass-image (accessed May 12, 2019).
66. 'Golf: Fans Lash out on Social Media after Golfing Great Body Shames Lydia Ko, *New Zealand Herald*, April 6, 2019, https://www.nzherald.co.nz/sport/news/article.cfm?c_id=4&objectid=12219936 (accessed May 20, 2019).
67. Ibid.
68. Kevin Norquay, 'At 21, Golf Supremo Lydia Ko is Humbled to be on the New Year's Honours List, *Stuff*, December 31, 2018, https://www.stuff.co.nz/sport/golf/109586727/at-21-golf-supremo-lydia-ko-is-humbled-to-be-on-the-new-years-honours-list (accessed May 22, 2019).
69. Michael D. Giardina, 'Global Hingis: Flexible Citizenship and the Transnational Celebrity', in *Sport Stars: The Cult of Sporting Celebrity*, ed. David L. Andrews and Steven J. Jackson, (London: Routledge, 2002), 211–27.
70. Parag Khanna, *The Future is Asian* (New York Simon & Schuster, 2019).

Disclosure Statement

No potential conflict of interest was reported by the authors.

Reading Tiffany Chin: The Birth of the Oriental Female Skater on White Ice

Jae Chul Seo, Robert Turick and Daehwan Kim

ABSTRACT
Tiffany Chin's emergence in figure skating, and the ways in which she was depicted by the media, can be understood as the birth of the oriental female skater on White ice. Figure skating has historically been viewed as a White sport, so Chin's success in that space created an opportunity for future Asian American skaters. To that end, the media's coverage of Chin offers insight into how the 'differences' of Asian American female skaters were initially registered, constructed, and communicated in a racialized and gendered way. This claim is supported through an understanding of how the background and history of American women's figure skating, the sport's traditional alignment with Whiteness, and a critical reading the media narratives surrounding Chin, combine to represent an American view that framed this Chin's successes as the birth of the oriental female skater.

Tiffany Chin was the first Asian American female skater to compete on a team representing the United States in a world championship or Olympic event. Chin won the 1981 World Junior Championships and made her senior debut at the U.S. Championships in the same year. Initially, after the media put her in the spotlight, she demonstrated her potential and established herself as an acknowledged leader among U.S. female skaters by placing fifth at the 1982 U.S. Championships, third in 1983, and second in 1984. Her successes earned her an invite onto the national team for the 1984 Winter Olympics, where Chin participated in the games as the youngest member at the age of sixteen. The following year, she won gold at the U.S. Championships and also earned a bronze medal at the World Championships. She never again performed as well as she had during the 1984–1985 competition seasons, something that was attributed to her troubling growth spurt and injuries. Chin qualified for, and was supposed to compete in, the 1988 Winter Olympics, but instead decided to retire and pursue a career in professional skating.

To that end, one might argue that the presence of Chin on ice, as well as the media narratives that attempted to cover and explain her success, can be understood as the birth of the oriental, female skater. More precisely, analyzing the media's narratives of Chin offer insight into how the 'differences' of Asian American female skaters were initially registered, constructed, and communicated in a racialized and gendered way. In support of this claim, this paper is structured according to three important topics: (1) a narrative of the history of American women's figure skating, (2) an account of media narratives of Chin, and (3) an interpretation that brings these two together and situates them in a historical context as the birth of the Asian American female skater.

The first section draws on written histories of the Winter Olympics and figure skating with a particular focus on Whiteness. We discuss the notion of the 'White American princess skater' as a way of making visible how the racialized and gendered aesthetics of Whiteness have become the dominant and invisible norm in the sport. In the second section, Mary McDonald and Susan Birrell's Reading Sport Critically Project method is utilized to detail the U.S. media narratives of Tiffany Chin, focussing on the ways in which those narratives described and portrayed her individual skating style, personal character, age/youthfulness, and her family.[1] To ground our interpretation of these narratives, in the final part of that section we lay out some significant contextual matters. In the third section, we situate the representation of Chin within the particular trajectory of White women figure skaters in the U.S. We argue that Chin signifies the birth of the oriental female skater by way of (1) the multi-cultural turn, and (2) oriental styles of representation, both of which emerged, were broadly current, and somehow established as a convention in 1980s U.S. popular culture.

Figure Skating as a Site of Whiteness

Whiteness refers to racial privilege, a standpoint from which Whites view themselves, others, and society, as well as a set of unmarked and unnamed cultural practices.[2] This strategic naming is a starting point for deconstructing the power of Whiteness, and it serve as a way to make it visible. According to Richard Dyer, 'as long as race is something only applied to non-White people, as long as White people are not racially seen and named [White or Whiteness] functions as a human norm'.[3] Thus, Whiteness should not be taken to refer to a set of certain natural characteristics possessed by a given ethnic group, but rather, as a social product constructed through various interrelations of power.

The ability to claim membership in or pass as White gives an individual access to racial privilege. This privilege includes the ability to receive favourable treatment and be noted as sophisticated, a distinction that will be discussed later in greater detail. Thus, as John Gabriel argues, Whiteness is a constellation of power, ideology, and/or space deployed by 'a set of discursive techniques... in the context of... cultural representation and instructional materialization'.[4] Taking this perspective, several scholars have examined the power of Whiteness, arguing that its power lies in its ability to render itself normal, invisible, unspoken, natural, universal, and privileged in many other ways that are not immediately obvious.[5]

In sport studies scholarship, critical studies of Whiteness emerged in the mid-2000s when some scholars began to seriously discuss it as a key concept for understanding social and racial relations, as well as cultural processes in the sporting world. As Stuart Hall reminds us, sport is a contested racial terrain.[6] Stated another way, it is not only a political site of struggle and resistance for athletes and People of Color, but it is also a culturally privileged site in which Whiteness as subjectivity is reproduced and reaffirmed in a particular way. Working from that perspective, over the past two decades, sport scholars have offered theoretical and methodological suggestions for studying Whiteness in sport.[7] These include works that discuss how Whiteness is infused in sport media texts on athletes and sporting events;[8] how particular sports have been constructed as racialized spaces or institutions that invisibly naturalize or universalize White ways of understanding and participating in sports;[9] and how Whiteness is entangled with other cultural practices and structures such as the polity, leisure, media, and others.[10]

In the context of Whiteness studies becoming more prevalent in sport studies, several scholars have examined the Winter Olympics and other winter sports as sites for studying Whiteness. As David Rowe notes, 'the [Olympics] Games were, in the first instance, Occidental'.[11] Ben Carrington also argues that the nature of modern sports has produced 'a homosocial space for the projection of White masculinist fantasies of domination, control and desire for the racialized "Other"'.[12] Furthermore, some sport historians, after thoroughly re-reading the writings of Pierre de Coubertin, have discussed the historical foundations of the Games and how the philosophy of Coubertin's Olympism is saturated with European ideas of racial humanism and colonial modernity.[13]

In his other writings, Coubertin highlighted how the superiority of White Europeans is clearly expressed in opposition to the inferiority of primitive and uncivilized peoples in Africa and to a lesser extent Asia. 'The Yellow men,' he writes in another essay titled *An Olympiad in the Far East*:

> ...seem to us to be admirably prepared to benefit from the athletic crusade that is taking shape. They are ready individually and collectively. They are ready individually because endurance, tenacity, patience, racial flexibility, the habit of self-mastery, of keeping silent, and of hiding pain and effort have shaped their bodies most effectively... For a while still, clearly, athletic Asia will grow and become strong where it is. Yet it is quite probable that contacts with the West will be made and, at Berlin in 1916, the Yellow teams will be able to show what they can do.[14]

Coubertin's ideas about race resonant across a few different sociological areas. The first would be social Darwinism in his belief that the White race is destined to take a leading role as the civilizing force in a global sporting world, while the Asian race is inherently inferior and might possibly be developed under White western paternalistic guidance. The second would be how Coubertin's discussion of Asia's growth fits within unilineal evolutionism, in that he highlights how they are moving from a primitive and uncivilized people to a more sophisticated society.

Scholars have also examined additional winter sports as sites for studying Whiteness. For instance, C. Richard King argued that the Olympic Games matter for

White power groups because they can function to reaffirm 'Whiteness as a source of pride, marker of civilization, and expression of naturalized superiority.'[15] Anthony Harrison also analyzed racial discourses circulating in the recreational communities of downhill skiing, and concluded that the sport is predominantly a social space for White people, as everyday racism works to restrict the participation and representation of Black skiers.[16] In addition, according to Kelly Poniatowski and Erin Whiteside, television commentaries of the Olympics represent White hockey players as 'having exceptional physical bodies, intellectual aptitude, and moral righteousness',[17] thus valorizing White heroism, morality, and privilege. Ann Travers explored women's ski jumping as an exclusionary site in which three key mechanisms of power, 'sex segregation, Whiteness, and class privilege', operated silently and unacknowledged.[18] She also noted that, like these other winter sports, figure skating is widely perceived as a White sport.

In the mid-1980s, when Tiffany Chin competed, there were not many non-White skaters in women's figure skating. The fact that few non-Whites were competing supports the notion that the sport was constructed as, and maintained to be, a site of Whiteness. There were, however, two non-White skaters in women's figure skating at the time when Chin competed. First, there was an African American female skater, Debi Thomas, who won a silver medal at the 1988 Olympics. Feminist scholars have argued that the media favoured the gold medal recipient, a White woman, over Thomas in terms of skating style. To be more specific, the media portrayed the White skater as an artist whereas her contemporary, Debi Tomas, was characterized as more of an athlete. Second, there was an Asian skater, Midori Ito, and she won the 1989 World Championships and the silver at the 1992 Olympics. The media portrayed Ito as a kind of Japanese threat, which mirrored concerns some had of a potential Japanese economic threat.[19]

This depiction of non-White athletes reflected a Euro-American centric trend in the sport in terms of at least three points: participants and organizers of the games had been predominantly White Europeans and Americans, the athletic and aesthetic characteristics of sport were largely drawn on European ideals of rationality and gentility, and the majority of the international events had been staged in industrialized countries located in Europe and North America.[20] The crucial point beyond these descriptive patterns is that figure skating matters to Whiteness. It has been a racially exclusionary site, space, and/or institution that is saturated with White cultural and physical supremacy. Ellyn Kestnbaum, noted that cultural meanings of figure skating 'have been shaped by the social practices and values of its founders, that is, primarily northern Europeans and North Americans of European ancestry from the upper-and upper-middle social/financial strata.'[21]

Along with these recognitions, a small number of scholars have made visible some particular aspects of Whiteness in women's figure skating. Elizabeth Krause argued that the media represented Tonya Harding as 'White trash' and that this construction illustrated the way in which the emphasized femininity of Whiteness is unmarked and reaffirmed through the marking of a different kind, Tonya's *flawed* Whiteness.[22] Tonya's and others that fall under the 'White trash' label, faults hurt the pure image associated with both her White identity and the sport of figure skating. For a sport that values purity and sophistication – figure skating is typically viewed as a sport reserved for the upper class – Tonya's actions damaged the pre-established norms associated with that space. Krause argued that those norms privileged certain identities (e.g. Whiteness and high-class), which had to become hierarchical because of her. This creation of Whiteness hierarchies allowed for Whites to place Tonya outside of 'proper' Whiteness.

In alignment with fitting the 'proper' ideal, in her ethnographic fieldwork on the Canadian site of amateur women's figure skating, Karen McGarry argued that Caucasian skaters such as Jennifer Robinson and Elizabeth Manley were viewed as a Canadian ideal of the feminine, while skaters of colour like Midori Ito and Surya Bonaly were valued for their exotic style while also being considered a threat to White femininity.[23] McGarry thus highlighted the hegemonic status of what she called 'a racialized aesthetics of Whiteness' as the dominant norm that functions in the production of gendered identities of the Canadian nation.[24] In part, this norm is created because, as McGarry opined, the majority of coaches, officials, and judges are trained within a particular 'white aesthetic' that privileges White, Euro-Canadian aesthetics as being pure, luminous, and beautiful. Lastly, she noted that skaters learn at an early age that aesthetics, demeanor, and personal appearance are key to one's success. Thus, they may feel pressured to conform to the White aesthetic, since nonconformity will not be rewarded.

In such works as these, figure skating has been recognized as a cultural site for promoting particular hegemonic ideals of White emphasized femininity. It is to this literature that we intend to make the 'racialized aesthetics of Whiteness' in women's figure skating historically visible, and begin by tracing a brief trajectory of media portrayals of some great American female skaters.

The Brief Trajectory of a White Princess Skater

Figure skating is one of a number of gendered aesthetic sports that are commonly judged as feminine. Although, as Gary Smith wrote, 'a splendid athletic performance rivals any great work of art',[25] sports have been predominantly constructed within a masculine naturalist aestheticism, with various aesthetic ideas, beliefs, and understandings of sports having also been gendered. This gendered perception of sport is not explained by biology, but is historically contingent, at least in the case of figure skating. As Mary Adams recently demonstrated, the sport evolved from being the almost exclusive pastime of upper-class men to becoming feminine.[26]

Essentially, from its earliest organization and formalization that figure skating was arguably a racialized site, both before and after it was feminized. Originally invented by and for upper-class gentlemen as a leisure activity, Adams writes that the sport was initially a kind of White masculine imperial project:

> The specific upper-class masculinity that shaped nineteenth-century English figure skating stemmed from a racialized world view that saw elegant activities like skating as symbols of 'civilized society,' an idealized community of interests that was seen as the exclusive domain of privileged White Europeans.[27]

In the late nineteenth century, when sport more generally increased in popularity as part of an overall expansion of leisure activities, women took to figure skating in local clubs. From there, the sport developed as a kind of gender-neutral activity with men and women skating together on relatively equal terms – the technical dimensions were no different and in some events they were allowed to compete against each other. This relative gender balance was broken in the 1930s and 1940s as figure skating came to be viewed as a feminine sport.

It was Sonja Henie's popularity and prominence that served as the most important factor contributing to the feminization of the sport.[28] She won Olympic gold medals in the 1928, 1932, and 1936 Winter Olympic Games, and ten consecutive World Championships from 1927 to 1936. Described as the 'Kewpie Doll',[29] Henie was a major force in figure skating, responsible for technical advances as well as developing a unique choreography combining athleticism, artistry, musicality, and balletic movements. She also brought stylistic advances to the sport, such as short skirts, White boots, and other fashionable accessories. After the 1936 Olympics, Henie retired from the sport, moved to the United States, and transformed herself into a film star in Hollywood. Her attractive imagery of youth and cuteness, combined with her amazing record of victories, transferred well onto the screen, and her films introduced figure skating as a popular form of entertainment to a large public.

Thus, Henie is an important historical agent figure in what may be called the birth of the White female skater and the emergence of a hegemonic process that emphasized the White femininity of the sport. Bettina Fabos stated that, 'The princess metaphor evolved out of 80 years of mass media coverage of women Olympic skaters.'[30] Adams also cited an excellent example of the media texts that employed the princess metaphor. A 1931 publication in *Skating* magazine described Henie accordingly:

> She is more than a skater, she is an artist… Her figures were executed almost flawlessly… Her free skating was the ecstasy of all beholders… Her opening spiral was done at terrific speed, with marvelous control, in fact so was her entire performances. Her Axel Paulsen was simply a dream and its landing extraordinary; I have never seen a better one. Her spins are astounding, for they are longer and faster than ever, and are finished on an inner back edge in beautiful positions. Miss Henie is unique in one thing, and that is an appealing attraction which is hard to describe in words. It is, perhaps, a combination of personality, charm, and perfection; but whatever it is, it blossoms forth to captivate her many followers.[31]

As the above narrative indicates, the media represented Henie as a visual icon, or face, of figure skating that embodied ideal types of feminine images. Not surprisingly, this style of representation echoes into the present day media.

What Henie represented was not only a gender ideal, but also a racially significant one in a crucial, initial moment when Whiteness and femininity combined in a particular way. According to Diane Negra, Henie's ethnicity, as much as her skating talent, was decisive to her stardom as her White image always operated as a thematic subtext for her persona.[32] Supportive evidence for this viewpoint can be read in a 1937 publication of *American Magazine* which stated, 'Sonja sleeps at least ten hours a night in a White bedroom, drives in a snow-White automobile, and dresses in White'.[33] In this way, what Henie signified was an ensemble of Whiteness and femininity in which her youth, skill, and foreign nationality contributed to constructing a certain kind of Whiteness.

In this respect, it might be argued that Henie's appearance and dominance on the ice, combined with the American public's enthusiastic according of her stardom, can be marked as the moment when what might be called 'the White princess skater' entered into the history of women's figure skating. According to Fabos, Henie was the first female skater to 'establish an image of [White] northern European beauties on ice',[34] and it was from this that an enduring princess metaphor for female Olympic skaters developed. Greatly influenced by the imagery developed around Henie, women's figure skating has churned out many such American White princess skaters portrayed as the protagonists of a fairy tale, such as: Tenley Albright, Carol Heiss, Peggy Fleming, and Dorothy Hamill. In what follows, we move to the culminating period in the construction of the American White princess skater by focussing on the latter two skaters, Fleming and Hamill.

Fleming won her first national championship in 1964 at the age of fifteen. Her success and potential initially hinged upon her technical proficiency. According to Kelli Lawrence, who has written a broadcast history of Olympic figure skating, 'what kept her on top ... was a solid arsenal of jumps executed with deceptively simple grace'.[35] As a darling of the international press, she was portrayed as 'doe-eyed, fragile, the leggy wisp, and America's shy Bambi',[36] or as 'a teenage beauty, a heartthrob, and a girl next door'.[37] Her performances were televised live on ABC with American audiences being captivated by her grace and beauty. As Lawrence argued, the phrase 'the Fleming effect'[38] spoke to this one skater's impact, for she made her sport a glamour event while she also became a marketing sensation.

Fleming's aura was recalled in a 1994 *Sports Illustrated* article, as the magazine produced a cover story honouring her as one of forty individuals who most significantly changed or advanced their sports, with the author noting that she launched the modern era of figure skating. Additionally, this story continued:

> Pretty and balletic, elegant and stylish, Fleming took a staid sport that was shackled by its inscrutable compulsory figures and arcane scoring system and, with television as her ally, made it marvelously glamorous ... On the ice she was stylish in a manner more reminiscent of ballet dancing than figure skating, and she was inoffensively sexy, teeming with femininity and energy.[39]

Fleming's combination of innocence, glamour, and prettiness earned her the favour of the figure skating establishment and the American media.

It was Dorothy Hamill who followed Fleming into the role of American ice princess. In the 1976 Olympics, she won the gold medal with all nine judges voting unanimously for her on the basis of her interpretation of the music, fluid skating, and infectious charm. At the age of 17, with her sweet face, winning smile and bobbed hairstyle, Hamill was instantly crowned as 'America's Sweetheart'.[40] During a televised ABC broadcast, Hammill mistakenly assumed that she was booed by the crowd. She preserved through the jeers and gave a gutsy and lyrical performance that was framed as a drama about Hamill's 'skating ambitions ... in terms of a fragile princess ascending a throne' and told via a crucial medium that portrayed her as 'a captivating ... character acting out her emotions and reaching for her dreams in a modern fairytale.'[41]

After the 1980 Lake Placid Olympics when U.S. figure skating was without a golden girl, the sport longed for the next American ice queen who would succeed Fleming and Hamill in time for the 1984 Olympics. It was at this time that a 16-year-old skater, Tiffany Chin, the daughter of a Taiwanese American father and a Taiwanese mother, competed for the U.S. and placed fourth. Going forward, the media paid a lot of attention to Chin, comparing her to former U.S. Olympians Peggy Fleming and Dorothy Hamill,[42] with particular focus on her promising future for the 1988 Olympics.

In what follows, more detailed is provided of the symbolic world of American women's figure skating in the 1980s, focussing especially on how the U.S. media represented the nation's first Asian American female skater. This was accomplished through the use of McDonald and Birrell's Reading Sport Critically Project method,[43] which focuses 'on a particular incident or celebrity as the site for exploring the complex interrelated and fluid character of power relations as they are constituted along the axes of ability, class, gender, and nationality'. They noted that media narratives are a useful source for reading sport because they proclaim a particular worldview through the production of important cultural signifying systems. The media narratives that were utilized in this investigation included major national newspapers/publications and commentary from televised sporting events. It is important to note that all of these sources are U.S.-based, thus the writers and broadcasters have a Western mindset that they applied in how they discussed Chin. To that end, the emerging narratives should be considered applicable only in the context of how the American media viewed and described Tiffany Chin. Of note, it is plausible that media texts from other nations will present a different narrative. Conversely, nations that were founded on European ideals, and share traditional American ideologies, may have a media that explained the phenomenon of oriental skaters on White ice similarly. In the context of this study, since our examination did not analyze non-U.S. based media texts, we can only attempt to explain the American media's coverage.

The Media's Representation of Tiffany Chin

On February 3, 1981, a young Asian American female skater appeared on the ice rink at the San Diego Sports Arena to compete in the U.S. National Championships. The skater was Tiffany Chin, a 13-year-old Taiwanese American from Toluca Lake, California, who had just won the World Junior Championship and was making her senior debut as the youngest skater in the senior competition. Capturing this moment of her presence and performance with a laudatory headline, 'Tiffany Chin, a Road to [the 1984] Olympics in Yugoslavia May Be San Diego Freeway', Chris Cobbs of *Los Angeles Times* penned, 'Her forte is athleticism—triple jumps and other taxing maneuvers'—and she's known as a daredevil. She has unusual strength but also is technically adept. One observer says she has "superb flow"'.[44] Additionally, Cobbs wrote that Chin was 'Described by her coach as a stubborn child with fantastic natural talent, Chin has expressive eyes, a mouth full of braces and a charming way', that 'she keeps her room neat, makes her own bed, has an easy time passing up junk food—"It doesn't appeal to many Orientals"—and looks at boys, distantly, as "friends"'. Furthermore, Cobbs wrote that 'Chin said the discipline demanded by her coach and her father, a mechanical engineer with a Ph.D. from the University of California-Berkeley, made it easy for her "not to get a big head"'.[45] Finally, Cobbs noted that if she makes it to the top that would represent a lift to all Orientals.[46]

The media accounts highlighted above reflect a particular form of representation in which Chin is constructed as a mixed iconography that revolves around her skating style, personal character, and her family. Taking these descriptions as a starting point, we developed the theme of 'media representations of Chin' and will explain why they can be interpreted as the birth of the oriental female skater. The media narratives of Chin can be summarized with three points: (1) she had a unique and distinctive style, including a very different skating style, (2) ideas about and attitudes towards her age and youthfulness were complex and ambivalent, and (3) her parents and family background were an important part of her profile.

First, the media represented Tiffany Chin as a distinctively unique and different skater, who had a natural talent for jumping, with an exotic, oriental appearance and attractiveness. Media accounts highlighted her athletic prowess, naming a new jump that she introduced after her – the 'Chin Spin'. For instance, Phil Hersh of the *Chicago Tribune* noted: 'The most obvious standard is the move... a move so original it is called the Chin Spin. Rocking and twirling, she creates the illusion of a hundred arms and legs all spinning at once'.[47] This unique jump, according to Randy Harvey of *Los Angeles Times*, made Chin 'a rare gem among American skaters'.[48] The piece continued, '[she combined] an artistic, graceful style with gravity-defying jumps and spins like no one else has before or since. At 16, she already had a spin named for her, the Chin Spin'.[49]

On the other hand, the media often introduced Chin as 'the first American with an Oriental background to qualify for a team representing the United States in the World championships or the Olympics'.[50] Along with this recognition, her artistic and graceful characteristics were often described as an image of the 'China Doll' or a distinctively 'Oriental' style. Noting that 'her exotic beauty... announced this country's superstar-to-be',[51] Richard Hoffer of *Los Angeles Times* emphasized the point that, 'in a sport where aesthetic appearance is vital, Tiffany, her dark Oriental features setting her apart from the other women, had all the required elements'.[52] Similarly, Neil Amdur of *New York Times* discussed Chin's exotic features and her artistry in relation to the metaphor of the China Doll:

> Tiffany Chin is not a figure-skating china doll, contrary to what some people have tried to suggest. Sweet-looking, yes. Artistic, definitely... But China doll? "It's a wonderful little phrase', John Nicks, Miss Chin's coach, said in recalling how a television announcer had tried to pin the nickname on her after an interview. 'But China doll is fragile and gives you the impression it's going to break. That's where the comparison ends. Tiffany can be pushed much harder than she looks. I don't hesitate to push her either, and she doesn't mind'.[53]

Her mother, Marjorie Chin, also often talked to the media about Chin's big brown eyes, which drew attention to how pretty her daughter was in terms of exotic beauty.[54]

A second important characteristic of the media narratives of Chin was a certain ambivalent attitude concerning her age and youthful appearance and features. In one version of this, the media framed Chin as a female skating prodigy, who still needed more time to become an ice queen. For example, before the 1984 Olympics, Neil Amdur of *New York Times* predicted that her age might be an issue noting that, 'if Miss Chin does not win a medal at these Winter Games because most judges... feel she is too young for such instant rewards, the groundwork will be dug for the future'.[55] This point about seniority, on the other hand, was mixed in a complicated way with concern for Chin being potentially a little ahead of her time.[56] Jane Leavy, a *Washington Post* writer expressed this saying:

> Chin, obviously, hasn't heard about too much too soon. 'The sooner the better', she said... In figure skating, danger lurks in winning too early, peaking too soon. Heights are hard to sustain. Four years ago, Elaine Zayak was the prodigy who couldn't miss in 1984. She is 11th after today's competition. 'Right now, it's (the 1988 Olympics) still a ways off', Chin said. 'It's my goal... I don't think I've peaked yet. I think I'm still rising'.[57]

In this way, Chin's young age of sixteen and her youthfulness caught the media's attention and became a topic for debate around two narratives in U.S. women's figure skating: 'too much too soon' and 'the sooner the better'.

The media also drew attention to Chin's family, portraying it as a kind of super-working unit of a docile, but disciplined daughter with well-educated, determined, and dedicated parents. Regarding her manners and personality, Chin was described as 'polite and smiles easily, but... displays little emotion [and speaks] of becoming desensitized'.[58] In the rink and at school, Chin was depicted as a hard-working, hard-training girl who had managed her gruelling daily schedule since she was eight. According to Janet Rae-Dupree of *Los Angeles Times*:

> [It] starts with practice in a North Hollywood rink at 6:30 a.m., continues with a few hours of class at Providence, and concludes with yet another practice at a Costa Mesa rink, which is nothing new to the teenager, who started her meteoric rise at the age of 8 by mimicking other skaters as they practiced. It leaves little time for the dating, movies, and dances that are the usual trappings of high school life, a factor she says she rarely considers.[59]

This image of Chin was further overlapped with representations of her parents as setting up a type of Asian American middle-class family. Focussing on their ethnic background, educational achievements, and professional status, the media introduced Chin's parents as, 'Always looking for investment possibilities, Marjorie is an astute businesswoman with a master's degree from USC. Her interests range from real estate, to a taco restaurant, to vending machines. She is opinionated and outspoken'.[60]

The media introduced Marjorie as a 'Dragon Lady' or 'Tiger Mom', who was 'fiercely protective of her child and unafraid to cuff her verbally, as tigers do more forcefully to teach their young'.[61] Along with Marjorie's stern discipline, her dedication to Chin was also highlighted. Pointing to the sacrifices that both mother and daughter had made and characterizing them as a 'different life style', Hersh of *Los Angeles Times* reported:

Marjorie began commuting four days a week between San Diego and Burbank, 260 miles round-trip, so that Tiffany could work with Carroll. Still in her pajamas, Tiffany slept in the back seat while Marjorie drove her to 6 a.m. lessons and then back to San Diego for afternoon elementary school classes... Sure, I don't get to do a lot of the things normal kids do, but I get to do the traveling and meeting new people and seeing different cultures that other kids can't get from school.[62]

In this way, Marjorie's style of mothering was a key factor in the media's understanding of Chin's family as an oriental family.

The Birth of the Oriental Female Skater

Media representations of Chin mark the initial moment that the oriental female skater was created in the history of U.S. women's figure skating. Since Chin's appearance on ice, this style of representation has become prevalent and almost formulaically applied to other skaters of oriental descent. For instance, Chin's image as a docile, but super-human like training machine is commonly seen in descriptions of Kristi Yamaguchi and Michelle Kwan as well. The common descriptors include not only the exotic implications of the oriental beauty or attractiveness, but also how their families were profiled as the middle-class California family. These rhetorical patterns closely resonate with discourses of the oriental female skater that were previously introduced, such as the model minority

Here, a discussion of the ways in which such patterns and styles of representation are contingent upon certain social, cultural, political, and historical contexts is warranted. As Thomas Foster argued, 'a historical articulation of textual practices... cannot be reduced to body of texts but has to be read as the articulation of a number of discrete series of events, only some of which are discursive'.[63] What is at stake here is the issue of what contextual factors contributed to the emergence of oriental female skaters as a cultural product of racial formation in the 1980s, and how this construction can be understood in relation to Kristi Yamaguchi and Michelle Kwan in the 1990s and to Asian skaters of the 2000s.

As key contextual factors in the emergence of the oriental female skater and recalling the major forces of American White supremacy, attention should be drawn to two particular ideas, discourses, or ideologies: the 'multicultural turn' that was widely spread in the early and mid-1980s of America, and the so-called 'oriental style', a genre of representation that became established in various forms and practices within U.S. popular culture in the 1980s. Furthermore, highlighting how multiculturalism is a national force of White American national ontology and discussing orientalism in relation to the historical force of the White American imperial frame are important within this conversation.

The Multicultural Turn on Ice

In order to discuss the multicultural turn that occurred on the ice, it is important to understand the immigration periods that influenced and impacted the nation as a whole. The history of Asian immigration to the United States has been generally understood as falling into five periods.[64] The first (1849–1882) was a time of heavy

Chinese immigration that began with the Californian gold rush, which was punctuated by anti-Chinese sentiments towards Chinese sojourners, prostitutes and coolie labourers, that ended with the Chinese Exclusion Act of 1882. The second (1884–1924) represented an 'initial period of Japanese immigration' marked by the arrival of sugar cane workers in Hawaii, and featured the increasingly anti-Japanese and anti-Asian movements that produced the Alien Land Acts of 1914 which prohibited noncitizens from owning land in California, and the Immigration Act of 1924 which excluded all Asian immigrants except for Filipinos. The third (1924–1952) was 'the period of Asian exclusion', the fourth (1952–1965) was 'the era of the McCarran Act' which eliminated all racial bars to immigration but replaced them with token quotas for most Asian nations. The fifth period (1965 to present) opened with the Immigration Act of 1965, which abolished all racial and ethnic quotas, and was an important statute for the rapid growth of Asian immigration that has contributed tremendously to the diverse and multicultural composition of the United States population.

The idea of multiculturalism has been deployed as one of the major themes through which to re-think and re-understand communities, societies, and nations, both culturally and politically. Despite its ubiquitous presence, the term multiculturalism is still an amorphous concept often used as a kind of umbrella notion whose meanings circulate in multiple ways.[65] For some conservatives, it is a new way of talking about 'Anglo conformity'.[66] For some liberals, it invites all racial or ethnic groups to compete equally in capitalist society, based upon the idea or belief that the structural level of social, historical, and cultural barriers can be modified or reformed.[67] For those in the middle, who may be more critically-minded, it might mean a descriptive fact of diversity in which five major groups of pan-ethnicity are organized and displayed like a spectacle, but one that covers up the power, privilege, and hierarchy of oppression vested in dominant groups.[68]

Per Anne-Marie Fortier's perspective, multiculturalism is a form of post/nationalist discourse, which refers to 'reworking of the nation as inherently multicultural'.[69] At the turn of multicultural era, however, it became impossible to imagine the nation without taking into account such key words as diversity, ethnicity, race, or minority cultures. Thus, in the context of the U.S., multiculturalism might refer to an idea, thought, or discourse that re-imagines or re-defines 'America' from a mono-cultural to a multi-cultural imagined community, a new nation that is and always has been inherently multicultural.

To a certain extent, multiculturalism seems to challenge dominant understandings of the modern nation, because it is a welcoming celebration of diversity and minority cultures that are embraced as crucial parts of the national culture. The problem is that it has been so loosely deployed that the issues of difference, struggle, and inequality rarely surface, but rather are dissolved into a palatable, colourful, and apolitical diversity. Thus, it has become common for many ethnic and minority groups to 'have their own national heritage/history month dedicated to celebrating and teaching about their culture and contributions to the nation'.[70] In the context of the U.S., this spectacle has a long been described using metaphors such as the 'melting pot' and the 'salad bowl'.

The melting pot model, or theory, might be understood as a form of cultural blending based upon the assimilationist ideology of Anglo-conformity. The metaphor hinges around a belief that all immigrants can or should become 'Americans' by emulating the standard or core values of White Anglo-Saxon Protestant culture. During the multicultural turn, which accompanied the diversity boom of the late 1980s and the early 1990s, the melting pot metaphor seemed to be displaced by a salad bowl which symbolized a new plural style of multicultural blending.[71] As a salad bowl consists of a mixture with many colourful ingredients, it is an appropriate metaphor for a multicultural society. It seems to advertise America as a space in which all different people can live in freedom and in pursuit of their dreams, all the while keeping their own culture and values, rather than as a pot in which multiple ingredients of race, ethnicity, and religion are melted or dissolved into one dominant culture. The salad bowl metaphor of American society has broad currency signalling that a belief in a certain level of acceptance, with respect to cultural diversity or difference, exists and that there is broad tolerance in terms of language, food, traditional customs, and other aspects of heritage.

It is within this metaphorical context of salad bowl, or re-emerged melting pot of America, that the media narratives of Chin as a marker for the birth of the Asian American female skater are situated. According to Mark Dyreson, the 'long history of making American Olympic teams into "emblems of the multiethnic fabric" or "a union of all races" reinvigorated melting pot stories in the 1980s and 1990s'.[72] Kristi Yamaguchi is suggested as a crucial example in his argument that 'the melting pot appeared … forcefully at the 1998 winter games in the person of Kristi Yamaguchi and other figure skaters'.[73] Then Dyreson goes further to argue that this melting pot vision continued to appear in the 2002 Salt Lake City Winter Games, at which Michelle Kwan was portrayed as among 'America's new Olympic diversity heroes'.[74]

In this respect, a solid argument could be made for including Chin into Dyreson's formulation, and make connections between her, Yamaguchi, and Kwan, using the trope of the model minority and the perception of the forever foreign Asian. In the cultural and political space of the neo-melting pot or salad bowl, the model minority thesis was also revived as an effective tool for the conservative policies of Ronald Regan administration that aimed to dismantle affirmative action and welfare programmes.[75] The 'family' especially was invoked as a core element of this notion. For example, it was deployed in overt racial comparisons that were made between the successes of Asian Americans and the failures of other ethnic minorities.[76] On the other hand, it was saturated with culturally based explanations of Asian American families whose differences from White American families were highlighted in a racially neutral or seemingly non-problematic way.

In regard to the term hybridity, Hall expressed a similar point in arguing that the concept should not be understood as 'a reference to the mixed racial composition of populations'.[77] These perspectives led us to conclude that difference is not based on certain inherent, natural, or static attributes, but it should be rather understood as an outcome of social, cultural, and political relations. Thus, a multicultural understanding of cultural plurality can function politically as a strategic tool for dominant groups to be able to control and manage the problem of difference and further sustain the hegemonic construction of mono-cultural America.

Chin's appearance on ice signalled the multicultural turn in women's figure skating during a time when economies of inclusion and exclusion began to oscillate between the nation and race. Of significant importance to this claim is a certain ambivalence embedded in the ways in which the media imagined, narrated, and represented 'race' within multicultural America. As an Asian American, Chin's 'Asian' side was dislocated or de-Asianized when the media positively framed her as a role model for other skaters. From the standpoint of White Americans, when the media focussed on her differences, however, the reverse happened and her Asian side was reaffirmed and highlighted through a certain process of de-Americanization. Thus, her American identity came across as fluid based on the journalist writing the article or narrating her contests.

The Oriental Girl on Ice

Considering American orientalism as a crucial force of the White American imperial frame, the U.S. media's representation of oriental female skaters should be questioned with what Hall called the 'discourse of the West and the Rest',[78] and Edward Said's 'imaginative geography of the Occident and Orient'[79] in mind. According to Hall, the U.S. is one with Western, White Europe, not Eastern Europe, because they share similar processes of historical development characterized as modernity, capitalism, industrialization, urbanization, and so on.[80] Although Said mostly discussed the relationship between the British and the French as the Occident, and the Middle East as the Orient, he also noted that the U.S. 'is much more likely to be associated very differently with the Far East (China and Japan, mainly) than it is with Europe'.[81] In this respect, the media narratives of Chin should be viewed as part of a larger formation of the ongoing historical process of the racialization of Asian American women as the Rest/Orient/Other.

The gendered constructions between the colonizer as a male and the colonized as a female have a long history, and the sexual language of imperialism has also long been apparent in West-East relations. According to Said, Orientalism was 'an exclusively male province... with sexist blinders',[82] in which the Orient was viewed with 'the escapism of sexual fantasy' or 'the freedom of licentious sex'.[83] Analyzing the writings of famous novelists and travellers such as Gustave Flaubert and 'Dirty Dick' Burton, Said argued:

> Just as the various colonial possessions... were useful as places to send wayward sons, superfluous populations of delinquents, poor people, and other undesirables, so the Orient was a place where one could look for sexual experience unobtainable in Europe... In time 'Oriental sex' was as standard a commodity as any other available in the mass culture, with the result that readers and writers could have it if they wished without necessarily going to the Orient.[84]

In this way, the Orient was not only gendered as a feminized entity which correlated with the conquest of the Oriental women, but it was also sexualized as the land of fantasy that seduced the Occidental with sexual desire, pleasure, and violence.

Situating the multicultural America of the 1980s within the history of American orientalism, attention should be drawn to certain conventional or formularized practices that were widely established in U.S. popular culture, which might be called the commodification of the oriental girl. To that end, the oriental image that Chin represented served as a kind of reservoir of exotic style and accessories fitted within the multicultural imagined space of women's figure skating. This is the argument that Jane Park[85] made in her discussion on the 'oriental style' of a newly emerged aesthetic product and Asian American cultural formation in Hollywood during the 1980s and early 1990s. She saw this as a kind of multicultural filmic language:

> [certain] kinds of oriental imagery – the invisible abject and the hyper visible feted – are reduced to decorative flourishes within the films... 'Oriental style' describes... the ways in which Hollywood films crystallize and commodify multiple, heterogeneous Asiatic cultures, histories, and aesthetics into a small number of easily recognizable, often interchangeable tropes that help to share dominant cultural attitudes about Asia and people of Asian descent.[86]

In women's figure skating, similarly, it is believable to think journalists, fans, and other important stakeholders were not concerned with the authenticity of the content nor the interiority of the imagery, but rather were attracted by the surface and certain visual economies of sexual consumption.

To better illustrate oriental imagery, it might be useful to introduce one passage frequently cited by various scholars[87] in Asian American studies. The article titled 'Oriental Girls' was penned by Sumi Cho in a 1990 *Gentleman's Quarterly*:

> Her face-round like a child's... eyes almond-shaped for mystery, black for suffering, wide-spaced for innocence, high cheekbones swelling like bruises, cherry lips ... When you get home from another hard day on the planet, she comes into existence, removes your clothes, bathes you and walks naked on your back to relax you ... She's fun you see, and so uncomplicated. She doesn't go to assertiveness training classes, insist on being treated like a person, fret about career moves ... She's there when you need shore leave from those angry feminist seas.[88]

As the passage portrays, the 'Oriental Girl' is supposedly small, submissive, exotic, and sexually active and eager to please, and by the 1990s this iconic imagery was already a popular caricature of sexual commodity for western White male consumption.

Various fields of U.S. popular culture such as the Hollywood, TV stations, and Broadway have played a crucial role in spreading the imagery of the oriental girl. In Hollywood, as Gina Marchetti described, Asian American women were often portrayed as a sexual servant or complement that is 'sexually available to the White hero'.[89] Kwan categorized such hyper-sexual/exotic characters of as 'the Oriental Woman', and argued that the 'ability and... willingness to serve as a sexual object is essential to her constitution'.[90] This image of the oriental girl/woman is also commonly seen in prime-time television, where Asian American women were often framed as rarely married and have active romantic lives with non-Asian male characters.[91]

The media representations of Chin and her skating arguably represent the moment when the oriental girl/woman was born into the multicultural site of women's figure skating. Like cinema, theatre, or musicals, the symbolic world of figure skating should be understood as an anthropological site in which the consumption of racial, sexual, and gendered differences are allowed and further identified within the politics of apolitical diversity.

The critical point being made here is twofold. The first, as mentioned previously, colonialist desire, fantasy, and gesture of the erotic Empire can be seen in the production of the oriental girl/woman on ice. Within these neo-colonial politics, Chin as the primitive subject and non-White, oriental female skater signifies an internally colonized object successfully assimilating herself into the controlled image of the oriental skater on ice. This practice or experience also further reaffirms the hegemonic status of White male sexual subjectivity. The second point is concerned with the way in which the notion of Yellow peril, or threat, is somehow automatically inscribed into the image of the oriental girl/woman in an aesthetically perilous way. This idea is informed by what David Morley and Kevin Robins called 'techno-orientalism',[92] which refers to an anti-Japanese sentiment that appeared in the domain of technology in the 1980s and the 1990s, when Japan's bubble economy was at its peak. The technologically advanced products of Japanese computers, Walkman devices, and video games were coined as a revival of the older Yellow peril with oriental technology conceived as a threat or fear of an Asiatic takeover of Western technological civilization. While techno-orientalism emerged as a response to an American crisis discourse of economy and technology, similar signs exist in women's figure skating, in what might be called sporting orientalism. That is to say, a prevalent form of anti-East Asian sentiment or racism was projected on Chin and other skaters of Yellow colour, whose bodies, aesthetics, and styles of skating were considered a threat to the White bodies, aesthetics and styles of U.S. women's figure skating.

Chin as a Trailblazer

Figure skating has historically served as a space that promoted Whiteness, as outlined in our discussion of how from its earliest organization and formalization the sport was a racialized and gendered site, both before and after it was feminized. In the 1930s and 1940s figure skating came to be a feminine sport with White women receiving the most media coverage and often being afforded celebrity status. The attention that these women received lead to the creation of the 'White Princess Skater' archetype that was frequently ascribed to the next rising White teenage figure skating star. The success of Tiffany Chin in the 1980s, and the manner in which her skating style, personal character, and her family were covered, reflected the pervasiveness of Whiteness in skating. As the multi-cultural turn was happening outside of the sport, Chin was propped up as a model minority member whose race was selectively emphasized/de-emphasized by media outlets. To that end, Chin had to combat Asian stereotypes due to her existence and success in a White space and sport.

Our research findings add to the race and gender discrimination in sport literature by describing the processes employed by historically dominant power groups (Whites;

media) as Tiffany Chin started to dominate a sport historically viewed as a White space. Following our methodological approach, future researchers can examine traditional White spaces, both in and outside of sport, that are struggling to explain and understand the entry and dominance of someone from an outside group. The potential for outside group members to become dominant stars in White sport spaces may rise as the United States continues to become more diverse. Thus, our findings and structure might serve as a starting point for deductive narrative analysis in future-related research.

As a trailblazer for Asian American skaters, the characteristics and qualities that were associated with Tiffany Chin have been formulaically placed on other oriental skaters. Future research should examine the continued perpetuation of racial and gender stereotypes encountered by Asian American female skaters, and offer suggestions that might help in facilitating positive social change. One area of potential change could be utilizing Chin as a case study to teach aspiring communication and journalist professionals about the power of the narratives that they produce. Those students could then utilize McDonald and Birrell's Reading Sport Critically Project method to examine other incidences where someone from an outside group – whether that be because of their race or gender – entered into and started to dominate a historically White or male space.

Notes

1. Mary G. McDonald and Susan Birrell, 'Reading Sport Critically: A Methodology for Interrogating Power', *Sociology of Sport Journal* 16, no. 4 (1999): 283–300.
2. Ruth Frankenberg, *The Social Construction of Whiteness: White Women, Race Matters* (Minneapolis: Routledge, 1993); Peggy McIntosh, 'White Privilege: Unpacking the Invisible Knapsack', in *Race, Class, and Gender in the United States: An Integrated Study*, ed. Paula S. Rothenberg (New York: Worth Publishers, 2004), 188–92.
3. Richard Dyer, *White: Essays on Race and Culture* (London: Routledge, 1997), 1.
4. John Gabriel, *Whitewashed: Radicalised Politics and the Media* (London: Routledge, 1998), 37.
5. Dyer, *White*; Gabriel, *Whitewashed*; Henry A. Giroux, 'Racial Politics and the Pedagogy of Whiteness', in *Whiteness: A Critical Reader*, ed. Mike Hill (New York: New York University Press, 1997), 294–315; Stuart Hall, 'The Local and the Global: Globalization and Ethnicity', in *Culture Globalization and the World System: Contemporary Conditions and the Representation of Identity*, ed. Anthony D. King (Basingstoke: Macmillan, 1991), 19–39.
6. Hall, 'The Local and the Global', 19–39.
7. Kevin Hylton, *'Race' and Sport: Critical Race Theory* (London: Routledge, 2009); C. Richard King, 'Cautionary Notes on Whiteness and Sport Studies', *Sociology of Sport Journal* 22, no. 3 (2005): 397–408; C. Richard King, David J. Leonard, and Kyle W. Kusz, 'White Power and Sport: An Introduction', *Journal of Sport & Social Issues* 31, no. 1 (2007): 3–10; Mary G. McDonald, 'Mapping Whiteness and Sport: An Introduction', *Sociology of Sport Journal* 22, no. 3 (2005): 245–55.
8. Michael L. Butterworth, 'Race in "the Race": Mark McGwire, Sammy Sosa, and Heroic Constructions of Whiteness', *Critical Studies in Media Communication* 24, no. 3 (2007): 228–44; Jaime Schultz, 'Reading the Catsuit: Serena Williams and the Production of Blackness at the 2002 US Open', *Journal of Sport and Social Issues* 29, no. 3 (2005): 338–57; Theresa Walton, 'Theorizing Paula Radcliffe: Representing a Nation', *Sociology of Sport Journal* 27, no. 3 (2010): 285–300.

9. Delia D. Douglas, 'Venus, Serena, and the Women's Tennis Association: When and Where "Race" Enters', *Sociology of Sport Journal* 22, no. 3 (2005): 255–81; John Kelly, 'Exclusionary America: Jackie Robinson, Decolonization and Baseball Not Black and White', *The International Journal of the History of Sport* 22, no. 6 (2005): 1036–59; Kyle W. Kusz, 'From NASCAR Nation to Pat Tillman: Notes on Sport and the Politics of White Cultural Nationalism in Post-9/11 America', *Journal of Sport and Social Issues* 31, no. 1 (2007): 77–88; Geoffrey Levett, 'The "White Man's Game?" West Indian Cricket Tours of the 1900s', *The International Journal of the History of Sport* 34, no. 7–8 (2017): 599–618; Theresa A. Walton and Ted M. Butryn, 'Policing the Race: U.S. Men's Distance Running and the Crisis of Whiteness', *Sociology of Sport Journal* 23, no. 1 (2006): 1–28.
10. Simon C. Darnell, 'Playing with Race: Right to Play and the Production of Whiteness in "Development through Sport"', *Sport in Society* 10, no. 4 (2007): 560–79; Jonathan Long and Kevin Hylton, 'Shades of White: An Examination of Whiteness in Sport', *Leisure Studies* 21, no. 2 (2002): 87–103; Mary G. McDonald, 'Dialogues on Whiteness, Leisure and (Anti) Racism', *Journal of Leisure Research* 41, no. 1 (2009): 5–21.
11. David Rowe, 'Image Projection and Gaze Reception: Mediating East Asia through the Summer Olympics', *International Journal of the History of Sport* 29, no. 16 (2012): 2231–43.
12. Ben Carrington, 'Cosmopolitan Olympism, Humanism and the Spectacle of Race', in *Post-Olympism? Questioning Sport in the Twenty-First Century*, ed. John Bale and Mette K. Christensen (Oxford: Berg, 2004), 4.
13. Seth Brown, 'De Coubertin's Olympism and the Laugh of Michel Foucault: Crisis Discourse and the Olympic Games', *Quest* 64, no. 3 (2012): 150–63; Carrington, 'Cosmopolitan Olympism, Humanism and the Spectacle of Race'; Dikaia Chatziefstathiou, 'Paradoxes and Contestations of Olympism in the History of the Modern Olympic Movement', *Sport in Society* 14, no. 3 (2011): 332–44; Michael R. Real, 'The Postmodern Olympics: Technology and the Commodification of the Olympic Movement', *Quest* 48, no. 1 (1996): 9–24; Rowe, 'Image Projection and Gaze Reception'; O. J. Schantz, 'Pierre de Coubertin's Concepts of Race, Nation, and Civilization', in *The 1904 Anthropology Days and Olympic Games: Sport, Race and American Imperialism*, ed. Susan Brownell (Lincoln: University of Nebraska Press, 2008), 156–88.
14. Pierre de Coubertin, 'An Olympiad in the Far East', in *Olympism: Selected Writings*, ed. Pierre de Coubertin and Norbert Müller (Lausanne: International Olympic Committee, 2000), 695–97.
15. C. Richard King, 'Staging the Winter Olympics: Or, Why Sport Matters to White Power', *Journal of Sport and Social Issues* 31, no. 1 (2007): 89–94.
16. Anthony K. Harrison, 'Black Skiing, Everyday Racism, and the Racial Spatiality of Whiteness', *Journal of Sport and Social Issues* 37, no. 4 (2013): 315–39.
17. Kelly Poniatowski and Erin Whiteside, '"Isn't He a Good Guy?": Constructions of Whiteness in the 2006 Olympic Hockey Tournament', *Howard Journal of Communications* 23, no. 1 (2012): 1–16.
18. Ann Travers, 'Women's Ski Jumping, the 2010 Olympic Games, and the Deafening Silence of Sex Segregation, Whiteness, and Wealth', *Journal of Sport and Social Issues* 35, no. 2 (2011): 126–45.
19. Abigail M. Feder, '"A Radiant Smile from the Lovely Lady": Overdetermined Femininity in "Ladies" Figure Skating', *The Drama Review* 38, no. 1 (1994): 62–78; Ellyn Kestnbaum, 'What Tanya Harding Means to Me, or Images of Independent Female Power on Ice', in *Women on Ice: Feminist Essays on the Tonya Harding/Nancy Kerrigan Spectacle*, ed. Cynthia Baughman (London: Routledge, 1995), 53–77.
20. King, 'Staging the Winter Olympics', 89–94.
21. Ellyn Kestnbaum, *Culture on Ice: Figure Skating & Cultural Meaning* (Middletown: Wesleyan University Press, 2003).
22. Stephanie Foote, 'Making Sport of Tonya: Class Performance and Social Punishment', *Journal of Sport & Social Issues* 27, no. 3 (2003): 3–17; Elizabeth L. Krause, '"The Bead of

23. Raw Sweat in a Field of Dainty Perspirers"': Nationalism, Whiteness, and the Olympic-Class Ordeal of Tonya Harding', *Transforming Anthropology* 7, no. 1 (1998): 33–52.
23. Karen McGarry, 'Passing as a "Lady"', *Genders Online Journal* 41 (2005), https://cdn.atria.nl/ezines/IAV_606661/IAV_606661_2010_51/g41_mcgarry.html (accessed February 14, 2019).
24. Ibid.
25. Garry J. Smith, 'The Noble Sports Fan', *Journal of Sport and Social Issues* 12, no. 1 (1988): 54–65.
26. Mary L. Adams, *Artistic Impressions: Figure Skating, Masculinity, and the Limits of Sport* (Toronto: University of Toronto Press, 2011).
27. Ibid.
28. Adams, *Artistic Impressions*; Bettina Fabos, 'Forcing the Fairytale: Narrative Strategies in Figure Skating Competition Coverage', *Sport in Society* 4, no. 2 (2001): 185–212; Kestnbaum, *Culture on Ice*.
29. Fabos, 'Forcing the Fairytale', 189.
30. Ibid.
31. Adams, *Artistic Impressions*, 146.
32. Diane Negra, *Off-White Hollywood: American Culture and Ethnic Female Stardom* (London: Routledge, 2001).
33. Ibid., 88.
34. Fabos, 'Forcing the Fairytale', 189.
35. Kelli Lawrence, *Skating on Air: The Broadcast History of an Olympic Marquee Sport* (Jefferson: McFarland, 2011), 38.
36. Lisette Hilton, 'ESPN Classic: Fleming Launched Modern Era of Figure Skating', *ESPN*, November 19, 2003, http://www.espn.go.com/classic/biography/s/Fleming_Peggy.html (accessed February 14, 2019).
37. Fabos, 'Forcing the Fairytale', 190.
38. Lawrence, *Skating on Air*, 37.
39. E. M. Swift, '35 Peggy Fleming', *Sports Illustrated*, September 19, 1994, 134.
40. Kestnbaum, *Culture on Ice*.
41. Ibid., 191.
42. Randy Harvey, 'Taking it on the Chin: In Skating, There's Some Things That You Don't Figure On', *Los Angeles Times*, January 25, 1989, D1.
43. McDonald and Birrell, 'Reading Sport Critically', 283–300.
44. Chris Cobbs, 'For Tiffany Chin, a Road to Olympics in Yugoslavia may be San Diego Freeway', *Los Angeles Times*, February 3, 1981, B1.
45. Ibid.
46. Ibid.
47. Phil Hersh, 'Show Time For Chin: Tiffany Adjusts to Spotlight, Pressure', *Chicago Tribune*, February 3, 1985, http://articles.chicagotribune.com/1985-02-03/sports/8501070292_1_marjorie-chin-national-figure-skating-championships-skaters (accessed February 14, 2019).
48. Randy Harvey, 'Taking it on the Chin: In Skating, There's Some Things That You Don't Figure On', *Los Angeles Times*, January 25, 1989, D1.
49. Ibid.
50. Neil Amdur, 'Outlook is Shinny and Goals are set for Tiffany Chin', *New York Times*, February 13, 1984, https://www.nytimes.com/1984/02/13/sports/outlook-is-shiny-and-goals-are-set-for-tiffany-chin.html (accessed February 14, 2019).
51. Richard Hoffer, 'The Comeback of Tiffany Chin: After Muscle Therapy, 3 Months Off, Young Skater Gives it Another Whirl', *Los Angeles Times*, December 14, 1985, B1.
52. Randy Harvey, 'Taking it on the Chin: In Skating, There's Some Things That You Don't Figure On', *Los Angeles Times*, January 25, 1989, D1.
53. Neil Amdur, 'Outlook is Shinny and Goals are set for Tiffany Chin', *New York Times*, February 13, 1984, https://www.nytimes.com/1984/02/13/sports/outlook-is-shiny-and-goals-are-set-for-tiffany-chin.html (accessed February 14, 2019).

54. Chris Cobbs, 'For Tiffany Chin, a Road to Olympics in Yugoslavia may be San Diego Freeway', *Los Angeles Times*, February 3, 1981, B1; Randy Harvey, 'Taking it on the Chin: In Skating, There's Some Things That You Don't Figure On', *Los Angeles Times*, January 25, 1989, D1; Phil Hersh, 'Show Time For Chin: Tiffany Adjusts to Spotlight, Pressure', *Chicago Tribune*, February 3, 1985, http://articles.chicagotribune.com/1985-02-03/sports/8501070292_1_marjorie-chin-national-figure-skating-championships-skaters (accessed February 14, 2019).
55. Neil Amdur, 'Outlook is Shinny and Goals are set for Tiffany Chin', *New York Times*, February 13, 1984, https://www.nytimes.com/1984/02/13/sports/outlook-is-shiny-and-goals-are-set-for-tiffany-chin.html (accessed February 14, 2019).
56. Jane Leavy, 'Only 16, Chin's Up and Coming', *Washington Post*, January 4, 1984, D3.
57. Ibid.
58. Randy Harvey, 'Taking it on the Chin: In Skating, There's Some Things That You Don't Figure On', *Los Angeles Times*, January 25, 1989, D1.
59. Janet Rae-Dupree, 'Skating Champ: Classmates Give Tiffany an Ovation', *Los Angles Times*, February 7, 1985, http://articles.latimes.com/1985-02-07/local/me-5282_1_tiffany-chin (accessed February 14, 2019).
60. Neil Amdur, 'Outlook is Shinny and Goals are set for Tiffany Chin', *New York Times*, February 13, 1984, https://www.nytimes.com/1984/02/13/sports/outlook-is-shiny-and-goals-are-set-for-tiffany-chin.html (accessed February 14, 2019).
61. Phil Hersh, 'Show Time For Chin: Tiffany Adjusts to Spotlight, Pressure', *Chicago Tribune*, February 3, 1985, http://articles.chicagotribune.com/1985-02-03/sports/8501070292_1_marjorie-chin-national-figure-skating-championships-skaters (accessed February 14, 2019).
62. Janet Rae-Dupree, 'Skating Champ: Classmates Give Tiffany an Ovation', *Los Angles Times*, February 7, 1985, http://articles.latimes.com/1985-02-07/local/me-5282_1_tiffany-chin (accessed February 14, 2019).
63. Jane Chi Hyun Park, *Yellow Future: Oriental Style in Hollywood Cinema* (Minneapolis: University of Minnesota Press, 2010).
64. Roger Daniels, 'American Historians and East Asian Immigrants', *The Pacific Historical Review* 43, no. 4 (1974): 449–72.
65. Virginia R. Dominguez, 'A Taste for the "Other": Intellectual Complicity in Racializing Practices', *Current Anthropology* 35, no. 4 (1994): 333–48; Avery Gordon and Christopher Newfield, 'Introduction', in *Mapping Multiculturalism*, ed. Avery F. Gordon and Christopher Newfield (Minneapolis: University of Minnesota Press, 1996), 1–16.
66. Gordon and Newfield, 'Introduction', 1–16.
67. Peter McLaren, 'White Terror and Oppositional Agency: Towards a Critical Multiculturalism', in *Multicultural Education, Critical Pedagogy, and the Politics of Difference*, ed. Christine Sleeter and Peter McLaren (Albany: University of New York Press, 1995), 33–70.
68. Angela Y. Davis, 'Gender, Class, and Multiculturalism: Rethinking "Race Politics"', in *Mapping Multiculturalism*, ed. Avery F. Gordon and Christopher Newfield (Minneapolis: University of Minnesota Press, 1996), 40–8; Stuart Hall, 'Conclusion: The Multi-Cultural Question', in *Un/Settled Multiculturalisms: Diasporas, Entanglements, Transruptions*, ed. Barnor Hesse (New York: Zed Books, 2000), 209–41; McLaren, 'White Terror and Oppositional Agency', 33–70.
69. Anne-Marie Fortier, 'Pride Politics and Multiculturalist Citizenship', *Ethnic and Racial Studies* 28, no. 3 (2005): 559–78.
70. Claire J. Kim, 'Imagining Race and Nation in Multiculturalist America', *Ethnic and Racial Studies* 27, no. 6 (2004): 987–1005.
71. Davis, 'Gender, Class, and Multiculturalism', 40–8; Gerda Lerner, 'Reconceptualizing Differences among Women', *Journal of Women's History* 1, no. 3 (1990): 106–22.
72. Mark Dyreson, 'Return to the Melting Pot: An Old American Olympic Story', *The International Journal of the History of Sport* 25, no. 2 (2003): 204–23.

73. Ibid., 213.
74. Ibid., 206.
75. Darrell Y. Hamamoto, 'Kindred Spirits: The Contemporary Asian American Family on Televison', *Amerasia Journal* 18, no. 2 (1992): 35–53.
76. Victor Bascara, *Model-Minority Imperialism* (Minneapolis: University of Minnesota Press, 2006).
77. Hall, 'Conclusion', 226.
78. Stuart Hall, 'The West and the Rest: Discourse and Power', in *Formations of Modernity*, ed. Bram Gielben and Stuart Hall (Cambridge: Polity Press, 1992), 184–227.
79. Edward W. Said, *Culture and Imperialism* (New York: Vintage, 2012).
80. Hall, 'The West and the Rest: Discourse and Power', 184–227.
81. Edward Said, *Orientalism: Western Representations of the Orient* (New York: Pantheon, 1978), 1.
82. Ibid., 207.
83. Ibid., 190.
84. Ibid., 190.
85. Park, *Yellow Future*.
86. Ibid., ix.
87. Sumi K. Cho, 'Converging Stereotypes in Racialized Sexual Harassment: Where the Model Minority Meets Suzie Wong', *The Journal of Gender, Race & Justice* 1, no. 1 (1997): 177–211; Peter Kwan, 'Invention, Inversion and Intervention: The Oriental Woman in the World of Suzie Wong, M. Butterfly, and the Adventures of Priscilla, Queen of the Desert', *Asian Law Journal* 5, no. 1 (1998): 99–137; Sunny Woan, 'White Sexual Imperialism: A Theory of Asian Feminist Jurisprudence', *Washington and Lee Journal of Civil Rights and Social Justice Law* 14, no. 2 (2007): 275–301.
88. Cho, 'Converging Stereotypes in Racialized Sexual Harassment', 191.
89. Gina Marchetti, *Romance and the "Yellow Peril": Race, Sex, and Discursive Strategies in Hollywood Fiction* (Berkeley: University of California Press, 1993), 2.
90. Kwan, 'Invention, Inversion and Intervention', 112.
91. Meera E. Deo, Jenny J. Lee, Christina B. Chin, Noriko Milman, and Nancy W. Yuen, 'Missing in Action: "Framing" Race on Prime-Time Television', *Social Justice* 35, no. 2 (2008): 145–62.
92. David Morley and Kevin Robins, *Spaces of Identity: Global Media, Electronic Landscapes and Cultural Boundaries* (London: Routledge, 1995).

Disclosure Statement

No potential conflict of interest was reported by the authors.

Disrupting the Nation-ness in Postcolonial East Asia: Discourses of Jong Tae-Se as a *Zainichi* Korean Sport Celebrity

Younghan Cho and Koji Kobayashi

ABSTRACT
This study explores how a *zainichi* (residing in Japan) Korean athlete reveals often-concealed postcolonial and post-Cold War tensions revolving around ethnic essentialism and nationalism in East Asia. The focus of the study is Jong Tae-se, a third generation *zainichi* Korean football player who has become a star in Japan, North Korea and South Korea. By examining media representations and online responses to Jong in South Korea as well as his autobiographies written in both Korean and Japanese, it is explained how Jong, as a *zainichi* Korean sport celebrity, both represents the arbitrariness of nation-ness and reproduces unresolved geopolitical and historical issues of postcolonial East Asia. Whereas his mobility, multilingual capability and fluid belongingness may signal changing dynamics of national-ness in East Asia, this analysis also reveals that his media discourses keep him tethered to anti-Japan and anti-communist sentiments. Such vicissitudes of the discourses around him attest that colonial and Cold War memories and historical wounds continue to be conjured in contemporary East Asia. Ultimately, this study discusses both the possibilities and the limits of a *zainichi* Korean subjectivity as a de-colonial tool for destabilizing national, colonial, and Cold War ideologies.

This study examines how a *zainichi* (residing in Japan) Korean athlete is reconfigured in postcolonial East Asia. By focussing on the discourses on Jong Tae-se,[1] a *zainichi* Korean football star, this research discusses how his subjectivity and representation provide an insight into the location of the 'invisible' cultural hybridity in disrupting the ethnic essentialism and nationalism within North Korea, South Korea and Japan. This study situates Jong Tae-se as an emblematic figure for destabilizing essentialist discourses of cultural and ethnic identities in the changing context of East Asia. In so doing, we seek an answer to the question: what are the politico-historical contexts of a *zainichi* Korean athlete interchangeably represented as North Korean, South Korean or Japanese and its implication to the ongoing restructuring of postcolonial and post-Cold War ideologies and identities in East Asia?

Jong Tae-se was born in Nagoya, Japan, in 1984 as a third-generation Korean resident. He holds permanent residency in Japan and also South Korean citizenship through his father, but obtained a travel passport from North Korea in order to play for the North Korean national team. Put simply, Jong is a South Korean citizen, a North Korean passport holder, and a permanent resident of Japan. Jong attracted national and regional attention by playing as a member of the North Korean national team in 2008, and leading the team to the 2010 World Cup. During the World Cup, Jong also attracted attention from global media due to his complicated background as a *zainichi* Korean who played for North Korea, a mysterious kingdom in the eyes of the world. His strong performances in both the qualifying and first rounds of the World Cup subsequently enabled him to play for several professional clubs in Japan and Germany. During the 2013 and 2014 seasons, he also played for the Suwon Samsung *Bluewings* in the South Korean professional football league (hereafter K-league).

Beside his professional career in South Korea, Jong enjoys a status of media celebrity by starring in several television entertainment programmes and also by featuring in many news broadcasts and documentaries. As a transnational sport celebrity, he seems to exemplify and embody the attitudes and identities of a new generation of *zainichi* Koreans, celebrated for his cultural diversity and bilingual capabilities.[2] Furthermore, as an athlete with high mobility and economic success, he often exemplifies flexible citizenship, one who neither belongs to any nation, nor is limited by fixed or essentialist notions of nationality.[3] However, Jong's choice of joining the North Korean national team in addition to his educational background in Japan provoked debates in South Korea over whether he is pro-North Korea and pro-Communist as the ideological division is firmly maintained. His visibility in the media inevitably brought public attention to his background and history as a *zainichi* Korean as well as to the origins of *zainichi* Koreans in East Asia more generally. This was the moment when his 'invisible hybridity' began to stimulate public discussions over unresolved politico-historic issues that are still lingering in East Asia.

In this context, *zainichi* Korean athletes not only represent contesting, multiple national identities that are subjugated by the new formation of East Asian cultural integration and interdependency, but also invoke the trauma of colonial and Cold War geopolitics in the region. Jong's multiple representations of nation-ness provide strategic sites for analysis of the arbitrariness of national media constructs, the fluidity of national identities, and the (dis)continuity of colonial and Cold War geopolitics.

Locating *Zainichi* Korean Celebrity in Postcolonial East Asia

> 'Impure' identity construction that is neither Japanese nor Korean in a full sense has been a serious issue for them. Their cultural expressions thus tend to deal with the agony and ambiguity about their own precarious lives in the social positioning as *zainichi* who are historically torn apart between the Japanese and Korean peninsula.[4]

While the term *zainichi* Koreans literally refers to the ethnic Korean residents of Japan, their historic origin traces back to Japan's occupation of the Korean peninsula from 1910 to 1945. Under colonial control, many Koreans migrated to Japan and were forced to assimilate as Imperial Japanese citizens, regardless of whether they came voluntarily or forcibly. For instance, Son Gi-jeong, a Korean runner, was forced to represent Imperial Japan under his Japanese name, Son Kitei, when he won a gold medal for Japan at the 1936 Berlin Olympics.[5] After the end of World War Two, many of the immigrant Koreans (about 650,000 out of the 2.4 million in total before 1945) decided to remain in Japan, which led to them losing their imperial Japanese nationality and being treated as foreign nationals. The Japanese government required the remaining Koreans to register as foreigners in 1946, thus enabling them to stay in Japan as permanent residents yet at the same time restricting their rights, such as the right to vote.[6]

During the Cold War period, *zainichi* Koreans formed two groups: the pro-North organization was called *Chongryon* while the pro-South organization was named *Mindan*. With support from the North Korean government, *Chongryon* was the dominant group until the 1970s, taking the lead in establishing *Chongryon* schools and nurturing the succeeding generation of *zainichi* Koreans by educating them in the Korean language, history, and identity. In the 1960s, a large group of *zainichi* Koreans also returned to North Korea under the repatriation programmes, which was regarded as a return to their homeland.[7] However, the normalization of South Korea-Japan relations in 1965 further complicated the political status and cultural identity of *zainichi* Koreans. The normalization officially announced that all of the *zainichi* Koreans would be regarded as South Korean, irrespective of their individual choices. After the normalization, South Korea under the Park Jung-hee regime sought to attract investment from *zainichi* Koreans, although the government was indifferent to supporting special schools for them in Japan.[8] This change facilitated a process for another wave of South Koreans to migrate to Japan for the purpose of finding jobs and attaining financial success. This wave of migrants was called 'newcomers' compared to the 'old-comers' who arrived in Japan before the end of World War Two.[9]

As South Korea surpassed North Korea in economic and political power, the influence of North Korea in Japan decreased, and the number of students who attended *Chongryon* schools also declined sharply. In 2010, there were 565,989 registered *zainichi* Koreans in Japan.[10] For both North Korea and South Korea, the issue of *zainichi* Koreans has served as a political maneuver to expose the ambiguous attitude of Japan towards its war responsibilities and express the unsettled postcolonial agony to the public, both internally and externally. Moreover, it reflects the ambivalence of colonial modernity brought by the Japanese imperial force to East Asia—which needs to be further examined for its (dis)continuation in the postcolonial context.[11] Put simply, the subjectivities of *zainichi* Koreans were produced as the result of both colonization and the Cold War, and, for a long time, abandoned, forsaken or marginalized by mainstream media in Japan, North and South Korea.

The concept of 'hybridity', developed by post-colonial theorists such as Homi Bhabha, Stuart Hall, and Gayatri Chakravorty Spivak, provides a useful starting point for understanding *zainichi* Koreans, and it is a theoretical challenge to locate *zainichi* Koreans in the historical and political context of East Asia.[12] Since hybridity is generally conceptualized to problematize essentialist notions of culture, ethnicity and identity, the concept is useful for articulating the struggles of *zainichi* Koreans to identify themselves between dominant and minority cultures – similarly to those of the colonized elsewhere. However, one may be able to point out a significant difference from the major postcolonial framework of white as colonizers and non-white as the colonized – that is, *zainichi* Koreans were subjects of colonialism by a 'similarly colored' colonial master. Contrary to the typical imperial and colonial theatre in the duality of West and non-West or white and non-white, postcolonial subjects, who were formerly colonial Koreans of Imperial Japan, were 'populated with peoples not utterly different from themselves in racial make-up and cultural interventions'.[13] As a result, unlike black and brown migrants in the nations of the former Western colonial masters, *zainichi* Koreans — especially those of second or later generations — are not easily identified as the Other by their physical appearance or skin colour. This enables *zainichi* Koreans to strategically hide their citizenship as Koreans and pass as Japanese by using Japanese names (*tsūmei* in Japanese) and using the Japanese language in public. Consequently, there has been political complicity between *zainichi* Koreans – who present themselves as Japanese to avoid everyday conflicts – and the Japanese media, that excludes the issues of *zainichi* Koreans to forgo unresolved postcolonial disputes between Japan and Korea, in constructing what may be called 'invisible hybridity'.

Despite the intended or unintended indifference of the Japanese mass media to the issues of *zainichi* Koreans, there has been some journalistic and academic work in Japanese on the subject.[14] The agony and ambiguity that *zainichi* Koreans feel has often been obscured within the mass media in Japan due to its sensitivity to the historical memories of the World War Two in relation to forced Korean labour, including sexual workers or 'comfort women'. As Naoki Sakai argues, 'it is in the sense of evading shame that the regime of *separation* between the Japanese and the Koreans sustains the colonial imagination for the Japanese'.[15] In South Korea, studies on *zainichi* Koreans are divided into two foci. The first considers the historic origins, legal status and social prejudices of *zainichi* Koreans in post-War Japan by examining important historic events such as the end of the World War Two, the South Korea-Japan summit talks in the 1960s, and the repatriation to North Korea.[16] By approaching *zainichi* Koreans as a minority in Japan, this trend often highlights the victimization of Koreans and postcolonial racism by the Japanese.[17] The second trend explores mass media representation of *zainichi* Koreans in South Korea in order to understand the hegemonic ideologies of the post-colonial and post-Cold War eras.[18] Under these frames, *zainichi* Koreans are represented and often stereotyped as national victims, half-Japanese, or the nouveau riche.[19]

While there are many *zainichi* Koreans who choose to keep their hybridity 'invisible', younger generations have been more open about their Korean roots and heritage especially since the new millennium. For instance, celebrities who have publicly pronounced their identities as *zainichi* Koreans include Kang Sang-Jung (an emeritus professor at the University of Tokyo), Song Jun Ui/Son Masayoshi[20] (founder and CEO of Softbank), and Cho Sung Hoon/Akiyama Yoshihiro (a mixed martial artist). Several feature films such as *Go* (2001), *We Shall Overcome Someday*

(2004), and the documentary *Our School* (2006) have vividly portrayed and represented *zainichi* Koreans' lives and struggles in contemporary Japan. Furthermore, the Korean Wave in Japan helped Japanese society and its people to approach South Korea and *zainichi* Koreans in a novel way, as well as increasing the amount of traveling and (returning) migration between South Korea and Japan. Consequently, the younger generation of *zainichi* Koreans, who are often called the 'post-*zainichi* generation',[21] show a change in manners and strategies in constructing their own identities. For instance, they often regard issues of nationality and naturalization as a personal choice or utilize their bi-cultural capabilities as cultural resources. In South Korea, this new approach highlights their cosmopolitan subjectivities, equipped with high mobility, linguistic fluency and economic competitiveness without reserving historic agonies and structural inequalities in both Japan and Korea. While there still exist prejudice and discrimination against *zainichi* Koreans in Japan, as manifested through the anti-Korean Wave and hate speech against *zainichi* Koreans and their schools, the emergence of the post-*zainichi* generation along with their increasing visibility both in mass media and everyday life makes it necessary to re-visit and examine the changing discourses on *zainichi* Koreans.[22]

Within the context of sport, *zainichi* Korean athletes were historically represented or treated by the mass media simply as Japanese citizens with Japanese names, thereby concealing their Korean origins and hybridity, and thus reproducing the mythologized homogeneity of Japanese-ness. For example, one of the most iconic sports stars in post-war Japan was Rikidōzan, a professional wrestler who was represented as 'the protector of Japanese virtue' in a series of matches against American opponents in 1954.[23] While it was largely obscured by mainstream media around the time, Rikidōzan was born in Korea as Kim Sin-rak under the control of Imperial Japan and adopted into a family in Japan with his Japanese name, Momota Mitsuhiro, before he came to be known as a sumō and then professional wrestler with the pseudonym Rikidōzan.[24] Moreover, baseball, as the most popular sport in post-war Japan, produced numerous *zainichi* Korean stars including Kim Kyung-hong/Kaneda Masaichi, Jang Hun/Harimoto Isao and Kim Eui Myung/Kanemura Yoshiaki. Nonetheless, given their racial resemblance, Japanese names and ability to speak fluent Japanese, the Korean roots and identity of many *zainichi* Korean athletes went unnoticed, and when they did disclose it publicly, their hybridity was often underplayed by mass media in the interest of reproducing cultural nationalism and the myth of ethnic purity. As William Kelly contends, '[i]n public, they were "Japanese", and this was done by insisting that whatever their blood-ethnic backgrounds they all shared the experience of coming up through baseball in the Japanese school system'.[25]

Although discussions on *zainichi* Koreans were historically kept on the margins in the context of sport, the 'invisible hybridity' of *zainichi* Koreans has been more widely exposed, questioned and politicized during the era of the post-*zainichi* generation. Especially when *zainichi* Korean athletes represent their nations, either North Korea, South Korea or Japan, their hybrid identities and representations have posed a threat to the homogeneous construction of their nation-ness or 'imagined community'.²⁶ In other words, their cultural hybridity reveals the *arbitrariness* of national representations and the *fluidity* of national identities, thereby destabilizing the modern political structures of nation-states within the context of postcolonial East Asia. For instance, football, as one of the most rapidly growing sports in East Asia, has served as an emerging site for many *zainichi* Koreans to explicitly display their hybrid identity and pursue a cosmopolitan desire to transcend the national borders in terms of both transnational mobility and stardom. Two vivid examples of such *zainichi* Korean football stars are Lee Chung-sung/Lee Tadanari and Jong Tae-se, whose expressive voices of cultural identity challenge the norm of 'invisible hybridity' embodied by preceding generations of *zainichi* Koreans. When Lee Tadanari became a naturalized citizen of Japan in 2007 in order to play in the 2008 Beijing Olympics as a member of the Japanese national football team, he chose his surname as 'Lee' over his Japanese surname, 'Ōyama', to represent the ethnic hybridity in his name. As he said, 'I wanted to prove that even a person named "Lee" could flourish as a member of the Japanese national team and give a hope [to other *zainichi* Koreans] by scoring a goal'.²⁷ On the other hand, Jong Tae-se chose to represent North Korea through his affiliation with *Chongryon* at the 2010 FIFA World Cup. The North Korean government issued him a travel passport, which satisfied FIFA's eligibility rules. The case of Jong's multiple representations is particularly pertinent to the understanding of how the mobility and identity of *zainichi* Koreans is both shaped and disrupted by colonial and Cold War geopolitics in East Asia.

Approaching Jong Tae-Se and His Discourses in East Asia

This study approaches a sport celebrity as a social construct and utilizes the discourses around a sport celebrity to illuminate emerging, dominant and even competing sentiments of a society and people in which the celebrity is positioned and constructed. Therefore, it regards sports celebrities like Jong Tae-se as emblematic individuals who are acting as 'channeling' devices for the 'negotiation of cultural space and position for the entire culture'.²⁸ In this approach, the media reportage and related discourses around Jong are not only about news or information transmission, but are also reflections of the desires, tensions, and agonies of its society and people more generally. In particular, the symbiotic relations between media and celebrity make it possible for news and stories of sports celebrities to rapidly spread across national and regional borders.²⁹

To explore the various discourses around Jong, this study collected the majority of its data from news media coverages of him and related online responses in South Korea, as well as his autobiographies written in both Korean and Japanese.³⁰ For the news media coverage, KINDS, a news search engine in South Korea was used to collect articles published between 2008 and 2013.³¹ By using his name as a keyword, about 1,400 newspaper and broadcast articles were found. Jong firstly appeared in Korean newspapers in 2008, when he joined the North Korean football team, and since then, he has sporadically drawn significant media attention. At the same time, this study explores the online responses to Jong and his media coverage from an online sports community.³² This online community originally consisted of South Korean Major League Baseball fans and later attracted fans of various other sports.³³ Jong's autobiographies that were examined included one book in Korean and two books in Japanese.³⁴ By examining his autobiographies along with media representation and public responses, this study reveals his own thoughts and desires, as well as recollected memories from multiple perspectives.

This study employs discourse analysis as a method, which is useful for analyzing the various representations of sport celebrities and the processes by which particular discourses are articulated within certain contexts in order to generate a set of knowledge and beliefs.³⁵ The study therefore aims to illuminate the competing media discourses as constructed by professional journalists, ordinary people, and the celebrity himself. Thus Jong Tae-se, a sport celebrity, was framed both as a media process coordinated by industry experts and journalists and as a commodity that was both consumed and produced by audiences, fans and the celebrity himself. This method then enabled us to examine the various narratives of Jong, which not only reflect particular social values and cultural norms that he embodied but also served as a collective battleground where conflicting ideologies were revealed, affirmed or negotiated.³⁶

Zainichi Korean Celebrity as National Arbitrariness

First of all, Jong Tae-se functions to destabilize an essentialist understanding of national belongingness, boundary and identity in postcolonial East Asia. For the past few decades, ethnic as well as national homogeneity has been regarded as an undeniable and indispensable decree for sustaining Japanese and Korean national cultures. While recent globalization and multiculturalism have debilitated people's entrenched belief in homogenous nationalism, the current changes are manifested through increased numbers of immigrants and diverse ethnic and national groups in their own society. Meanwhile, the emergence of Jong Tae-se as a regional celebrity provided an opportunity for East Asian society and its people to raise a query against ethnic and national essentialism.

As soon as Jong Tae-se debuted as a member of the North Korean football team in 2008, he drew attention from South Korean media. Not only his *zainichi* background but also his choice of joining the North Korean team elicited media scrutiny as well as curiosity from the South Korean public. His debut as a member of the North Korean team in an international sporting event symbolizes the multiplicity or even arbitrariness of national belongingness.

Such a unique status may be exceptional and temporal, but it also signals the malleable and flexible nature of nationality. In her discussion of multiple-passport holders, Aihwa Ong suggests the term 'flexible citizenship' to refer to 'the cultural logics of capital accumulation, travel, and displacement that induce subjects to respond fluidly and opportunistically to changing political-economic conditions'.³⁷ At a glance, Jong seems to exemplify a flexible citizen who has multiple cultural resources, high mobility, economic success and fluency in different languages. He also played for many professional teams in Japan, South Korea and Germany while responding to the media interviews in Japanese, Korean, and English, depending on the country where the interviews took place.[38] Indeed, one news article highlights 'his excellency in foreign languages of speaking English, Japanese, and even Portuguese'.[39]

Contrary to the model of flexible citizenship, however, Jong was forced to choose one nationality at any particular occasion, and his enforced choice as opposed to his right to hold multiple nationalities, paradoxically reflects the predicament of a *zainichi* Korean in the new millennium. Because of his education background and cultural influence from a *Chongryun*, it is reported that 'Jong's home town is North Korea, although he has South Korean nationality. In his youth, he had to attend a *Chongryun*-affiliated school... so North Korea, not South Korea, is placed in his heart'.[40] In 2008, however, Jong also represented Japan as a member of the All-Star team of the Japan Professional Football League (hereafter J-league) for the match against the All Stars of the K-league. Jong described his experience of playing on the Japanese team as a strange fate.[41] Furthermore, Jong was even regarded as a South Korean when he played as a member of the Samsung *Bluewings* in the K-league. Contrary to other international imports, who are registered as foreign players in the K-league, he was registered as a domestic player because the Samsung *Bluewings* strategically attempted to avoid exceeding the quota for international players. His nationality came to elicit another controversy when he, as a member of the Samsung *Bluewings*, participated in another international event, the Asian Federation Cup (hereafter AFC). If his nationality was registered as South Korean for the championship league of the AFC, he would automatically lose his eligibility to play for the North Korean national team. This legal controversy was resolved when the AFC issued a statement that 'Jong's dual citizenship as North Korean and South Korean is approved'.[42] As such, his different nationalities, controversies, as well as ad-hoc decisions by multiple entities reveal the very arbitrariness of nation-ness.

Jong's case resonates with the changing sentiments among the third-generation *zainichi* Koreans, many of whom gradually came to regard national identity as a matter of personal choice rather than as an essential asset or pre-given destiny. In his discussion on the post-*zainichi* generation, Lie suggests that for third-generation *zainichi*, 'the idea that nationality should be the last redoubt of ethnicity is not as compelling as it was for the previous generation', so 'the decision to naturalize [into Japanese] is a matter of individual choice'.[43] As previously mentioned, Lee Tadanari has become a naturalized citizen of Japan. As rising football players and third-generation *zainichi*, both Jong and Lee envisioned themselves playing for national teams and eventually reached this goal - but on different teams. On November 15, 2011, they met on the same pitch for the first time, each representing a different nation for a 2014 World Cup Asian qualifier match in Pyongyang, North Korea. The event represented a historic moment in which the contrasting choices – and identity struggles – of two *zainichi* Korean football players crossed paths under heightened political tensions between North Korea and Japan over the issues of abductions and missile tests.

In his autobiography, Jong maintained that he held his central identity as a *zainichi* Korean and refused to be categorized into one fixed nationality as expressed both in Japanese and Korean:

> People can change beliefs, interests and lifestyles, but they cannot change or betray their own roots. I am *zainichi* when I play as a star striker, and I am *zainichi* when I am

made redundant by a team. As I said earlier, wherever I go, wherever I live, *zainichi* is *zainichi*.[44]

Ultimately, my root is *zainichi*, which I cannot run away from. It depends on me whether *zainichi* is something to be proud of or not. It is a critical match for me whether I live up to the *zainichi* identity as my root.[45]

Rather than limiting himself into one national identity, he often opted for embracing a transnational, or inter-Asian, subjectivity. In a television documentary in South Korea, he expressed his thoughts as follows:

I want to transcend national boundaries. I do not limit myself into such a small world such as South Korea, North Korea or Japan... I regard myself as a complicated being who mediates these countries in a good balance. I wish to fulfill such a role.[46]

Likewise, in his autobiography, Jong noted how the perception of his nationality and ethnicity had been shifted throughout his career:

When I joined Kawasaki Frontale (J-league team), people often went 'North Korea? Zainichi? What do you mean?', 'Can you speak Japanese?', 'When did you come to Japan?' I was recognized as a Korean. As I established my professional career, I became known more as *zainichi*. This recognition spread over North Korea and even South Korea ... when I played for North Korea in the East Asian Football Championship and World Cup qualifiers. And when North Korea won a ticket to the World Cup, I became a household name throughout Asia and indeed Asia's Jong Tae-se.[47]

In his mind, the issue of nationality and even naturalization may be overcome by establishing, embracing and embodying a hybrid *zainichi* identity. As such, while the controversies over his nationalities and representations demonstrate the arbitrariness of nation-ness in East Asia where essential nationalism is still tenacious, Jong's multiple national belongings certainly function to destabilize ethnic essentialism and nationalism in each nation-state.

Zainichi Korean Celebrity as Living History

Jong Tae-se's presence in the media enables East Asia to revisit the historic origins and traumatic experiences of *zainichi* Koreans. Jong functions as an embodiment of history that brings the origins, struggles, and living conditions of *zainichi* Koreans into the present tense. As such, the postcoloniality of East Asia becomes more visible than ever through his personal story which inevitably conjures up not only Japanese colonial occupation but also the Cold War division into the context of contemporary East Asia.

As soon as Jong Tae-se was selected for North Korea, the South Korean media and people instantly paid attention to him. However, Jong was not the first *zainichi* Koreans who became a national member of the North Korean team: he was, in fact, the third player from the J-league after Ahn Younghak and Lee Han-Jae.[48] Calling him 'a monster striker', a news article raised public attention to Jong for his performance on the field as well as the complicated background of his nationality, ethnicity and eligibility.[49] Because many South Koreans were ignorant of the origins, legal status, and current condition of *zainichi* Koreans, they became very curious about and then surprised by his personal story and motivation behind his choice of North Korea as his national team, as evidenced by the following online responses:

> WJ: Korean diasporas in Japan stand at the crossroads among North Korea, South Korea, stateless, or Japan with a lot of pain. Many of them select North Korea due to loyalty and attachment, and Jong is one of them.[50]

> Meme: complicated and surprising facts behind Jong Tae-se's nationality... It is Japan where he was born and his friends live... It is South Korea that his family's nationality belongs to... it is North Korea that he plays for as his homeland. Jong has become a young man with such a complicated story. His story is embedded with suffering from Japanese colonial occupation and national grief of separation between North and South.[51]

Accordingly, his choice became a hot issue in the online community. Many online members did not know the background of *zainichi* Koreans, and some accordingly expressed their confusion over Jong's decision. Some of them did not even know that the second and third generation *zainichi* Koreans still hold South Korean citizenship.

> Game: According to the ruling of FIFA, is it possible for Jong Tae-se to play for the South Korean soccer team? His grandfather, father, and he all have South Korean nationality.

> Kalia: His identity is simply a *zainichi* Korean, and he chose North Korea simply for the purpose of playing soccer in the World Cup.

> Ahn: To me, his identity is inclined towards North Korea due to his education.[52]

Due to the media speculation on his background and identity, Jong came to represent not only his own personal story but also the historic experience of *zainichi* Koreans more generally to the contemporary South Korean society. Similar to any sporting events between South Korea and Japan, Jong's story induced South Korea, a former colony of Japan, to face its past under Japan's imperial control with an emotional grudge.[53] In so doing, Jong functions as 'one instance of the way in which the spectre of history seems more than ever to intrude on public life'.[54]

Jong's celebrity status at the 2010 World Cup created a 'vortex effect' around him, which Garry Whannel refers to as the growth in range of media outlets and the vastly increased speed of circulation of information.[55] Particularly, his crying scene during the first pre-game ceremony of the World Cup was viewed by global audiences and football fans, which sparked widespread curiosity over the reasons for his tears.[56] Related media reports and video clips helped reveal historic wounds and the complicated history of *zainichi* Koreans for many.[57] In a short period of time, Jong became 'the focal point of a wide range of intersecting discourses – the central point of a vortextual process'.[58] Several broadcasters also made special programmes that highlighted the lives of Jong and other *zainichi* Korean athletes in Japan.[59]

Jong Tae-se is not only conscious of his *zainichi* identity but also straightforward with his complicated background and issues of nationality. He particularly highlighted his personal and collective agonies in Japan and the ethnic education that he received in his youth, as expressed in Korean:

> When (international) reporters ask me questions on non-sports issues, including political ones, I am ready to embrace them. When I respond to these questions with sincerity and in their languages, I can do away with stereotypes about me or Chosun.[60]

> My grandfather migrated to Japan during the colonial period, and settled down against unfair discrimination, and my parents, following his will, sent me to 'our school' in which I was educated as a person from Chosun for 16 years... such experiences gave me national attachment, national spirit, and conviction as one of the people of Chosun, even though I live in Japan.[61]

In speaking to Japanese audience, Jong explained the struggles in his early life with respect to the inflexible rules of nationality:

> I attended the *Chongryon* school, learned about North Korea for its positives and negatives, and held a long-standing dream to represent a North Korean team. I couldn't think about anything else. I can tell you that my patriotism is very strong. My nationality is, actually, South Korean. I had a strong contradiction in my mind – why is it South Korea even though I went to the *Chongryon* school and support North Korea? I was thinking at the time, if I could become a member of the North Korean national team, I would be willing to change my nationality.[62]

Despite his invisibility in terms of physical appearance or skin colour, Jong Tae-se's hybridity or postcoloniality was made highly visible and inerasable by his own narrative and expressive voice on his identity, education, and choice of North Korea to play for a national team. This is the complexity of invisible hybridity of *zainichi* Koreans as postcolonial subjects.

Zainichi Korean Celebrity as a De-Cold War (Im)possibility

The discourses on Jong Tae-se in East Asia show that *zainichi* Koreans are still caught between ideological tensions that originated from the division of the Korean peninsula during the Cold War. Jong Tae-se and his discourses were inevitably influenced by relations between North and South Korea, and in 2013 he was seriously involved with a pro-North controversy in South Korea, which was the latest manifestation of anti-communism or McCarthyism in the post-Cold War period. The ideological battle over Jong reflects that a spectre of the Cold War still lingers around *zainichi* Koreans as well as postcolonial East Asia.

During the Cold War, including the Korean War (1950-1953), the two Koreas became the most dangerous and hostile enemies, and as such, *zainichi* Koreans are separated by the dividing ideological line. To *zainichi* Koreans, as Sonia Ryang describes, their political identification 'became a fierce battleground for expatriate politics during the Cold War'.[63] In Japan and South Korea, *zainichi* Koreans who were affiliated with or educated under *Chongryon* were easily demonized as pro-North Korean groups and individuals. While the Cold War ended in the early 1990s, the Korean peninsula remains divided by ideological collision, and in Japan North Korea remained a major external threat due to its kidnapping of Japanese citizens during the 1970s and its later nuclear missile tests.[64]

With respect to the ideological divide, although Jong initially struggled to fit in with the communist/socialist culture of the North Korean national team, he openly appreciated it in the form of a critique towards capitalist societies such as South Korea and Japan:

> All the coaches and players [of the North Korean team] have affectionate eyes. So, I want everyone to understand that it is completely different from 'the image of North

Korea' that people often have, because the players are really genuine human beings. I am often asked about what the North Korean national players live for. They don't live for money. I always suggest how special they are as this kind of human beings.[65]

Jong's personal goal and trip to North Korea are akin to the story of An-Seong, the protagonist of the popular *zainichi* film *Pacchigi* (2004), who decided to be repatriated to North Korea in the 1960s with a dream of playing football in the North Korean team in the World Cup. While An-Seong's decision of repatriation was presented as apolitical in the name of football,[66] Jong's life seems to have fulfilled the dream of the *zainichi* protagonist. In this sense, and figuratively speaking, Jong's accomplishment of his personal goal through football may signal a possibility of overcoming the Cold War trauma that has haunted the lives of *zainichi* Koreans for decades.

However, Jong's time in South Korea has never been smooth. Rather, his reception shows that *zainichi* Koreans are still tethered to the Cold War ghost. Jong has constantly been under scrutiny by the media over his connection, attachment and loyalty to North Korea.[67] The issue became salient particularly when relations between South and North Korea turned more hostile. As a case in point, in anticipation of the 2010 World Cup, a large telecommunications company in South Korea prepared a commercial featuring Jong Tae-se and Park Ji-sung, captains of each Korean team, but military tension between the two Koreas forced the company to cancel the airing of the commercial.[68]

The ideological battleground around Jong reached a new level in 2013 when he played in South Korea as a member of the Samsung Bluewings in the K-league. *Daily Best*, an ultra-conservative online community incited ideological demonization by branding him as the Reds or North Monster.[69] More specifically, *Daily Best* mobilized a campaign against him by stating that 'It is crazy to select a monster from North Korea to be all star players in K-league'.[70] Ideological attacks against Jong reached their peak when he was accused of violating the National Security Law in the summer of 2013. At the time, the political landscape of South Korea was filled with pro-North controversy, which repressed progressive and pro-North politicians and their parties. Jong was accused of being on North Korea's side because of an interview he did in 2010 where he said, 'I respect Kim Jong-il absolutely and I like to believe and follow him whatever happens'.[71] He was indicted by a conservative organization that claimed that 'Jong Tae-se praised the *Juche* ideology of Kim Il-sung and played soccer for the North Korean regime under the influence of his education with *Chongryon*'.[72]

While the legal investigation over his alleged pro-North stance elicited public reaction, people in the online community expressed diverse opinions concerning him. One member suspected that Jong could be a spy for North Korea, and that the South Korean government should therefore either punish or deport him.

Heat: I am sure that Jong Tae-se is the Reds ... .I think Jong should be reported.[73]

Giant: I think Jong Tae-se needs to clarify his position ... He has to explain why he had such an interview [praising a leader of North Korea], but is now playing for the Samsung *Bluewings*.[74]

On the other hand, another pointed out that the current situation was similar to McCarthyism, and even argued that the National Security Law, a remnant of the Cold War, should be abolished.

> Letoile: Given the controversy over Jong Tae-se, it is time to abolish the National Security Law, which is contradictory to Constitution.[75]

Simultaneously, diverse and competing opinions over the controversy and the National Security Law hint at a possibility of rupturing the Cold War ideological structure. In this sense, Jong Tae-se embodies and represents both the vulnerability and disjuncture of the Cold War ideological structure in postcolonial East Asia more generally.

Zainichi as an Inter-Asian Subjectivity (and Decolonial Method)

Our analysis of Jong and his discourses shows that he exemplifies the malleability and multiplicity of identities that further contribute to de-stabilizing reified, monolithic and homogenous understandings of nationality, citizenship and ethnicity. Simultaneously, his presence conjures up colonial and Cold War memories, historical wounds, as well as the current predicaments of *zainichi* Koreans. The symbiotic relations between media and celebrity further contribute to promulgating public knowledge and historic debates over the issues of *zainichi* Koreans. In this vein, Jong exemplifies the duality of sport celebrities in East Asia. While he, like many other sport celebrities, represents global mobility, cosmopolitan identities, and profitable commodities, he is often articulated through national and regional disputes, rules and imaginaries that have been shaped by the post-colonial and post-Cold-War conditions in East Asia.[76] Furthermore, our analysis suggests construing the multiplicity and fluidity of *zainichi* Korean identity in relation to the possibility of inter-Asia subjectivity. Jong represents an embodiment of historic baggage that reminds people of the imperial/colonial and Cold War history, and the continuing wounds and discrimination, in postcolonial East Asia. Also, his entanglement with the pro-North controversy in South Korea indicates that *zainichi* Koreans are still caught within anti-communism ideologies of the Cold War and anti-North Korea sentiments. At the same time, he symbolizes the potential for dismantling essentialist ideology and discourse of nation-ness in East Asia. As Jong describes his identity as a *zainichi* Korean, he does not necessarily belong to any of South Korea, North Korea or Japan; rather, as a transnational sport celebrity, he is able to traverse the national borders and to connect with more than one country through his multi-lingual and multi-cultural resources. As such, Jong's case provides an opportunity to facilitate de-colonial thinking towards the construction of inter-Asia subjectivity. De-colonial thinking embraces the idea that 'coloniality is constitute, not derivative, of modernity', which helps to 'understand how the colonial matrix of power was constituted, managed and transformed'.[77]

The arbitrariness of Jong's changing nationalities as well as his desire to transcend the national borders may indicate a potential to approach *zainichi* Koreans for de-colonial thinking as well as practices in postcolonial East Asia. Jong's self-identification with the inter-Asia subjectivity enables him to provide a similar but more nuanced answer to the question of where *zainichi* Koreans belong. Additionally, the wide range of media coverage and programmes about him and other *zainichi* Koreans made the invisible hybridity more visible for people across East Asia to re-visit the shared past history in a vivid and newly fashioned way. Such re-cultivated understandings of *zainichi* Koreans, as Tessa Morris-Suzuki suggests, enable us to produce 'feeling and imagination as well as pure knowledge' and to 'help to determine how we act in the world'.[78] The understanding of *zainichi* Koreans as inter-Asia subjectivities ultimately contributes to the ongoing discussions on diaspora and diverse minorities that do not fit into the rigid boundaries of nation-states as well as historical and contemporary relations of East Asian nations. To conclude with Jong's words, 'I was born in Japan. North Korea is my national team, and South Korea is my home country. I have cultural backgrounds crossing three nations, and I honestly think that each of them is part of my body'.[79]

Notes

1. In this paper, Korean and Japanese names are ordered with family names first followed by given names in accordance with their convention.
2. David L. Andrews and Steven J. Jackson, 'Introduction: Sport celebrities, public culture, and private experience', in *Sport Stars: The Cultural Politics of Sporting Celebrity*, ed. David L. Andrews and Steven J. Jackson (New York: Routledge, 2001), 1–19.
3. Aihwa Ong, *Flexible Citizenship: The Cultural Logics of Transnationality* (Durham: Duke University Press, 1999), 6.
4. Koichi Iwabuchi, 'When the Korean Wave Meets Resident Koreans in Japan: Intersections of the Transnational, the Postcolonial and the Multicultural', in *East Asian Pop Culture: Analysing the Korean Wave*, ed. Beng Huat Chua and Koichi Iwabuchi (Hong Kong: Hong Kong University Press, 2008), 254.
5. William W. Kelly, 'Japan's Embrace of Soccer: Mutable Ethnic Players and Flexible Soccer Citizenship in the New East Asian Sports Order', *The International Journal of the History of Sport* 30, no.11 (2013): 1235–46.
6. Choi Youngho, 'Zaeil Chosunin, Hankukin Sahoiui Bonkuk Locality' [Zainichi, and the hometown locality of its Society]. *Locality Humanities* 1 (2009): 259–97.
7. Kim Kwiok, 'Bundankwa ChunChengui Disapora' [Diaspora of division and war], *History Criticism* 91 (2010): 53–93.
8. Kim Taesik, 'Nooka Diaspora-rul Philyoro Haneukak' [Representation of Zainichi in the Korean films], *Japan Criticism* 4 (2011): 224–47.
9. Shin Sojung, 'New Comer-wa Zainichi-ui Kwanke Yonkoo' [The relation between new comer and Zainichi], *Japanese Culture Studies* 31 (2009): 245–70.
10. 'Ministry of Internal Affairs and Communications (2011)'. *Seifu tōkei no sōgō madoguchi*, http://www.e-stat.go.jp/SG1/estat/List.do?lid=000001074828# (accessed August 26, 2011).
11. Younghan Cho, 'Colonial Modernity Matters? Debates on Colonial Part in South Korea', *Cultural Studies* 26, no.5 (2012): 645–69. Hyunjung Lee and Younghan Cho, 'Introduction: Colonial Modernity and Beyond in East Asian Contexts', *Cultural Studies* 26, no. 5 (2012): 601–16.
12. Homi K. Bhabha, *The Location of Culture* (London: Routledge, 1994); Stuart Hall, 'Cultural Identity and Diaspora' in *Identity: Community, Culture, Difference*, ed. Jonathan Rutherford (London: Lawrence & Wishart, 1990), 222–37. Gayatri Chakravorty Spivak, *A Critique of Postcolonial Reason: Toward a History of the Vanishing Present* (Cambridge, MA: Harvard University Press, 1999).
13. Leo Ching, 'Yellow Skin, White Masks: Race, class, and Identification in Japanese Colonial Discourse', in *Trajectories: Inter-Asia Cultural Studies*, ed. Kuan-Hsing Chen (London: Routledge, 1998), 66.

14. Chiba Naoki, *Gurōbaru supōtsu ron* [Discourse of global sports] (Osaka: Designegg, 2014); Fukuoka Yasunori, *Zainichi kankoku/chōsen jin: Wakai sedai no aidentiti* [Zainichi Koreans: The identity of a younger generation] (Tokyo: Chuokoronsha, 1993); Kang Sang-Jung, *Zainichi* (Tokyo: Kodansha, 2004); Chung Daekyun *Zainichi kankokujin no shūen* [The end of *Zainichi* Koreans] (Tokyo: Bungeishunju, 2001); Ueda Masaaki, *Rekishi no naka no "zainichi"* [*Zainichi* in history] (Tokyo: Fujiwara Shoten, 2002).
15. Naoki Sakai, 'From Area Studies Toward Transnational Studies', *Inter-Asia Cultural Studies* 11 no 2, (2010): 271, emphasis in original.
16. Kim, 'Bundankwa'; Seo Kyungsik, *Eoneoui Kamokseseo* [Prison of language], trans. Kwon Hyoktae (Seoul: Tolbaegae, 2011). Yoon Guncha, *Gyochakdeon Sasangui Saekye* [Contemporary history of theory], trans. J. Park (Seoul: Changbi, 2008).
17. Lee Jungeun, 'Sikmin Jeakookkwa Junjeng and Diaspora', *Korea Sociology* 45, no. 5 (2011): 169–97.
18. Cho Kyunghee, 'Hankuk Saheoui Jaeil Chousnin Insik' [Zainichi as proper noun], *Yellow Sea Literature* (2007): 46–75.
19. Kwon Hyoktae, 'Jaeil chosuninkwa Hankuk Saheo' [Zainichi and South Korean society], *History Criticism*, no 78 (2007): 234–67.
20. In this paper, where appropriate, when names of *zainichi* Koreans are mentioned, they are firstly presented with their Korean names, followed by their Japanese names (or *tsūmei* in Japanese).
21. John Lie refers to the post-*Zainichi* generation as 'ethnic Koreans who are ready to embrace their Japaneseness, including Japanese citizenship.' See John Lie, Zainichi (Koreans in Japan): *Diasporic Nationalism and Postcolonial Identity* (Berkeley: University of California Press, 2008), 134.
22. Lie, *Diasporic Nationalism and Postcolonial Identity*.
23. Kelly, 'Japan's Embrace of Soccer', 1238.
24. Okamura Masashi, *Rikidōzan: jinsei wa taiatari, butsukarudakeda* [Rikidōzan: Life is about tackling, only about striking] (Minerva Shobō, 2008).
25. Ibid., 1239.
26. Benedict Anderson, *Imagined Communities: Reflections on the Origin and Spread of Nationalism* (London: Verso, 1983).
27. Motokawa Etsuko, 'Lee Tadanari, ajia kappu no rakkībōi o mezashite [Lee Tadanari: Towards a lucky boy of the Asian Cup]', *Sportsnavi.com.*, 2011, http://sportsnavi.yahoo.co.jp/soccer/japan/2011/text/201101150006-spnavi_1.html (accessed August 18, 2011).
28. Andrews and Jackson, 'Introduction', 19.
29. David Rowe, *Sport, Culture and the Media: The Unruly Trinity*, 2nd ed. (Buckingham: Open University Press, 2004).
30. Unless noted otherwise, news articles, online commentaries as well as biographies that are written in Japanese or Korean are translated into English by the authors.
31. KIDS is accessed on www.kinds.or.kr. The collection of news media coverage shares the data of the research from Cho Younghan, 'Hankuk Sahui Je 3 Saedae Jaeil Chosun-in Danron Yonkoo [Discourses of the third generation of Zainichi Koreans in South Korea]', *Korea Cultural Studies* 33 (2017): 211–45.
32. The website of MLBPARK is www.mlbpark.com.
33. Younghan Cho, 'Materiality of an Online Community: Everyday Life of Global Sport Fans in South Korea,' in *The Routledge Handbook of New Media in Asia*, ed. Larissa Hjorth and Olivia Khoo (New York: Routledge, 2015), 130–40.
34. Jong Tae-se, *Jong Tae-se ui Noonmoo* (Seoul: Renaissance, 2012); Jong Tae-se, *Zainichi Damashii!* [The soul of *zainichi*!] (Tokyo: NHK Shuppan, 2011); Jong Tae-se, *Kabe wo kowasu!!* [Breaking the wall!!] (Tokyo: Iwanami Shoten, 2010).
35. Norman Fairclough, *Discourse and social change* (Cambridge: Polity Press, 1992).
36. Greame Turner, *Understanding celebrity* (London: Sage Publications, 2004).
37. Ong, 'Flexible Citizenship', 6.
38. *Daily Economics*, January 31, 2012.

39. SBS, June 9, 2010.
40. *Daily Economics*, May 30, 2008.
41. *Hangyerae*, July 17, 2008.
42. *Yonhap News*, February 1, 2013; *Herald Economics*, February 1, 2013.
43. Lie, *Zainichi*, 146.
44. Jong, *Zainichi damashii!*, 194–5.
45. Jong Tae-se, *Jong Tae-se ui Noonmool* (Seoul: Renaissance, 2012), 184
46. 'Jong, Tae-se, I am a striker of "Chosun"', SBS, July 24, 2010.
47. Jong, *Zainichi damashii!*, 196.
48. *Kyunghyang Shinmoon*, June 14, 2007.
49. *Kyunghyang-shin*, February 19, 2008
50. A reply to a posting from MLBPARK on June 25, 2008, http://mlbpark.donga.com/bbs/view.php?bbs=mpark_bbs_bullpen&idx=60691&cpage=2&s_work=search&select=stt&keyword=%C1%A4%B4%EB%BC%BC (accessed January 10, 2019).
51. A posting from MLBPARK on June 16, 2010, http://mlbpark.donga.com/bbs/view.php?bbs=mpark_bbs_bullpen09&idx=503610&cpage=7&s_work=search&select=stt&keyword=%C1%A4%B4%EB%BC%BC (accessed January 10, 2019).
52. A posting and replies from MLBPARK on June 16, 2010, http://mlbpark.donga.com/bbs/view.php?bbs=mpark_bbs_bullpen09&idx=503351&cpage=8&s_work=search&select=stt&keyword=%C1%A4%B4%EB%BC%BC (accessed January 10, 2019).
53. Victor D. Cha, *Beyond the Final Score: The Politics of Sport in Asia* (New York: Columbia University Press, 2009).
54. Tessa Morris-Suzuki, *The Past within Us: Media, Memory, History* (London: Verso, 2005), 4.
55. Garry Whannel, *Media Sport Stars: Masculinities and Moralities* (London: Routledge, 2002).
56. As well as live-broadcasting of the game, various versions of Jong Tae-se's crying scenes can be found on YouTube. One clip has been viewed about 800,000 times, https://www.youtube.com/watch?v=NsOubeMN7eQ (accessed February 11, 2019).
57. *Korean Economics*, June 16, 2010; *Money Today*, June 16, 2010.
58. Whannel, *Media Sport Stars*, 207.
59. Examples include 'Jong Tae-Se, I am a striker of Chosun' (SBS, July 24, 2010), 'Football and Three Homelands' (MBC, 27 August 2010), and 'I am a Korean' (SBS, January 1, 2012).
60. Jong Tae-se, *Jong Tae-se*, 149.
61. *Hangyerae*, July 3, 2008.
62. Jong, *Kabe wo kowasu!!*, 24–5.
63. Sonia Ryang, 'Introduction. Between the Nations: Diasporas and Koreans in Japan', in, *Diaspora Without Homeland: Being Korean in Japan*, ed. Sonia Ryang and John Lie (Berkeley: University of California Press, 2009). 8.
64. John Lie, 'The End of the Road? The Post-Zainichi Generation. Between the Nations: Diasporas and Koreans in Japan', in *Diaspora Without Homeland: Being Korean in Japan*, ed. Sonia Ryang and John Lie (Berkeley: University of California Press, 2009), 168.
65. Jong, *Kabe wo kowasu!!*, 39.
66. Ichiro Kuraishi, '*Pacchigi!* And *Go*: Representing Zainichi in Recent Cinema', in *Diaspora Without Homeland: Being Korean in Japan*, ed. Sonia Ryang and John Lie (Berkeley: University of California Press, 2009), 107–20.
67. 'Why does Jong Tae-se become a member of North Korea?', *Hangyerae*, July 24, 2010.
68. On March 26, 2010, *Cheonam*, a corvette of the South Korean Navy sank in the Yellow Sea, killing 46 seamen. The, South Korean government pointed to a North Korean torpedo as the cause of the sinking, https://www.theguardian.com/world/2010/apr/22/north-korea-cheonan-sinking-torpedo (accessed January 10, 2019).
69. *Seoul Economics*, May 31, 2013.
70. *E-today*, May 1, 2013.
71. *Kookmin Ilbo*, June 3, 2013.

72. *Joongang Daily*, June 20, 2013.
73. For the discussion on Jong in the online community, http://mlbpark.donga.com/mlbpark/b.php?&b=bullpen&id=2417729&m=search&query= (accessed January 6, 2019).
74. For the discussion on Jong in the online community, http://mlbpark.donga.com/mlbpark/b.php?&b=bullpen&id=2434388&m=search&query= (accessed January 6, 2019).
75. For the discussion on Jong in the online community, http://mlbpark.donga.com/mlbpark/b.php?&b=bullpen&id=2422739&m=search&query= (accessed January 6, 2019).
76. Rowe, *Sport, Culture and the Media*.
77. Walter D. Mignolo and Catherine E. Walsh. *On Decoloniality: Concepts, Analytics, Praxis* (Durham: Duke University Press, 2018), 4.
78. Morris-Suzuki, *Past in the Present*, 24.
79. Jong, *Kabe wo kowasu!!*, 55.

Disclosure Statement

No potential conflict of interest was reported by the authors.

Funding

This study was supported by the Hankuk University of Foreign Studies Research Fund.

The Absent Savior? Nationalism, Migration, and Football in Taiwan

Tzu-hsuan Chen and Ying Chiang

ABSTRACT
A surge of interest in football has surfaced in the past few years in Taiwan. Many fans credit it to Xavier Chen, a Belgium born French-Taiwanese footballer. Chen lives mostly in Belgium and has a distant connection with Taiwan. His Mandarin efficacy is very limited. Yet he is still being hailed as the savior of football. Despite being a member of the Belgium Under-19 national team, Chen's tie with Taiwan was unearthed by a local football fan, who later became his agent, in the computer game franchise 'Football Manager'. He was recruited and later naturalized as a Taiwanese citizen and debuted for the national team in 2011. Chen, nicknamed 'The Noble Prince of Football', has been a very unique sport celebrity in many regards. His educational background, composure, masculinity and 'noble' image are all represented in a very different way, vis-a-vis conventional, native-born Taiwanese athletes. This research adopted critical discourse analysis to examine the coverage from major Taiwanese media outlets, from his debut in 2011 until one year into his retirement, to argue that the representation of Xavier Chen as a de-territorialized, nationalistic athlete embodies Taiwan's desperate attempt for recognition and assistance from international society through the sport of football.

> He could choose for Belgium. His mother is Belgium [sic]. His father is Taiwanese. And he chose Taiwan.
>
> Mark Uytterhoeven (Actor & KV Mechelen board member)[1]

Taiwan has long been ridiculed as a desert of football by the nation's own sports fans. Baseball, a relatively marginal sport in the global context, is the nation's favorite spectator sport and carries the most nationalistic implications. While Taiwan's baseball teams constantly rank in the top five in the world, their football never enjoys the same fanfare off the field and in 2016 the national team plunged to 191st in FIFA's world ranking. Although Taiwan had its glory days in Asian football by way of winning two gold medals in men's football in the Asian Games in the 1950s, the achievement was actually accomplished by Hongkongers under the alliance of 'democratic China'. Even more embarrassing, that part of history is barely recalled by most Taiwanese.[2]

However, a surge of interest in football has surfaced in the past few years. Many fans credit this to Xavier Chen,[3] a Belgium-born French-Taiwanese footballer, and even call him the 'savior' of Taiwanese football. Chen lives mostly in Belgium and has remote connections with Taiwan. His Mandarin is very limited. When he agreed to play for Taiwan in 2011, his then 96-year-old grandfather had to teach him stroke by stroke to sign his Chinese name. As a Belgium national Under-19 representative, he confessed that whether playing for Belgium or Taiwan is equally meaningful.[4] He flew back to Belgium immediately without a prolonged stay after getting his Taiwanese ID and passport. Indeed, he only visited Taiwan once before playing for the nation. How can a person be so strange to his 'homeland' yet be regarded as a savior?

For a nation desperately seeking exposure and recognition in the midst of diplomatic predicaments and threats imposed from China, Xavier Chen is reminiscent of the 'Linsanity' phenomenon caused by the Harvard-graduate Taiwanese-American NBA player Jeremy Lin in 2012.[5] Compared, however, to the global popularity of basketball in general and the NBA in particular, football is not a mainstream sport in Taiwan. However, for football fans there, Xavier Chen was regarded as the bridge reconnecting the isolated nation to the world via the globe's most popular sport. This paper examines Xavier Chen and his influence as an intriguing example of a sport celebrity and his embodiment of the ever-complicated relationship between nationalism, migration and football in Taiwan.

Sport and Migration

With globalization and transnational migration getting more and more intense in the past few decades, sport as a cultural terrain is not immune from the trend. Modern sport started spreading across the globe with Eurocentric imperialism in the nineteenth century and initiated a pattern of standardization, institutionalization, rationalization and globalization[6] Sport labour migration has become a hallmark in sport globalization. Under the circumstances, athletes migrating across borders obscure traditional definitions of boundary and ignite debates on politics, economics, culture and race. According to Joseph Maguire, Grant Jarvie, Louise Mansfield, and J.M. Bradley, there are four types of sport immigrants: pioneers, settlers, nomads, and returnees. Pioneers promote 'their' sport with missionary passion. These migrants helped establish football as a global game as the British Empire expanded. Baseball in Taiwan is also a cultural heritage left by Japanese colonization between 1895 and 1945. Settlers, as the name suggests, settle where they provide their service. Foreign players in professional leagues are these sort of 'mercenaries' who choose the place which offers the best economic return for their sporting skills. As for nomads, they stop for a shorter period of time for their work and could be viewed as 'cosmopolitan strangers'. In the end, these sport migrants could end up going back to their homelands and become returnees in order to extend their career. For example, Brazilian footballer Romario chose to spend his last playing days in Campeonato

Brasileiro Série A after spending years in countries such as the Netherlands, Spain, Qatar, the United States and Australia.[7]

However, Maguire et al's ideal-type categorizations fail to meet the needs of a much more dynamic and complicated sport migration in the contemporary world, especially in terms of its nationalistic and cultural implications. In the baseball-crazy East Asian region, Chan-ho Park (South Korea),[8] Ichiro Suzuki (Japan)[9] and Chien-ming Wang (Taiwan)[10] all emigrated and represented their respective homelands as 'proxy warriors' in Major League Baseball. All these players stayed in the U.S. for more than a decade. Yet, their ties with their homeland were still much stronger than those with the U.S. It is difficult for them to fit in any of the categories.

By contrast with professional athletes who migrate as laborers pursuing the best economic interest in exchange for their sporting skills, naturalized athletes who represent countries other than their original homeland raise different discussions and have become a looming issue for international sport federations. Jansen, Oonk, and Engbersen sampled 45,000 athletes between the 1948 London Olympics and 2016 Rio Olympics from Argentina, Australia, Brazil, Canada, France, the United Kingdom, Italy, the Netherlands, Spain, Sweden and the United States in order to discover a longitudinal trend.[11] There were 167 athletes from these eleven countries who had swapped countries via the five following principles in obtaining a new nationality:1) right of soil (*jus soli*), 2) right of blood (*jus sanguinis*), 3) right of residence (*jus domicilii*), 4) right of marriage (*jus matrimonii*), and 5) right of talent (*jus talenti*). The final principle involves the flow of money and 'skills' or 'human capital', which also functions as a currency in today's global market for highly skilled foreigners.[12] This could lead towards marketization of citizenship in international sport as countries compete for talent. The protagonist of this essay, Xavier Chen, in addition to his apparent blood tie with Taiwan, obtained his Taiwanese citizenship *de facto* via this last principle by being paid more handsomely than his compatriots by Taiwanese Football Association.

Sport and Nationalism

Under the ever-intensifying pace of globalization, sport, as an economic and cultural vehicle has been intertwined with the global network. National borders may be blurring in some cases, but the relationship between sport and nationalism nevertheless remains strong.[13] According to Bairner, 'sport and nationalism are arguably two of the most emotive issues in the modern world.' Sport is usually taken as a vehicle for the expression of national affections and identities, and 'is clearly linked to the construction and reproduction of the national identities of many people.'[14] Hoberman also discusses the different relationships between sport and political ideologies, and describes a 'sportive expressionism' in which sport can be taken as a kind of 'dramatic performance'.[15] He suggests that 'sportive expressionism can employ the heroic-athletic individual in an agonistic state or the rhythmic choreography of the mass'.[16] In other words, elite athletes are important symbols of nationalism. 'National sporting teams, composed of the best players born within certain national boundaries become the focus of powerful, if unrealizable, fantasies.'[17]

They are thus represented as 'proxy warriors' for nationalistic pride.[18] But Hoberman also argues that 'sportive nationalism is not a single generic phenomenon. On the contrary, it is a complicated sociopolitical response to challenges and events, both sportive and non-sportive that must be understood in terms of the varying national contexts in which it appears.'[19] While this research is about a unique football player who embodies the sporting nationalism of Taiwan, a country with a multi-colonized history, equivocal national identities and ambiguous forms of nationalism, nevertheless Bairner argues that despite the different nationalist political activities, we 'share certain assumptions and rely, to a greater or lesser degree, on telling stories about the past, constructing national mythologies, and, in some cases, inventing traditions'.[20] Xavier Chen embodies the diplomatically isolated Taiwan's collective anxiety and the yearning of 'being seen' by the international society.

Sport Nationalism in Taiwan: A Persistent Double Anxiety

As Ying Chiang and Alan Bairner observe, 'It is impossible to capture the idea of sport in Taiwan without an understanding of Taiwanese nationalism and vice versa.'[21] Nationalism has become the foundation of the construction of the identity, imagination and practice of sport in Taiwan. From the nineteenth century in societies such as China, Hong Kong and Taiwan, there was a collective humiliating self-identity as 'the sick man of East Asia'. Indeed it was a term that Chinese thinkers reinvented to amplify a series of Chinese national crises since the Opium Wars. However, over time the term was considered, in the words of Jui-sung Yang, as 'purely a contemptuous criticism on the Chinese body from the evil West ... [Thus}, many Chinese enthusiastically believe that victory in international sports games is the best way to 'wipe up the national humiliation resulting from the "Sick man of East Asia"'.[22]

With its multiple colonial history, Taiwan has to various degrees inherited Spanish, Dutch and Japanese culture since the seventeenth century. In terms of sport, it was the Japanese who brought its modern forms to the island and instilled these through its colonial apparatus during the early twentieth century. Following the defeat of Japan in the Second World War, Taiwan was handed to China. It then became the base for the Kuomintang (KMT) after its defeat by the Communists in mainland China in 1949. It also received substantial military and economic aid from the US during the Cold War.[23]

Among these historically significant influences, China (People's Republic of China, or PRC) is the most complex figure to Taiwan. They are on the one hand linguistically, racially and culturally proximate and economically interdependent, yet politically opposite and militarily hostile on the other. In the early years, the KMT still clung to the slim hope of restoring the sovereignty of the Republic of China (ROC) over the mainland. But their refusal to accept Taiwan as the official name in sport and other international contexts was proof of enduring hostility. However, with political tides changing and the chances of 'restoring' the ROC on the mainland becoming next to impossible, Taiwan had to accept the bizarre and compromised name of Chinese Taipei under the terms of the Lausanne Agreement in 1981.[24] Thus

Taiwan inherited not only the 'Sick man of East Asia' sentiment shared by all ethnic Chinese, but also endured political isolation after the Chinese Civil War to the extent that it has perhaps become an 'Orphan of Asia'. Indeed, there are currently only seventeen countries in the world with official diplomatic ties with Taiwan, and most of these are shaky and prone to pressure from China.[25] This 'double anxiety' became the *raison d'être* for sport in Taiwan. Moreover, Taiwan's dominant totalitarian regime did not offer fertile ground for sport. Martial Law was imposed in 1949 and not lifted until 1987. Freedom of speech and public gatherings were severely restricted. Sport was therefore never a focus for community unity or local identity. Under these circumstances it developed in a highly opportunist fashion, especially when it was required to serve nationalistic purposes.[26]

Elite sport has subsequently become a significant vehicle for achieving national goals in Taiwan, including a shared national identity.[27] According to Chiang and Chen, Taiwanese as a whole lack self-assurance and must be recognized by their significant others. For most Taiwanese, those who achieved great accomplishments in international sport and kindred fields became 'the glory of Taiwan' – a phrase that has become common in contemporary Taiwanese media coverage. 'Regardless of how trivial the issue, the Taiwanese appear desperate for every chance to prove their existence and worth'.[28]

The most researched aspect of sport and nationalism in Taiwan is baseball which started as a Japanese colonial project and became the national game of Taiwan.[29] Chen claims that baseball has served as a vehicle for national identity since the success of Taiwanese Little League teams in the United States during the 1970s.[30] The success of Chien-ming Wang, arguably the greatest Taiwanese player in Major League Baseball, is also regarded as having important implications for nationalism.[31]

By contrast, Chin-feng Tong has stated that 'Taiwan is a well-known football desert',[32] a commonly shared identity among its fans and press. As of December 2018, Taiwan (as Chinese Taipei) was the 124th-placed nation on the FIFA World Ranking. As Chiang explains, "FIFA World Cup was the synonym of football for most Taiwanese. Most Taiwanese watch and care about football only once every four years."[33] Other than the excitement ignited by the mega-spectacle of the World Cup, most of the time football fandom was the combination of anxiety and sometimes humiliation. In her work, Chiang focused mainly on the gender implications of the media representation of Taiwanese female football fans. However, the media commentaries and coverage of the 2014 World Cup still constructed a male-centered, melancholic national sentiment. Participating in the World Cup was portrayed as a solemn and sorrowful dream to Taiwan and its Asian neighbors.[34]

This background highlights the uniqueness of Xavier Chen. In an island that rarely cares for football, a mix-raced, half-we-half-they savior was portrayed as coming from Europe in the hope of rescuing a sport and generating enough exposure for a land overshadowed by the rise of China.

Sporting celebrities such as Chien-ming Wang, a former New York Yankees pitcher,[35] former number one female golfer Yani Tseng[36] or Taiwanese American NBA player Jeremy Lin[37] were all dubbed 'Glory of Taiwan'. The first two athletes are unquestionably 'genuine' Taiwanese. They became household names and symbols of nationalistic identity with their athletic excellence and unquestionable Taiwanese origin. Jeremy Lin, on the other hand, posed an intriguing case, especially *vis-à-vis* Xavier Chen. Lin kept himself in a gray zone and was reluctant to take sides in the tension and controversy between Taiwan and China. As he said in an interview with *Sports Illustrated*, 'I just try to stay out of all that stuff'.[38] But with the growing popularity of 'Linsanity', Jeremy Lin's American citizenship became an awkward reminder of the legitimacy of Taiwanese national emotions projecting on him. The puzzling question of 'is Jeremy Lin a real "glory of Taiwan" or are we the "free-riders" of Linsanity' continues to haunt the nation and reflects the schizophrenic essence of Taiwanese sport nationalism.[39] Unlike Lin, Xavier Chen is unwaveringly Taiwanese in this regard. Even though he lives in Belgium most of the time and played professionally in China for three seasons, his willingness and ultimate decision to represent Taiwan was never in doubt. But like Lin, Xavier Chen rarely appears in Taiwan. However, his nine international caps for Taiwan is something Lin never achieved. For Taiwanese people, Chen is both an insider and an outsider. His ambiguity embodies Taiwan's schizophrenic attempt at international recognition. On one hand, he is more 'one of us' than Jeremy Lin. On the other hand, he is European, a distant but aspiring Other. With Chen being a bridge, especially with his mix-raced look and elite educational background, this kind of elasticity for Taiwanese identity can be constructed. After his retirement, he stayed in Belgium. A savior, after all, is supposed to stay at a distance and not be among his followers who continuously ask for miracles.

In order to build a contextual understanding of Xavier Chen's rise and to establish his mythical status as a football celebrity in Taiwan, qualitative critical discourse analysis was used to examine media stories and triangulate findings in the context of Taiwanese culture, social and historical background.[40] The texts were collected from June 6, 2010, the day Chen debuted in the Taiwanese major press, to December 31, 2018, six months after his final appearance in Taiwan, when he was promoting his documentary *Dreamers: Last Shot - Xavier Chen*. Data were collected from three major newspapers in Taiwan including *United Daily*, *Apple Daily* and *The Liberty Times* and their online databases by using the keywords Xavier Chen and Chang-yuan Chen (陳昌源, his Mandarin name). The following discussion offers both a chronological analysis of news coverage of Chen and an examination of mass media representation and embodiment of an anxious and precarious nation's collective expectation for a 'savior' in order to find a slim silver lining in the shadow of the rising rival – China.

A Savior Cometh

First of all, the 'football savior' is referred to by two names in the Taiwanese press. Xavier is his French name and is more often written as *Xia Wei Yeh* (夏維耶), a phonetic transcription, in Taiwan. He also has a Mandarin name, Chang-yuan Chen, which was given to him by his grandfather. Chen is a common Chinese family name. The character *chang* in his given name means 'prosper', and *yuan* 'origin'. Even his given name perfectly presages a mythical savior coming from the outside to prosper in his country of origin. However, in his memorandum of understanding with the Chinese Taipei Football Association (CTFA), he demanded that the name printed on the back of his jersey be Xavier instead of Chen, a Chinese name so common that he shares it with another 2.6 million Taiwanese people (out of a population of 23 million), in order to highlight his uniqueness.[41]

Calling Xavier Chen a sport migrant may be a misnomer. After all, he does not seem to fit into any of the four categories identified by Maguire et al.[42] He certainly was not a football trailblazer in Taiwan. He did not settle in Taiwan. He never really had to be a nomad, other than when he played for the Chinese Super League for Guizhou Renhe from 2013 to 2015. He, from Belgium's perspective, never had to return because he never really left. This is especially true considering he now works for the Belgian sports channel Proximus11, a job he took up immediately after his retirement as a player. Perhaps, from a Taiwanese perspective, he is an absentee, a sport migrant that never really has to migrate - an absent savior that never had to settle down.

Like every mythical savior with an appropriately dramatic origin story, the discovery of Xavier Chen was also one of seemingly fateful coincidence. Chia-ming Chen, the then-public relations director of the Chinese Taipei Football Association, who later became his agent in Taiwan, found out about Xavier Chen through the computer game franchise *Football Manager*. The game is known for its ultra-realistic and detailed database that accurately mirrors real-world football. While what most fans could do is to assemble a winning team in videogames, Chia-ming Chen pushed the dream further beyond the cyber terrain. He wanted his 'real' national team to be more competitive, and a shortcut to reviving Taiwanese football would be to recruit established oversea players. While he was playing *Football Manager*, he started searching for players with common Chinese surnames on the game's database of football players. He soon found a player named Chen playing for the top-flight Belgian club KV Mechelen. That is how the 'savior' was first spotted. However, his last name alone was not enough to make him a convenient recruit for Taiwan. First of all, his genealogy had to be established. This part of the obstacle was removed later, after it was confirmed that his grandfather Keng-sun Chen was a Taiwanese diplomat stationed in Brussels, Belgium. Keng-sun's son Jean studied at the Catholic University of Louvain where he met his future wife, Frenchwoman Sabrina, who gave birth to their son Xavier in 1983. After confirming his ethnicity, Taiwan had to face some challenges in recruiting him, as China also showed interest.[43]

When Xavier Chen was first covered by Taiwanese media, he was represented as a total outsider. The reporter in question realized that he somehow had to spin the story from an angle other than football, seeing that Taiwan was a football desert and readers were not entirely interested in football players. This is apparent in the way the story starts by likening Chen's appearance to that of Hollywood star Keanu Reeves. Connecting Chen with an established and famous celebrity that Taiwanese fans thought he resembled could raise more interest in him as a player and increase interest in football in Taiwan in general. At the time of this interview, Chen was still reluctant to take up the position of representing Taiwan:[44] 'Taiwan is my father's country. I've kept it in my mind always. Representing Taiwan? It would be interesting. But I will put the Belgium league as my top priority. I am not in a hurry to make decisions.' The distance between Xavier Chen and Taiwan was further demonstrated by his inability to speak Mandarin: 'The third generation Taiwanese Xavier speaks fluent English, French and Flemish but can only say 'hello' and 'thank you' in Mandarin. He could not even properly pronounce his own Chinese name.'[45] Even though Xavier Chen was raised partly by his grandparents, they rarely mentioned China or Taiwan and never thought of teaching him Mandarin. He had only visited Taiwan once when he was ten years old before his official 'homecoming'. The distance between Xavier and Taiwan or China, according to his own account, was due to his grandfather's painful memories of the Chinese Civil War and being exiled to Taiwan with the defeated Chiang Kai-shek and his depleted KMT government. Furthermore, as a diplomat, he had to witness firsthand the struggle and failure of the Republic of China. Therefore, Keng-sun Chen preferred to have his grandson grow up as a European. He himself eventually left Belgium to return to Taiwan after Xavier grew older.[46]

After Taiwan's enthusiastic campaign to recruit him, along with encouragement from his relatives in Taiwan, Chen eventually elected to play for Taiwan. His €1,000 appearance bonus per match was not very substantial, considering that his annual salary with KV Mechelen was €700,000. In a press conference, he told reporters: 'Many people asked me why Taiwan? They are weak in football. After watching some DVDs, I think the team is not that bad. I want to help the team.' He also explained that playing for China was something that never crossed his mind. It was his decision to honor his grandfather and side with Taiwan instead of China, a rival more powerful in almost every way, be it political influence, economic prowess or football.[47]

Eventually, it was blood that motivated Xavier Chen to make the decision to 'follow grandfather's footsteps.'[48] In his documentary *Dreamers: Last Shot - Xavier Chen*, he described what happened:

> So when I told my father and my grandfather 'Taiwan wants me to play for the national team.' They were very amused. They were really happy and they said 'Yeah! Let's go!' ... For me it was like an honor for my family to play for the national team of Taiwan. I felt that my grandfather was very happy that I returned there. This is also why [it is] important for my choice to play for national team.

He soon made his international debut as part of the Taiwanese national team in a match against Malaysia in the 2014 World Cup qualifier on July 3, 2011 and immediately made an impactful first impression. He scored the game-winning penalty kick. Although Taiwan was eliminated from the 2014 World Cup qualifiers by scoring fewer away goals, the then-record of 15,335 inspired fans witnessed the historical moment of Chen's debut for the Taiwanese national team at Chung San Stadium in Taipei.

Other than his stellar performance on the field, Chen also won over Taiwanese fans through his heartwarming comments in the press. Compared to his previously hesitant attitude, he had completely embraced his new-found identity before his international debut for Taiwan:

> Playing for the national team is an important experience for any football player. Even if the team is not very strong, donning the kit itself is a dream. Like Jong Tae-Se who

burst into tears when hearing the national anthem in last year's World Cup, Xavier looks forward to his debut for Taiwan. 'I want to hear the anthem. It must be very touching.' He says that he would ask his father to teach him how to sing it, 'it's too quick for me to sing but, at least, I have to know the meaning. When it plays, I want to feel it personally.'[49]

After his debut game for Taiwan, he ran to the bleachers and gave his jersey to his then-96-year-old grandfather and happily took photos with his fans with the Taiwanese flag around his shoulders. This night gave birth to a new generation of football fans dubbed the 'Xavier Generation'.[50]

As is fitting for a 'mythical savior', the epic conclusion of Xavier's football career in Taiwan has ensured that his name will go down in Taiwanese football history. The stage could not have been more perfect. After the brilliant matches he played for Taiwan, Xavier Chen announced that he would retire after the AFC Asian Cup qualifier in 2017 versus Bahrain, who were 50 places higher than Taiwan in the FIFA world ranking at the time. The match was held on Taiwan's National Day, The Double Ten (October 10) Day. His perfect cross found team captain Po-liang Chen in the 6-yard box and registered the assist on the game-tying goal in the 89th minute. Taiwan later scored the decisive goal during the added time to defeat Bahrain 2-1. This match has been called the most improbable victory in Taiwanese football history. Once again, Xavier Chen was the hero of the match and retired from international football on an incredibly high note.[51]

His status of 'savior' was further elevated with the release of his documentary *Dreamers: Last Shot - Xavier Chen* in the summer of 2018. Even though it was just a limited release and the filmmakers actually lost money in making it, this does not detract from Xavier Chen's legacy. On the contrary, the fact that this documentary was produced is a noteworthy achievement. In Taiwan, only a few elite athletes have had their autobiographies published, let alone a full-length feature documentary. The documentary revealed that his chronic injury of a stress fracture on his left leg had resurfaced weeks before his final match, and that he had to inject painkillers to allow him to continue playing on the pitch. The image of his pained expression during his treatment was circulated on the internet and has become part of Taiwanese football history's timeless imagery.

From Noble (Confucian) Prince to Progressive Advocate

Xavier Chen's rise to fame and continuous legacy through only nine international matches drew to a perfect conclusion after his defining role in the match against Bahrain on National Day. Ever since his debut, he has been called the 'Noble Prince of Football' by the mass media. This nickname was not just inspired by his handsome looks but also his graceful disposition and notable educational background compared to his fellow footballers. He got his bachelor's and master's degrees in law at Université Libre de Bruxelles and is a certified to be a notary public.[52]

With such a unique educational background *vis-à-vis* fellow European or South American football players, Xavier Chen resonates with Taiwan's Confucian tradition in which studying and academic achievement outranks other personal qualities. As a Chinese saying goes, 'everything is low-class work except academic study' (*Wan ban jie xia pin, wei you du shu gao*).[53] Being a descendant of a Taiwanese diplomat, it is obvious that academic achievement was a priority in Xavier's upbringing. As Jean Chen, Xavier's father, explained in *Dreamers: Last Shot - Xavier Chen*:

> We never thought he'll become a professional football player. He made that decision after graduating from university. We had a pact saying if you want to become a professional player, you have to spend 5 years in the university and obtain that diploma in law. Then you can choose between being a lawyer or a football player ... We are most content with the fact that apart from football, he also has a university degree.

In their examination of the 'Linsanity' phenomenon in Taiwan, Chiang and Chen argue that Jeremy Lin's Harvard degree is an important element of the Linsanity fever.[54] They further argue that 'intellectualism' is the basis of the Taiwanese cultural system.[55] Jeremy Lin, a Harvard graduate who has achieved remarkable success in basketball, has subverted the stereotype of athletes in Taiwan. However, this kind of 'subversion' actually further prioritizes academics over sport accomplishments in an implicit fashion.

The excerpt above also shows that it is not only Xavier Chen's academic achievements that have made him a role model of Confucian values. It is also his filial piety that earned him the title of 'noble prince'. He did not refuse his parents' request to first obtain a university degree before making any career decisions. Instead, he chose to fulfill the conditions his father had set and 'appease' his ancestors before pursuing his football aspirations.

Xavier Chen not only demonstrated his gentle demeanor by obeying his parents, but he was also a leader by example. He was captain of the national team for the first time on October 9, 2015, but, his field-general presence and leadership off the field had impressed Taiwanese players and fans even before the captaincy. When Taiwan played against Cambodia in the international friendly on October 8, 2014, Chen was noticeably absent from the match. He later explained that this was due to the controversy surrounding his unprecedented €1,000 appearance bonus and additional perks, which were not applicable to his teammates but promised when the CTFA recruited him. In his announcement, he called for building a strong system that attracts quality overseas players to represent Taiwan. Also, he stated that he would still be willing to play for Taiwan if his terms were to be met in the future. If necessary, he would find his own sponsors to cover his appearance bonus instead of the CTFA. Nevertheless, he asked fans to root for Taiwanese football and revolutionize Taiwanese football together.[56]

If Taiwanese athletes were to refuse to play for the nation, they would immediately be labeled as traitors and ungrateful. However, that was not the case for Chen. Since he represented 'modern' and 'world-class' football, his demands were viewed as progressive and as a driving force for Taiwanese football to get on the right track by progressive fans. Throughout the whole controversy, it was obvious that most fans blamed the CTFA for their failure in keeping up with the modern world of football.[57]

Xavier Chen later escalated his demands by calling for better treatment of his fellow teammates. Prior to his protests, the Taiwanese national team football players were only given a 200NT (6.5 USD) 'allowance' per day during training sessions by the Sports Administration. Appearance bonuses for matches were not guaranteed, and even if there were some incomes, they usually came as a bonus or incentive, especially after few and far between victories. However, with Xavier Chen's high-profile presence and his calls for fair treatment, the players' perilous situation was exposed and subsequently led to more support from fans. Since then, national team players have started to get better treatment, with the CTFA responding by promising 30% of the box-office revenue as their appearance bonus soon after Chen's protest. After years of struggling and with new leadership in place at the CTFA, appearance bonuses for the national team were finally institutionalized after Chen's retirement. The players now receive as much as 150,000NT per match. The fight Xavier started eventually bore fruit.[58]

For fans in Taiwan, Xavier Chen is not only a role model for traditional Confucian values, but he was also a driving force for bringing the outdated institution of Taiwanese football up to international standards. It first appeared as though he was defying the traditional moral hierarchy by standing up against the CTFA, however, the CTFA was scandal-ridden at the time, justifying Chen's 'disobedience'. The then-CTFA President Chen-yi Lin was prosecuted for fraud in 2015. Fans were overwhelmingly against the corrupt organization, which contributed to framing Xavier as the savior versus the villainous CTFA.

> *Weizi left him; Jizi was enslaved by him; Bi Gan admonished him, and died for it. Confucius said, "There were three good men in the Yin."*
>
> Quote from 'Weizi', *Analects*

According to 'Weizi', Chapter Eighteen of the Confucian Classic *Analects*, there are three benevolent ways to disobey tyrants. Although they appeared to be an act of rebellion, Chen's protests were actually regarded as ethical and loyal to the state and the people. His role in the reform of Taiwanese football practices exemplified the virtue of leadership.

By following the traditional Confucian value of filial piety and obeying his father's will, Chen was equipped with a western education on law, which certainly aided him in the fight against the CTFA for the fair treatment of Taiwanese football players. His personality of "globalness" empowered him furthermore to take on the role of 'savior' against the corrupted local CTFA. Throughout this fight, Chen exhibited a humble but firm attitude, which further established his image as savior, composed of both Confucian qualities and a progressive, global mindset on and off the field.

A Savior Crossing the Strait

Ever since his debut in 2011, Xavier Chen has become the most-known footballer in Taiwan. His performance and ethnicity quickly caught China's attention. Prior to the winter transfer window of 2013, Chen transferred from KV Mechelen to Guizhou Renhe of the Chinese Super League for one million euros and then signed a three-year extension with the team.[59] He stated that one of the reasons he elected to play in China was the convenience of traveling when playing for Taiwan. Even though China is Taiwan's political rival in almost every way, this was a reasonable career decision for any football player. One of the most obvious reasons for Chen playing for a Chinese team is that there is no established professional league in Taiwan. Consequently, playing in China is an obvious choice for skilled Taiwanese football players who aspire to prolong their career, and not just because they share the same language and similar cultural customs, but also because Taiwanese players do not have to compete with other international players for recruitment in Chinese football teams. Since the 2009 season, Taiwanese, Hongkongese and Macanese players have been categorized as *'ne-yuan'* (domestic reinforcement) instead of *'wai-yuan'* (foreign reinforcement) in Chinese football. Under this policy, each team is allowed to register one *ne-yuan* in addition to four non-Asian international players and one Asian player (The 4 + 1 Rule). Under this favoured condition, Taiwanese players are exempt from fierce competition with other potentially more talented and polished foreign players and are more likely to be signed by Chinese football clubs than before. From the perspective of football, it was a friendly and welcoming policy, as it allowed Taiwanese players to develop in a more mature and competitive environment. Even members of independence-leaning Taiwanese ultras applauded the Taiwan-friendly policy as they believe that it can 'make our national team stronger.'[60] Politically speaking, however, it does echo the PRC's One China Policy as it virtually treats Taiwan as identical to the PRC's two Special Administrative Regions.

While Taiwan continues to struggle with China in the international political arena, their athletes often operate under the radar and become an awkward reminder of their country's predicament in relation to their rapidly rising rival. Of the approximately thirty Taiwanese basketball players who played or are currently playing in China, none of them have been reported on in any significant manner. Even if their stories occasionally surface in mass media, they all focus on personal performance. National identity is a topic that is rarely touched upon.[61] Xavier Chen and his China experience is no exception. Even with his caliber, his performance in the Chinese Super League was never covered by the mainstream press in Taiwan. Among the three major newspapers, there were no stories featuring his on-field performance during his three-year tenure with Renhe. Only *Apple Daily* ran a story ('Leaving the Chinese Super League for Belgium. Xavier: No Friends') of his departure when the contract expired in 2015: 'Xavier says that he does not have any friends in China. [He] can't get used to the life there. He stayed in a hotel for three years and misses home a lot.'[62] It is obvious that football in China is not what Taiwanese football fans care about, even when it comes to Xavier Chen. This one very short story expresses Xavier Chen's negative experience and even projects animosity towards China.

What Xavier Chen embodies can also be translated as him being 'our' savior. 'You Chinese should keep your hands off of him' seems the general sentiment. After losing the battle for his service in 2010, the Chinese press jeered his choosing Taiwan over China and commented that he did so because he feared competing against Linpeng Zhang, the starting right back for the Chinese national team.[63] The story was denied by Xavier's Taiwanese agent, who commented it as 'sour grapes' from China.[64]

Overall, in his nine international caps for Taiwan, as a right back, he scored three goals, which outnumbers his two goals scored in the professional career, a total of 252 matches, and was mostly known for shutting down his opponents' left wing attacks. Could someone who played only nine games and only ever occasionally showed up in the nation really be regarded as a 'savior' for a particular sport? Well, if the backdrop is a football desert, then even just a few drops of rain could be regarded as a miracle.

Assessing the 'Absent Savior's' Impact on Taiwanese Nationalism

As previous studies suggest, an important element of Taiwanese sport nationalism is recognition from their significant 'others'. Xavier Chen, on one hand, is one of their own, but on the other, he is also this significant other. With his Taiwanese father and European upbringing, he is the perfect mixture for a nation seeking redemption from its harsh political and diplomatic reality amid the rise of China vis-à-vis a globally popular sport.

On the field, Chen was a legend. His Taiwanese international career was impeccable, mythical even. From his debut in 2011 to his finale on National Day in 2017, Xavier Chen scored more international goals than during his club career. Fighting through an injury and delivering a game-changing assist in the match against Bahrain resulted in one of the most historic imageries in Taiwanese football. Off the field, he struck a perfect balance of representing Confucian values but also transforming himself into a progressive advocate and being a spearhead and spokesperson for the reform of Taiwanese football.

Taiwan's quest for skillful, yet well-educated, noble-mannered athletes who embody traditional qualities and international charisma did not stop with Xavier's retirement. After all, Taiwan is still facing a dire international political reality. Recruiting athletes that fit Xavier Chen's profile is a convenient shortcut and an instant rescue from outside. It did not take long for Taiwan to find Xavier Chen's successor. Will Donkin, a youth football player currently in the academy of Crystal Palace, definitely resembles Xavier Chen in both talent and ethnicity. With a Taiwanese mother and British father, the 17-year-old also has a rare educational background for a football player having attended the renowned Eton College. He has already been dubbed 'Taiwanese Messi' by the *Sun* even before his international debut.[65]

For Taiwan, the quest for a savior is a desperate yet inevitable move for them to cope with the predicament they are in. With the political situation with China and the football predicament, Taiwan was unlikely to win any victories. Xavier Chen being both a 'we' and a 'they' perfectly met the prerequisite of a 'savior'. His on-field performance ignited a passion for football in a once-football desert. Off the field, he shouldered the burdens of being a savior for a homeland he rarely inhabits, by way of being virtually absent.

Notes

1. Quoted from Dreamers: *Last Shot - Xavier Chen*, released by Gear Film Corp. in 2018.
2. Tzu-hsuan Chen, 'Taiwan-Hong Kong United: A Socio-Historical Analysis on the Alliance of Taiwan and Hong Kong Football'. *Asia Pacific Journal of Sport and Social Science* 6, no. 3 (2017): 216–30.
3. This article adopts western convention of name order, namely, a given name followed by a family name, except for well-known historic figures such as Chiang Kai-shek that are written in reverse order.

4. Yu-lung Ma, 'Representing Belgium or Taiwan? Xavier: Equally Honorable', *United Daily*, June 9, 2010, B4.
5. Ying Chiang and Tzu-hsuan Chen, 'Adopting the Diasporic Son: Jeremy Lin and Taiwan Sport Nationalism', *International Review for the Sociology of Sport* 50, no. 6 (2015): 705–21.
6. Joseph Maguire, 'Globalization and Sport: Beyond the Boundaries?' *Sociology* 45, no. 5 (2011): 923–9.
7. Joseph Maguire, Grant Jarvie, Louise Mansfield, and J. M. Bradley. *Sport Worlds: A Sociological Perspective*, (Champaign, IL: Human Kinetics, 2002). Chapter 2.
8. Rachael Miyung Joo, '(Trans)national Pastimes and Korean American Subjectivities: Reading Chan Ho Park', *Journal of Asian American Studies* 3, no. 3 (2000): 301–28.
9. Yuka Nakamura, 'The Samurai Sword Cuts Both Ways: A Transnational Analysis of Japanese and US Media Representations of Ichiro', *International Review for the Sociology of Sport* 40, no. 1 (2005): 467–80.
10. Tzu-hsuan Chen, 'From the "Taiwan Yankees" to the New York Yankees: The Glocal Narratives of Baseball', *Sociology of Sport Journal* 6, no. 29 (2012): 546–58.
11. Joost Jansen, Gijsbert Oonk, and Godfried Engbersen, 'Nationality Swapping in the Olympic Field: Towards the Marketization of Citizenship?' *Citizenship Studies*, 22, no. 5 (2018): 523–39.
12. Ibid., 526
13. Alan Bairner, *Sport, Nationalism, and Globalization: European and North American Perspectives*, (Albany: State University of New York Press, 2001), 1.
14. Ibid.
15. John M. Hoberman, *Sport and Political Ideology*, (Austin: University of Texas Press, 1984), 7.
16. Ibid., 12.
17. Ali Bowes and Alan Bairner, 'England's Proxy Warriors? Women, War and Sport', *International Review for the Sociology of Sport* 53, no. 4 (2018): 394.
18. Ibid.
19. John M. Hoberman, 'Sport and Ideology in the Post-Communist Age', in *The Changing Politics of Sport*, ed. Lincoln Allison (Manchester: Manchester University Press, 1993), 18.
20. Bairner, *Sport, Nationalism, and Globalization*, 5.
21. Ying Chiang and Alan Bairner, 'Women, Sport and Gender Politics in Taiwan', in *Women, Sport and Exercise in the Asia-Pacific Region*, ed. Gyozo Molnar, Sara N. Amin and Yoko Kanemasu (London: Routledge, 2018), 21.
22. Jui-sung Yang, 'Imaging National Humiliation: "Sick Man of East Asia" in the Modern Chinese Intellectual and Cultural History', *Journal of History* no. 23 (2005): 43.
23. Meredith Jung-En Woo-Cumings, 'National Security and the Rise of the Developmental State in South Korea and Taiwan', in *Behind East Asian Growth: The Political and Social Foundations of Prosperity*, ed. Henry S. Rowen (London: Routledge, 1998)
24. Yi-Ling Huang and Chen-Huei Wang, 'Chinese Question in the Olympic Movement: From the Perspective of Taiwan', *The International Journal of the History of Sport* 30, no. 17 (2013): 2052–68.
25. Zhuoliu Wu, *Orphan of Asia* (New York: Columbia University Press, 2008).
26. Tzu-hsuan Chen and Alan Bairner, 'Crossing the Penalty Area? The Dynamics of Chinese/Taiwanese Football', in Softpower, Soccer, Supremacy: The Chinese Dream, ed. J.A.Mangan, Peter Horton, Tianwei Ren (Bern: Peter Lang, in press)
27. Chiang and Bairner, 'Women, Sport and Gender Politics in Taiwan', 21.; Chiang and Chen, 'Adopting the Diasporic Son', 708.
28. Ibid., 705
29. Andrew Morris, *Colonial Project, National Game: A History of Baseball in Taiwan* (Berkeley: University of California Press, 2010).
30. Chen, "From the "Taiwan Yankees" to the New York Yankees', 549.
31. Chang-de Liu, 'The Development of Baseball's International Division of Labor and the Transformation of Sporting Nationalism in Taiwan', *Taiwan: A Radical Quarterly in Social Studies*, no. 70 (2008): 33–77.

32. Chin-feng Tong, 'Football Desert and "Made in Taiwan"', *Yazhou Zhoukan* (Asian Weekly), July 20, 2014, http://www.yzzk.com/Cfm/Content_Archive.Cfm?Id=1404963841280&Docissue=2014-28 (accessed October 15, 2018).
33. Chiang, 'The Representation of Women and Gender Implications of 2014Fifa World Cup in Taiwanese Print Media', 50, no. 1 (2017): 95 – 111.
34. Ibid.
35. Chen, "From the "Taiwan Yankees" to the New York Yankees, 550.
36. Yu-chu Wang, and Tzu-hsuan Chen, 'Golf, Nationalism and Gender: An Analysis of Media Representation of Yani Tseng', *Taiwan Journal of Sports Scholarly Research* 60 (2016): 73–96.
37. Chiang and Chen, "Adopting the Diasporic Son'.
38. Albert Chen, 'The Politicization of Jeremy Lin', *Sports Illustrated*, December 17, 2012, 56.
39. Chiang and Chen, 'Adopting the Diasporic Son.
40. T.A. van Dijk, *Discourse as Structure and Process* (London: Sage, 1997).
41. Chia-ming Chen, 'Several Untold Stories of Xavier', *Sports Vision*, October 17, 2017, https://www.sportsv.net/articles/45687 (accessed October 15, 2018).
42. Maguire, Jarvie, Mansfield, and Bradley, *Sport Worlds*. Chapter 2.
43. Hao Ma, 'Xavier: China FA's Invitation Too Casual. No Place for Me with Linpeng Zhang', *Sina Sport*, May 21, 2013, http://sports.sina.com.cn/n/2013-05-21/12016580236.shtml (accessed October 28, 2018).
44. Yu-chien Wang, 'Playing for Taiwan Xavier: Very Interesting', *Apple Daily*, June 6, 2010, https://tw.sports.appledaily.com/Daily/20100609/32573139/.
45. Ibid.
46. Te-yu Chen, 'Xavier: A Home So Far, yet So Close', *Apple Daily*, June 21, 2018, https://tw.appledaily.com/headline/daily/20180621/38049192/.
47. Yu-hsin Yang, 'Xavier in Taiwan Jersey; 40000NT Per Match', *United Daily*, June 5, 2011, B4.
48. Shih-hung Yeh, 'World Cup in Taiwanese Jersey? ID Short for Xavier', *Liberty Times*, May 26, 2011, http://sports.ltn.com.tw/news/paper/495400 (accessed October 15, 2018).
49. Yu-hsin Yang, 'Listening to Anthem Like Crazy. He Wants to Play with Emotions', *United Daily*, June 5, 2011, B4.
50. Tzu-hsuan Chen, Leftfield: *Insights of the Game from a Sport Sociology* (Taipei: Linking Books, 2019), 199.
51. Cheng-hung Wu, 'Comeback Win for Taiwan; Perfect Farewell for Xavier Chen', *NowNews*, October 10, 2017, https://www.nownews.com/news/20171010/2622424/
52. Chun-dai Chen, 'Curtain Falls for Nobel Prince of Football; Xavier: 'Thank You, Taiwan!', *The News Lens*, June 14, 2018, https://www.thenewslens.com/article/97730. Also from Xavier Chen's official website, http://www.jovanholder.be/xavierchen/bio.html.
53. Junwei Yu, and Alan Bairner. 'The Confucian Legacy and Its Implications for Physical Education in Taiwan', *European Physical Education Review* 17, no. 2 (2011): 219–30.
54. Chiang and Chen, 'Adopting the Diasporic Son', 717.
55. Ibid., p.717.
56. Liu and Lih, 'Some Thoughts Regarding Xavier's Refusal of Playing in East Asian Cup', *Sports Vision*, November 6, 2014, https://www.sportsv.net/articles/3898#_ftn1 (accessed October 28, 2018).
57. Chia-ming Chen, 'Several Untold Stories of Xavier'.
58. Hung-bin Li, '150,000NT Appearance Bonus for the National Football Team. Women too.', *ChinaTimes.com*, January 11, 2019, https://www.chinatimes.com/realtimenews/20190111003359-260403?chdtv
59. Yu-hsin Yang, 'Chen Bids Farewell to Belgium New Season in Chinese Super League', *United Daily*, December 21, 2012, B4.
60. Interviewed on May 13, 2015 by the authors with Taiwanese football ultras. Notes in possession of the authors.

61. Jia-Yang Hu and Tzu-Hsuan Chen, 'Media's Representations of the Nationalistic Implications of Taiwanese Basketball Talents' Migration to China', *Mass Communication Research*, no. 135 (2018): 93–138.
62. Yu-chien Wang, 'Leaving Chinese Super League for Belgium. Xavier: No Friends', *Apple Daily*, November 12, 2015, https://tw.sports.appledaily.com/daily/20151112/36894745/. (accessed October 28, 2018).
63. Ma, 'Xavier: China FA's Invitation Too Casual. No Place for Me with Linpeng Zhang'.
64. Chia-ming Chen, 'Belgium Star Made in Taiwan', 2013, http://Ginola.Pixnet.Net/Blog/Post/142894656. (accessed October 28, 2018).
65. Andrew Richardson, 'Crystal Palace Fans Excited as Academy Star Will Donkin, 16, Makes International Debut', *The Sun*, November 17, 2017, https://www.thesun.co.uk/sport/football/4934607/crystal-palace-academy-will-donkin-international-debut/ (accessed November 8, 2018).

Disclosure Statement

No potential conflict of interest was reported by the authors.

Funding

This article was funded by Ministry of Science and Technology, Taiwan [Grant ID:106-2410-H-179-005-MY2].

ORCID

Tzu-hsuan Chen http://orcid.org/0000-0003-0620-1527

The Heroic White Man and the Fragile Asian Girl: Racialized and Gendered Orientalism in Olympic Figure Skating

Chuyun Oh

ABSTRACT
Intersecting performance studies and critical sports studies, this article analyzes the North American media coverage of South Korean figure skater and the gold medalist Yuna Kim at the 2010 Winter Olympics in Vancouver. While North American newspapers and NBC (US) and CTV (Canada) broadcasts acclaim Kim's athletic achievements onstage, they also infantilize and Orientalize Kim as an exotic, fragile, and dependent Asian girl. Contrarily, the media highlights the role of her Canadian coach Brian Orser offstage as a heroic white man. It dramatizes and sympathetically identifies with him by nostalgically recalling the 'Battle of the Brians'. When Kim's Koreanness is invisible and conflated as hypervisible ethnic Other, Asian/Asian Americanness, her athletic competency is negated under the name of Orientalism that fetishizes, romanticizes, and thus, reinforces the racialized and gendered hierarchies between the heroic white man and the fragile Asian girl. Nevertheless, Asian/Asian American female athletes' increased visibility opens a liberatory space for re-visiting Asian and Asian Americanness – Pan-Asian identity – at the glocal Olympic stage.

A middle-aged white man in a black suit stands back-to-back with a young Asian woman. He wears a confident smile with his arms crossed over his chest. The woman is clad in tight white pants and high-heeled boots. She slightly tilts her hips and leans back while flirtatiously forming her fingers into guns in front of puckered lips. This scene appears in a 2010 television commercial for Samsung air conditioners. The models are Yuna Kim, an internationally-known South Korean female figure skater, and her coach Brian Orser, a Canadian figure skater and two-time Olympic silver medalist in 1984 and 1988.[1] Influenced by Kim's short programme to the James Bond Medley at the 2010 Vancouver Winter Olympics, where she won the gold medal, the characters resonate with typical images from the movie series – a seductive Bond girl and James Bond.

In the era of glocalization, the global flow directly influences local sports, and vice versa.[2] Athletes praised for their skills are now transformed into global sports celebrities via transnational media, and their local success often leads to global success in other countries.[3] Since the late 1990s, Asian sports celebrities such as Chan Ho Park, former South Korean baseball pitcher for the Los Angeles Dodgers, and Yao Ming, former Chinese basketball player in the National Basketball Association, have transcended the geographically fixed notion of nationality.[4] Kim is one of the most notable Asian sports celebrities today and is included on Forbes' list of the world's highest-earning female athletes, with US $14 million earnings in 2014.[5]

Sports celebrities are not free from racialized and gendered postcolonial ideology. Their 'flexible citizenship' demonstrates the internalized racial and gender hierarchy in glocalization.[6] In Korea, white men are prioritized over non-white male and female athletes;[7] Dutch football coach Guss Hiddink, who served the Korean national team at the 2002 World Cup, and Kim's coach Orser quickly became celebrities in Korea and received honorary citizenship, while Dang Ye-Seo, born in China, a naturalized South Korean female table tennis player and an Olympic medalist, struggled for eight years to obtain Korean citizenship while confronting repeated criticism.[8]

Previous research on Kim has addressed the Korean media's representation of 'Queen Yuna', a source of national pride against her rival Japanese figure skater Mao Asada;[9] conventional gender roles in advertising;[10] a non-sexualized, heroic, competitive single woman serving neoliberal nationalism;[11] and upward class mobility and ethnic identity symbolized by the 'Korean dream' against postcolonial anxiety.[12] Rachael Miyung Joo analysed the U.S. media's portrayal of Korean female athletes as 'exotic Asian sexuality' but did not provide a detailed analysis of Kim's case.[13] Despite racialized and gendered influences on figure skating,[14] and Kim's global sports celebrity status, there is scarce literature on her media representation outside Korea. Furthermore, the movement of the body is not a mere spectacle but a cultural text where racial and gender identities are negotiated and contested.[15] Dance, such as ballet, played a significant role in the development of the movement vocabularies and aesthetics of figure skating.[16] The performative aspects of Kim's figure skating, however, are often overlooked.

An analysis performed at the intersection of performance studies and critical sports studies through the lens of Orientalism renders these overlooked spaces visible and offers new insights into the meaning of Asian sport celebrities. Edward Said's concept of Orientalism is relevant given the emergence of neocolonial imperialism at the Olympics with the propaganda of 'the war on terror' that frames non-whites as Other during the post-racial era.[17] Representation is a central process of reinforcing Orientalism in sports.[18] The ways in which the North American media represents Kim's short and free skating programmes at the 2010 Vancouver Olympics expose the contours of contemporary Orientalism. Her short programme featuring her Bond girl character provides 'one of the sport's iconic images'. It exemplifies an Orientalist consumption of Kim, disclosing the invisibility of her Koreanness in contrast to the hypervisibility of her Asianness.[19]

The Orientalization of Asian and Asian American Figure Skaters

Said developed the term Orientalism amid his research on the Middle East and Europe, in which the former is constructed as an exotic, deviant, inferior feminine

Other by the imperialist gaze of Western colonizers.[20] Orientalism is a 'systematic discipline' wherein white Euro-American cultures manage and produce the Orient.[21] In a North American context, the 'Orient' mainly refers to East Asia (Japan, China, and Korea).[22] The Olympics is not a neutral exhibition of sports but a battlefield staging racialized, gendered, and ethnicized national ideologies.[23] Orientalism in sports produces false racial inferiority, which is used to justify Western dominance.[24] At the Olympics, white masculinity is represented as the dominant, universalized, hegemonic heroic figure, while racial, ethnic, and gender minorities are portrayed as the exotic Other, including the exoticization and feminization of Asia, which reinforces gendered and ethnicized hierarchies.[25] Jackie Hogan's 2009 study found that female athletes are marginalized as 'internal Others' compared to dominant male athletes who often embody national identities.[26]

Figure skating is crucial to sports celebrity studies because of its highly gendered and racialized representation of conventional femininity. Along with rhythmic gymnastics and synchronized swimming, it is viewed as a 'feminine sport', as opposed to the likes of football, baseball, and hockey.[27] From the late eighteenth century, however, figure skating was men's social activity in Europe that denoted a privileged class and refined aristocratic masculinity, also emphasized in elegant dancing and fencing.[28] It was not until the 1920s, with its inclusion in the Olympics, that figure skating became a dominant sport for women.[29] Norway's Sonja Henie and Canada's Barbara Ann Scott, who became sports celebrities in the mid-twentieth century, exemplify the emergence of 'ideal' femininity in figure skating,[30] which favours a youthful but sensual, slim, light-skinned, heterosexual-looking, and above all, Eurocentric notions of white femininity while marginalizing non-white athletes.[31] Light skinned Europeans and Americans dominated the field until the 1990s, when Asian and Asian American skaters, such as China's Chen Lu and Chinese American Michelle Kwan, began to take the world stage.[32]

Asian/Asian American women fit into the stereotypical feminine image of figure skating.[33] However, according to Yamamoto, their bodies are coded 'as a site of spectacularized differences that mar[k] the boundaries of normative whiteness'.[34] Asian American athletes have been framed as perpetual 'foreigners' or 'threats' to the 'white nation' symbolized by white masculinity.[35] Regardless of their U.S. citizenship, Asian American athletes are conflated as a homogeneous ethnic group and are represented as 'mysterious, dark, dangerous' exotic Other.[36] In this Orientalist reductionism, Asian and Asian American women are juxtaposed with sexually stereotypical images, such as the Lotus Blossom, China Doll, Madame Butterfly, and Geisha Girl.[37]

The Orientalization of Asian American female figure skaters is more evident when compared to white Americans. Asian Americans are positioned as 'nationally American but racially Asian'.[38] The cases of Japanese American Kristi Yamaguchi compared to Nancy Kerrigan in 1992 and Chinese American Michelle Kwan compared to Tara Lipinski in 1998 exemplify this racialization. Yamaguchi was often mistaken as Japanese,[39] while Nancy Kerrigan was commonly referred to as 'America's ice queen' and 'Grace Kelly' on the ice.[40] In the 1998 Nagano Olympics, Kwan won the silver, and Lipinski, a blonde, blue-eyed American, won the gold.

MSNBC reported that 'American beats out Kwan'.[41] The organization apologized shortly after, explaining that it was an 'error that may have been interpreted to state that U.S. figure skater Michelle Kwan was not American'.[42] Although Yamaguchi and Kwan brought medals to the U.S., they were positioned as 'less American than their more visibly white American teammates', who were adored as typical 'girl[s] next door' and received much more favourable rewards and endorsements.[43]

In this continuous process of Othering, the ethnic specificity of Asian Americans is erased. Their ethnicities (e.g., Japanese, Chinese, Korean, and Taiwanese) are often invisible and homogenized as the Orient. *Skating* magazine, the official publication of the U.S. Figure Skating Championships, used 'oriental' to describe Taiwanese American Tiffany Chin and Yamaguchi: 'Chin wore an exquisitely beaded black dress, reminiscent of an oriental flower garden'. Five years later, the magazine wrote: 'Dressed in an oriental style, red-wrap-front dress and skating to a selection of oriental flavor music, Kristi took the ice with assurance'.[44]

Media representations of Kim's Vancouver Olympic performances reveal how the Orientalist gaze operates in contemporary North American cultures.[45] Using the anthropologist Clifford Geertz's method of 'thick description' to read televised and print accounts of Kim's body as a cultural text, including her gestures, movements, facial expressions, and interactions with the audience and with her coach provides a fairly inclusive overview of the Orientalist constructions of her virtuoso Olympic triumph for North American audiences.[46]

The Orientalist Gaze on Kim

The North American news media applauded Kim's artistic and technical achievements, calling her 'Queen Yuna'.[47] For her free skate to Gershwin's 'Concerto in F', the *Los Angeles Times* reported: 'Never have athlete and artist been more perfectly balanced than they are with Kim'.[48] The *New York Times* described her triple jumps as 'natural as breathing' and her performance as 'airy', 'ethereal', and 'floating'.[49] *CNN* complimented her 'elegance' and technique as 'ethereally beautiful and outwardly perfect'.[50]

As in ballet, lightness and easiness – meaning artistry – are key to figure skating and are inseparable from athletic competency.[51] It is not surprising that the media describes Kim as a dancer. The *New York Times* wrote that she: 'performed with such ease, she looked as if she were dancing on a stage in ballet slippers - not skating on a slick sheet of ice'.[52] *The Atlantic* noted: 'She engaged with the music with the sophistication of a prima ballerina', a description it followed by noting the 'ruthlessness' of the attack of an athlete who 'breaks the will of her competitors.'[53] The *Korea Times* wrote that Kim's performance was 'a remarkably charismatic dance' with 'flexibility and powerful energy'.[54]

The media coverage of Kim's short programme to the James Bond Medley, however, reveals a different nuance, emphasizing her character itself. *ESPN* reported: 'When the rowdy cheers finally faded, she simply took her spot at the end of the rink, slowly unfurled one arm, cocked her index finger like a gun and turned her head to give the judges a sly, seductive smile'. *Cleveland* wrote: 'She played the Bond Girl to the hilt, rubbing her hand up one thigh while she was in front of the judges, fixing them with a flirtatious look'. *Reuters* begins with sensationalizing Kim: '"You're beautiful", yelled one male fan seconds before the medley of James Bond theme music started up, while plenty of others waved home-made banners declaring "Mysterious Bond Girl Yuna"'. The *Los Angeles Times* reported that 'Skating to a musical medley from James Bond films – including, appropriately, "Goldfinger", in which the villain loves only gold – the reigning world champion was sassy, speedy and just plain scintillating'. Other articles used 'sexy pizzazz', 'sensuality', and 'flirty, winking Bond girl' to portray Kim's performance.[55] Descriptive words like 'villain', 'sexy', 'sassy', 'seductive', and 'flirtatious' go beyond athleticism or artistry and resonate with the stereotypical characteristics of the mysterious, dangerous, exotic Oriental Other.

The Heroic White Man and the Fragile Asian Girl
U.S. Media: NBC[56]

Sports are not immune from the colonial history wherein white men are positioned as civilized and benevolent dominant groups.[57] NBC commentaries articulate the process of Orientalizing Kim in comparison to her white male coach, Orser. The first male commentator (M 1) opens remarks on Kim's short programme by addressing Orser: 'Awaiting her introduction, final words from the coach, Brian Orser, two-time silver medalist competing for Canada'. Standing on the ice, Kim quickly drinks water. The camera moves behind the coach, potentially reproducing his gaze. M 1 continues, 'The coach is in Toronto. Brian is saying because he has been to the Olympics twice, she is leaning on him a little bit for this experience'. The commentators do not share any direct quotes from Kim. Instead, what they heard from Orser characterizes and represents Kim's inner status. The descriptive framework of Kim awaiting and heeding the 'final words' of her coach casts a passive element to her performance, as if it would be a mere embodiment of his instruction. By using the coach's first name, the commentators create emotional proximity to him through which the audience would identify with Orser.

The commentators also imply Kim's emotional susceptibility. As she begins to glide toward the centre of the rink, a female commentator (F) says, 'When this draw happened, everyone was concerned for her, and yet she and Brian, *both* (original emphasis) were thrilled with the draw because she is one heck of a competitor and she has fire and ability and she just wants to go out there and prove who's the best'. The 'draw' refers to the order, in which Kim performed after Asada, her longtime rival. M 1 continues, 'Well, who better to prove than James Bond. That's her character [laugh] in the short programme'. Based on these commentaries, although 'everyone was concerned', things turned out okay because '*both*' Kim and Orser accepted the order. The assurance that '*both* were thrilled' implies that Kim alone would have been intimidated by this, and that her positive reaction was a direct result of Orser's. Orser's opinion works as a confirmation and reassurance of the rightness of the order and of Kim's readiness for her performance. In this rhetorical construction, the agency of Kim's performance does not fully belong to her but instead yields to Orser.

Kim does receive full recognition from the commentators for her performance. As she begins her routine, the second male commentator (M 2) says, 'Be the first two jumping passes, and the rest of it she owns. Good speed going into this'. The mood changes as Kim smiles, showing decorative gestures influenced by the Bond girl character like finger guns. Commentator F says, 'She has such a wonderful quality of strength and sensuality with the little … flirt [laughter] thrown in there too'. The commentaries acclaim Kim's athleticism complemented by her 'sensuality' and 'flirt[atiousness]'. When Kim completes her programme, the commentators praise her success, saying 'Queen Yuna' and 'what a performance'. Watching the slow-motion replay, they acclaim her flawlessness and say that they want her 'to get full credits for everything'.

Yet offstage, Orser is the central figure of their interest. The replay video ends by showing the coach. Excitedly watching Kim, he closes his eyes, lifting both arms with a determined face. The commentators laugh sympathetically in response to this scene. Kim and Orser are shown sitting in the kiss-and-cry area. M 2 says, 'I don't know how many people in the world could coach this woman with everything that she has on her for her country. It's just a magnificent job grounding her and giving her what she needs', implying that Orser is uniquely able to deal with the pressures facing professional athletes, and that Kim would not be the same without his help. The phrase 'grounding her' suggests that without Orser, Kim would be emotionally insecure and possibly unable to achieve the same results. In this rhetoric, although the commentaries give full credit to Kim for her performance onstage, they simultaneously imply that her competency relies on her coach's intervention and confirmation before and after the performance.

Canadian Media: CTV[58]

CTV places even more emphasis on Orser and Canada than NBC. As it uses the same visual source, this section focuses only on its commentaries. A male commentator (M) opens by addressing Orser: 'Final words from one of Canada's great skating heroes'. He then introduces Kim: 'She is the most popular athlete in her country. Korean flags everywhere here. She was trained in Canada and the goal here in Vancouver, one word: gold'. A female commentator (F) follows: 'She is a star in Canada, too. I think she's won a lot of hearts here by training here and being with Brian Orser', directly attributing Kim's popularity to Orser.

Watching the programme, the commentators applaud Kim's competency, saying that her jump has 'great speed' and that 'the coverage and the quality' of her movements are more aesthetically pleasing than those of Asada. When Kim finishes, M exclaims, 'Holy smokes! Who says these kids can't handle the pressure?' and asks, 'Did you see your old buddy Brian Orser on the boards?' with a laugh. He continues, 'He skated every step with her'. F responds, 'This would be such a victory for Brian if Yuna Kim were to win the gold here because it's the gold that he feels has slipped from his hands'. When Kim's final score is announced, M says, 'It's a world record ... Look at Brian'. During the slow-motion replay, F highlights the backstage process:

> Watching Brian while he was watching Yuna, now we know where she gets her fantastic body movement from [laughs]. Brian Orser was telling me the other night that she was fussing around with her triple flip a little bit [...] all he had to say was, 'How old were you when you landed your first triple flip?' And she said, 'Eleven years old'. He said, 'So, what's your problem?' [laughs].

Orser is clearly the focus of the commentary here. The commentators begin by introducing 'Canada's great skating hero' and finish by again explicitly drawing attention to him, telling viewers to 'Look at Brian'. Like NBC, CTV represents Kim's story through Orser's words. The commentators are more interested in how Orser reacts to Kim's performance than in the performance itself, 'watching Brian while he was watching Yuna' and noting that 'he skated every step with her'. They share personal conversations with Orser, referring to him as an 'old buddy' and calling him by his first name like NBC. In addition, they attribute Kim's performance to Orser, quipping that she gets her 'fantastic body movement from' him. Orser, however, did not choreograph her programme; that role belongs to David Wilson, another former Canadian figure skater who choreographed Kim's performances from 2007 to 2014. By positioning Orser at the centre of the narrative, these commentaries build a sense of emotional attachment and personal proximity to him. They identify with him more than with Kim, and credit him for the medal that 'slipped from his hands'.

On the contrary, Kim is infantilized and called a 'kid'. There is no age limit at the Olympics;[59] given the significance of physical ability in sports, medalists include athletes as young as 13 years old.[60] Kim was 19 in 2010, which is surely too old to be called a kid, a somewhat idealistic condition as an athlete. The word choice reveals a prevalent assumption that female skaters should be young, or at least look young, to maintain the status quo of sports that prefer a display of conventional masculinity; this is referred to as the 'girlification' of female figure skaters, who are understood to be 'just girls' at best.[61]

The opening and closing remarks of sports commentaries create a framework for contextualizing the performance of an athlete. NBC and CTV's introductory and closing remarks reinforce the existing racialized and gendered hierarchy – the young, Asian female disciple who desperately needs her male coach in order to perform well, submissively listening to the legendary, heroic, experienced white male's 'final words' before the competition and awaiting his approval at the end.

Sympathetic, Fetishized Racial and Gender Hierarchies

Nations are 'discursive constructs' that operate through a strategic process of inclusion and exclusion.[62] Videos on the official Olympics channel and Korea's official Olympics channel, SBS, provide a different interpretation of Orser's role compared to the NBC and CTV broadcasts.[63] On the Olympics channel, Orser barely says anything to Kim before the performance. Instead, the camera captures Kim blowing her nose while Orser watches. He quietly gazes into her eyes and slightly nods, smiling supportively. Then he lowers his fists twice, briefly saying an encouraging word, which seems to be the only explicit verbal comment, and holds his fist in front of his chest. Kim appears preoccupied with her upcoming performance and is looking down, too focused to respond to his encouragement. As she puts down her tissue with a final sigh, she quickly gives Orser a perfunctory smile and leaves before he finishes his final gesture of holding his fist. The SBS, commentators do not show or say anything about Orser at all. The coverage begins with Kim making a ritual blessing, the Catholic sign of the cross, which conveys a sense of solitude. The following commentaries focus on her lonely athletic and emotional struggle. Contrarily, NBC and CTV include more narratives about Orser's fame and work behind the scenes, while excluding the competitive, independent aspects of the athlete. Indeed, Orser was aware of the Western media's fascination with him, saying that it is 'a bit of an insult to [Kim]' when people ask him whether he is finally going to get a gold medal.[64]

It was more comfortable for NBC and CTV to credit Orser for Kim's success. Athletes who competed with Kim at the 2010 Olympics included Canada's Joannie Rochette, who won bronze, and America's Rachael Elizabeth Flatt, who placed seventh. By framing Kim through the eyes of Orser and giving credit to him, she is viewed not necessarily as a competitor or a threat to whites but as a girl who achieves her 'fairytale' dream thanks to practicing in Canada with its national hero.[65]

The Battle of the Brians

The NBC and CTV commentaries not only idealize Orser but present him as a sympathetic figure. His previous experience as a champion is transported into coaching. An athlete's experience in the field, however, does not guarantee coaching skills.[66] Not all previous medalists have been successful coaches. For example, Brian Boitano, the gold medalist at the 1988 Calgary Olympics, has coached but has not found notable achievement in that role. In 2006, Orser first met Kim at the Toronto Cricket Skating and Curling Club when he had just started teaching.[67] He had extensive experience conducting skating clinics but not coaching.[68] By that time, Kim could already do a triple flip-triple combination.[69] She 'was virtually [Orser's] first student as a professional coach'.[70] Choreographer Wilson explained Orser's hesitancy: 'Brian got thrown into a situation, like fast-tracking big time — Coaching 101 ... Yuna was like his first real student. Can you imagine?'[71]

This is not to diminish the coach's role. A skater's success would not be possible without collective teamwork, including a choreographer, coach, family, physical therapist, counselor, and more. Orser and Wilson both credit Kim's coaching team – which included David Wilson and Tracy Wilson, the 1988 Olympic bronze medalist – for Kim's gold medal, which 'turned Kim into a star'.[72] Kim also acknowledged that Orser 'really knows what I feel in the competitions' due to his previous experience at the Olympics and said that if she got the gold medal, she 'would dedicate it partly to Orser'.[73]

Even though teamwork is crucial in generating an athlete's success, the North American media tended to overtly dramatize Orser by comparing Kim and Asada with the 'Battle of the Brians', a reference to the rivalry between Orser and Boitano, the American gold medalist at the 1988 Winter Olympics in Calgary.[74] Orser received the silver, losing to Boitano by 0.1 points. Orser also lost to America's Scott Hamilton, the gold medalist in the 1984 Olympics. Orser is thus not only a beloved, familiar sports star but also a figure who draws sympathetic, warm support from North American audiences, called 'a good guy'.[75] The *New York Times* wrote that Kim 'came into these Olympics well aware that the unexpected can happen here', referring to the story of the Brians. *The Telegraph* also implied it: 'Orser knows all about the danger of complacency'.[76] The *Chicago Tribune* stated: 'Maybe it's because Brian Orser 'skates' along with South Korea's Yuna Kim as she performs her figure skating programs, doing little hops and turns as he stands behind the rink boards. Or maybe it's because he came so frustratingly close to two Olympic gold medals.' The paper then interviewed Dorothy Hamill, the 1976 Olympic Champion, who said: 'I want Brian Orser to win … Isn't that terrible? … I'm cheering for him as much as Kim'. Orser is portrayed as a fading legend who now 'stands behind the rink boards' skating along with his protege. One might ask whether the same level of empathy would have been accorded if he was not white or North American.

Kim, as racial Other, takes an ambiguous position between the cultural and geographical proximity of the U.S. and Canada. By juxtaposing Kim and Asada's rivalry with that of the Brians, Orser's loss is remembered, dramatized, and further sympathized. For U.S. audiences, a white Canadian man would be closer and more comfortable to identify with than an Asian woman. Also, Orser lost twice to U.S. champions, which would evoke sympathy toward him. As a nation that is culturally proximate to the U.S., Canada often benefits from American hegemony.[77] As long as Kim is subordinated under Orser's shadow, her success would not provoke North American audiences' nationalism and instead would mitigate any tension.

The Fetishization of the Asian Woman–White Man Relationship

Kim and Orser's relationship received more attention than that of other athletes and their coaches. NBC barely addresses coaches during the 2010 Olympics. For Johnny Weir, the American male figure skater with Norwegian ethnicity, his coach, Galina Zmievskaya, a light-skinned, dark blond Ukrainian-American female, did not receive any attention, even though she speaks to Weir at length, nearly 20 seconds, before his performance.[78] In Asada's short programme, NBC does not mention her coach. The commentary starts and finishes by addressing the athlete.[79] In Asada's long programme, the camera zooms in on only her face while sitting in the kiss-and-cry zone.[80] For the short programme of Rachael Elizabeth Flatt, a blond, white female and the U.S. champion, NBC does not mention her white male coach.[81]

One might argue that the media focus on Orser because of a closer mentorship or friendship that might exist between the two. However, compared to other athletes who often hug their coaches for a long time and even cry after their performances, Kim seems tranquil in the NBC and CTV footage. On NBC, when Kim skates off the ice, Orser tells her, 'Wow, I am so proud of you' and gives her the blade guards. Kim responds, 'Yeah, so good' in a perfunctory manner. They do not exchange prolonged eye contact, meaningful words, or long and emotionally charged hugs. In the kiss-and-cry area, there is no dramatic moment. Kim waves her hands, wearing a big bright smile as she looks at the camera, as she would do for commercial endorsements, and greets the audience cheering behind her. When her score is announced, she and Orser briefly hug. Their relationship seems professional and neutral.

Orser is not the main focus in the case of other athletes he has coached. For Yuzuru Hanyu, a male Japanese gold medalist at the 2014 Winter Olympics, NBC mentions Orser only once after the performance: 'Brian Orser is coach, congratulating him with a big smile and fist bump'. Orser displays much more affection with Hanyu than with Kim, such as frequent smiles, hugs, and conversation, but the commentators do not emphasize these. While waiting for his final score, a Japanese woman sits next to Hanyu, but the commentators never mention her or Orser.[82]

The Orientalist construction of Asian/Asian American women is completed in relation to white men: racially and sexually marked submissive Asian women are fetishized by and needed in service of white men.[83] The North American media's fascination with Kim and Orser opens room to question whether the same focus would have occurred if the coach had been a non-white male and Kim had not been a young Asian woman.

An ABC documentary begins with Orser speaking on behalf of Kim, including on her personality, childhood, training process, and even her emotional struggle.[84] Then the film shows an interview with Kim via a voiceover translation in English that says, 'When Brian told me "You are ready", someone might see an insignificant statement. But not to me. He really gives confidence and that makes me believe in myself'. However, what Kim actually says in Korean – heard in the background – is not about her coach but about her childhood training experience and expectations. The English voice also sounds higher, softer, and more girlish than Kim's actual voice speaking in Korean.

Despite the North American media's portrayal of Kim as a dependent, fragile girl, as a professional athlete, she had amassed notable achievements from an early age and seemed to be mentally prepared for her performance. In an interview with *ESPN*, she said that 'I had waited a long time for the Olympics … I had ample time to practice and prepare, so I wasn't shaky or nervous just because it was the Olympics. I was able to relax and enjoy the competition'.[85] She continued that she felt 'very comfortable' at the Olympics, just as in other competitions.[86] Orser also frequently mentioned that Kim is naturally a 'very fierce' competitor and would be 'unstoppable' as long as she skates to her capability.[87]

(In)visible Koreanness, Hypervisible Asianness – Pan-Asian Identity

Visibility is not power for those who are already marginalized socioculturally, as it can reinforce existing stereotypes and objectification.[88] Kim is not Asian American but Korean, an ethnic and racial majority in Korea. Under Orientalist rhetoric, however, her Koreanness is invisible, while her Asianess is hypervisible. A Bond girl character would be exotic to Korean audiences and to Kim as well, for it is an imported idea based on Western movies. It is possible that her choreographer – who is not Korean – intentionally employed a stereotypical image of an Asian woman to better target Western audiences. Indeed, Kim's previous routines included *Miss Saigon* (choreography by Wilson) and *Reflection* (choreography by Orser), songs from Disney's animated film *Mulan*, where the main characters are Vietnamese and Chinese, respectively. *Miss Saigon,* in particular, portrays stereotypical imagery of Asian women in North America.[89] Kim's performances in these instances exemplify the recirculated racialized and gendered Orientalism and reductionism that erases the ethnic specificity of Koreans in glocalization.

Korean media also projects Orientalism. Describing Kim as 'a perkier version of Lucy Liu' and similar to Maria Sharapova, the *Korea Times* wrote that with her 'camera-friendly appearance', Kim's 'superb athletic ability gives men an excuse to stare at the television screen'. Liu and Sharapova are some of the most sexualized female celebrities, the former especially known for her stereotypical Oriental image. Here, Kim is not only objectified via the voyeuristic gaze but also conflated with the Orientalist imagery of Asian/Asian Americanness, a potential moment of self-Orientalism, that internalizes the Western gaze and Orientalizes itself as Other.

Meanwhile, Kim herself exhibits a more ambiguous attitude toward Asianness. She has noted that her role model was Michelle Kwan. In an interview with *NBC*, Kim said, 'I almost memorized her long programme because I watched it over and over'.[90] Because Kim is a pioneer in figure skating in Korea, it may have been harder for her to find a Korean role model. Kim was possibly drawn to Kwan not only because of her superior skills and artistry but also Kwan's race that is more identifiable and proximate to Kim.

In an interview with *Time*, Kim was asked whether her long programme at the 2014 Winter Olympics, titled 'Homage to Korea' based on traditional Korean music, was 'a bit of a risk'.[91] She agreed, 'because to non-Asians, Chinese, Japanese and Korean music could easily sound the same'.[92] Kim declined several times choreographer Wilson's suggestion to present a Korean theme because she was 'worried about the global reception'. For her, 'Homage to Korea' was for her Korean fans: 'Honestly, I don't think it spoke to the international judges as effectively'. Kim was aware of the invisibility of Koreanness and a Korean cultural theme on the global stage. Being a past Olympic champion perhaps gave her room to explore Koreanness for Korean audiences, even if it was likely less marketable to international audiences.

Increased visibility of Kim on the world stage seems to elevate invisibility of Koreanness and hypervisibility of Asianness. Kwan and Yamaguchi are frequently compared with Kim and invited for interviews to judge her skating.[93] While the two are some of the best figure skaters in the U.S., it is equally possible that non-Asian athletes could have been invited. Comparing Kim with Russia's Adelina Sotnikova, the gold medalist at the 2014 Olympics, *CNN* wrote 'While an East-West split wasn't apparent in the battle between Tara Lipinski's triple loop-triple loop combination and Michelle Kwan's ability to make judges weep, it remained unclear who favored technique and who performed artistry'.[94] Both Lipinski and Kwan are Americans, but race/ethnicity engenders dichotomy; 'technique' refers to Sotnikova and Lipinski – white, light-skinned athletes – and 'artistry' implies Kwan and Kim, Asian and Asian American athletes.

Nevertheless, this increased visibility opens space for re-visiting Asian and Asian Americanness – pan-Asian identity. The emergence of Asian and Asian American figure skaters denotes a changing climate at the Olympics and challenges – albeit subtly – the gendered and ethnicized discourse. For example, Yamaguchi was the 'only woman who explicitly represented the athletic achievements [and] hard-won athletic excellence' at the Salt Lake City 2002 Olympic Games' opening ceremony.[95] In 2018, two of the three U.S. Olympic women's figure skating team, Mirai Nagasu and Karen Chen, were Asian Americans. Some of the 'brightest ice skating stars' in the world today are Asians and Asian Americans, sparking what some have called an 'Asian American skating renaissance'.[96]

To make this possible, Asian and Asian American athletes have built a supportive community and inspired each other to survive in a field once dominated by white Europeans. Yamaguchi has said that her idol was Tiffany Chin and has credited previous Asian American skaters for her success: 'She made me believe that I'm like her and made me believe that I could be like her someday. Hopefully, I was able to create the same kind of feeling for others [and] help open the door to Asian American skaters'.[97] 2017 U.S. champion Karen Chen said that Kim was her inspiration: 'I have always looked up to her … I have done everything in skating, like flawlessly, and her emotion, and her feelings … I want to be able to experience the same thing'.[98] As Asian American skater Kwan was a role model to Kim, now Kim is inspiring the next generation of Asian American skaters.

Towards the Audacious Hope of Dancing on the Ice

Figure skating is a contested site of sporting racialized, ethnicized, and gendered Orientalism with postcolonial influences. By intersecting performance studies and critical sports studies, a richer analysis of the North American media coverage of Kim's performances at the 2010 Olympics, including official footage aired on NBC (U.S.) and CTV (Canada), and newspapers, documentaries, and interviews emerges. The media applauds Kim's athletic and artistic achievement onstage while exoticizing the sensuality of her Bond girl character. Offstage, it infantilizes Kim as a fragile, submissive, emotionally dependent girl and represents her through Orser's perspective. It identifies with him, develops emotional proximity, and eventually constructs the narrative of Orser as a heroic white man through which credibility and the ultimate reward belong to white masculinity. The racialized and gendered hierarchy - the heroic white man and the fragile Asian girl - is fetishized and idolized. It also sympathizes with and further dramatizes Orser by comparing Kim and Asada with the 'Battle of the Brians'. Kim's success, thus, is not considered the threat of an exceptional Asian but instead serves white masculinity as the medal that 'slipped from [Orser's] hands'. The ice becomes a site of strategic exclusion and the inclusion of invisible Koreanness operating for the sake of hypervisible Asian/Asian Americanness under Orientalism.

The increasing visibility of Asian and Asian American female figure skaters, however, denotes a promising structural change through which they create a mutually supportive pan-Asian community against white hegemony. Figure skating is one of the few fields where what women do matters more than what men do, which opens an opportunity to make a liberating statement for female athletes.[99] While visibility is a double-edged sword, it is still possible to dream for these athletes to shine neither as Oriental princesses nor as a service to the white nation, but as individuals who find their voices and achieve their audacious hope of dancing on the ice.

Notes

1. This article follows the Western convention for the name order, such as Yuna (given name) Kim (surname), and Mao (given name) Asada (surname).
2. Younghan Cho, 'The Glocalization of US Sports in South Korea', *Sociology of Sport Journal* 26, no. 2 (2009): 320–4.
3. Younghan Cho, 'Asia Seupocheu Selleobeuriti Saenggakagi Jeonjiguhwawa Idongseong-Simingwon-Jeongcheseongui Maengnageseo' [Sports Celebrity in Asia: Mobility, Citizenship and Identity in the Age of Globalization], *Media & Society* 19, no. 1 (2011): 10; Nammi Lee et al., 'South Korea's "Glocal" Hero: The Hiddink Syndrome and the Rearticulation of National Citizenship and Identity', *Sociology of Sport Journal* 24 (2007): 286, 291.
4. Cho, 'Sports Celebrity', 25.
5. Bryan Armen Graham, 'The Sad, Perfect End of Kim Yuna's Figure-Skating Reign', *The Atlantic*, February 22, 2014, https://www.theatlantic.com/entertainment/archive/2014/02/the-sad-perfect-end-of-kim-yunas-figure-skating-reign/283986/ (accessed January 1, 2019).
6. Cho, 'Sports Celebrity', 27; Younghan Cho, 'Wolgyeonghaneun Asian Seupocheu Selleobeuritiwa Yudongjeok Simingwon' [Migrating Sports Celebrity and Flexible Citizenship: Media Representations of Tang Yeo-so during the 2008 Beijing Olympics in South Korea and China], *Korean Society for the Sociology of Sport* 27, no. 4 (2014): 217–41; Jinsook Kim, 'Why We Cheer for Viktor Ahn: Changing Characteristics of Sporting Nationalism and Citizenship in South Korea in the Era of Neoliberal Globalization', *Communication and Sport* 7, no. 4 (2019): 488–509.
7. Yeomi Choi, 'Major League Baseball and Racialized Masculinities in Korean Digital Media', *Communication and Sport* XX(X): 1–20.
8. Cho, 'Sports Celebrity', 27.
9. Yoon Kyung Lee and Soo Young Jung, 'Han, Il Inteonet Poteol Saiteuui Seupocheujeoneollijeum Bigyo Yeongu: Gimyeona Seonsuwa Asada Mao Seonsue Daehan Neibeowa Yahujaepaen Nyuseureul Jungsimeuro' [A Comparative Analysis of Sports Journalism on 'Naver' and 'Yahoo Japan' News on Yuna Kim and Mao Asada], *Speech and Communication* 16 (2011): 105–42.
10. Jung Woo Lee and Joseph Maguire, 'Road to Reunification? Unitary Korean Nationalism in South Korean Media Coverage of the 2004 Athens Olympic Games', *Sociology* 45, no. 5 (2011): 853.
11. Hye-Jin Oh, '"Kwin"ui sangsangnyeokgwa "tumyeonghan sinche": Bakgeunhyewa gimyeonareul tonghae bon "singgeul yeoseong"ui singgyulleoriti' [Queen's Imagination and Transparent Body: The Singularity of Single Women Represented by Park Geun-hye and Yuna Kim], *Culture and Science* 78 (2014): 144–52; Sang Woo Nam, Hanjoo Kim, and Eunha Koh, 'From National Sister to National Hero: Media Discourse on the Rise and Success of Kim Yuna', *Journal of Korean Sports Sociology* 23, no. 2 (2010): 61–85.
12. Chuyun Oh, 'Nationalizing the Balletic Body in Olympic Figure Skating', *Sport in Korea: History, Development, Management*, eds. Dae Hee Kwak, Yong Jae Ko, Inkyu Kang, and Mark Rosentraub (New York: Routledge, 2017), 119–32.
13. Rachael Miyung Joo, '"She Became Our Strength": Female Athletes and (Trans)national Desires', in *The Korean Popular Culture Reader*, ed. Kyung Hyun Kim and Youngmin Choe (Durham, NC: Duke University Press, 2013), 258.
14. Bettina Fabos, 'Forcing the Fairytale: Narrative Strategies in Figure Skating Competition Coverage', *Sport in Society* 4, no. 2 (2001): 185–212.

15. Ann Cooper Albright, *Choreographing Difference: The Body and Identity in Contemporary Dance* (Middletown, CT: Wesleyan University Press, 2010), xiv, xiii.
16. Mary Louise Adams, 'The Manly History of a "Girls' Sport": Gender, Class and the Development of Nineteenth-century Figure Skating', *The International Journal of the History of Sport* 24, no. 7 (2007): 886.
17. Fan Hong, 'Epilogue: Nationalism, Orientalism and Globalization: The Future of the Asian Games', *Sport in Society* 8, no. 3 (2005): 515–519; Jackie Hogan, 'Staging the Nation: Gendered and Ethnicized Discourses of National Identity in Olympic Opening Ceremonies', *Journal of Sport and Social Issues* 27, no. 2 (May 2003): 117; Jessica W. Chin and David L. Andrews, 'Mixed Martial Arts, Caged Orientalism, and Female Asian American Bodies', in *Asian American Sporting Cultures*, ed. Thangaraj Stanley I. et al. (New York, NY: New York University Press, 2016), 152–79; Simon C. Darnell, 'Orientalism through Sport: Towards a Said-ian Analysis of Imperialism and "Sport for Development and Peace"', *Sport in Society* 17, no. 8 (2014): 1001, 1006; Thomas R. Chung et al., 'Asian American Sporting Cultures', *Contemporary Sociology* 46, no. 2 (2017): 246.
18. Darnell, 'Orientalism', 1004.
19. Jack Gallagher, 'Choreography Legend David Wilson A Man in Demand', *The Japan Times*, August 21, 2018, https://www.japantimes.co.jp/sports/2018/08/21/figure-skating/choreography-legend-david-wilson-man-demand/#.XQMkltMzYfE (accessed June 15, 2019).
20. Edward W. Said, *Orientalism* (New York: Pantheon Books, 1978).
21. Darnell, 'Orientalism', 1004.
22. John B. Weinstein, 'The Orient on Ice: Transnational Cultural Portrayals by Asian and Asian American Figure Skaters', *Transnational Performance, Identity and Mobility in Asia* (2018): 145.
23. Hogan, 'Staging the Nation', 100.
24. Darnell, 'Orientalism', 1003.
25. Hogan, 'Staging the Nation', 100–1, 107, 112.
26. Jackie Hogan, *Gender, Race and National Identity: Nations of Flesh and Blood* (New York: Routledge, 2008); Miyoung Oh, 'South Korea's Gendered Nationhood: A Case Study of Heavyweight Weightlifter Jang Mi-ran', *Asia Pacific Journal of Sport and Social Science* 4, no. 3 (2015): 237–50.
27. Adams, 'The Manly History', 873-874; Russell Field, 'Artistic Impressions: Figure Skating, Masculinity, and the Limits of Sport', *Histoire Sociale/Social History* 45, no. 90 (2012): 419.
28. Adams, 'The Manly History', 878.
29. Field, 'Artistic Impressions', 420.
30. Ibid.
31. Chin et al., 'Martial Arts', 160; Fabos, 'Fairytale', 189, 192, 198.
32. Weinstein, 'The Orient', 143.
33. Chin et al., 'Martial Arts', 160.
34. Traise Yamamoto, 'In/Visible Difference: Asian American Women and the Politics of Spectacle', *Race, Gender & Class* 7, no. 1 (2000): 43.
35. Chin et al., 'Martial Arts', 160–1; Yamamoto, 'In/Visible', 45, 47.
36. Chin et al., 'Martial Arts', 155–7.
37. Yamamoto, 'In/Visible', 47.
38. Jae Chul Seo, 'Yellow Pacific on White Ice: Transnational, Postcolonial and Genealogical Reading of Asian American and Asian Female Figure Skaters in the US Media' (PhD diss., University of Iowa, 2014), iii.
39. Hiromitsu Inokuchi and Yoshiko Nozaki, '"Different than Us": Othering, Orientalism, and US Middle School Students' Discourses on Japan', *Asia Pacific Journal of Education* 25, no. 1 (2005): 61–74.
40. Ellyn Kestnbaum, 'What Tanya Harding Means to Me, or Images of Independent Female Power on Ice', in *Women on Ice: Feminist Essays on the Tanya Harding/Nancy Kerrigan Spectacle*, ed. Cynthia Baughman (New York: Routledge, 1995), 53–77.
41. Yamamoto, 'In/Visible', 54.

42. Ibid.
43. Chin et al., 'Martial Arts', 160.
44. Weinstein, 'The Orient', 145.
45. To examine how the Orientalist gaze operates in Kim's media representation in North America, this study employs a textual analysis of select North American broadcast and newspaper sources from the 2010 Vancouver Olympics. This data includes NBC and CTV video commentaries, articles from *ESPN*, *Time*, the *New York Times*, the *Los Angeles Times*, and *CNN* - and other supplementary interviews and documentaries. For broadcast resources, I focus on NBC and CTV because they were the official Olympic broadcasters in the U.S. and Canada respectively. I use descriptive analysis to study Kim's body as a cultural text, including her gestures, movements, facial expressions, and interactions with the audience and with her coach.

    For newspaper analysis, the search keywords were 'Yuna Kim 2010 Vancouver Olympics James Bond Girl' and 'Yuna Kim 2010 Vancouver Olympics free skate', retrieved in January 2018. I found ~80 articles for the first and 200 for the second category. The period covered was from January 1, 2009, to December 30, 2015. This includes Kim's first Olympic season, which began on October 15, 2009 at the 2009–10 ISU Grand Prix of Figure Skating in Paris, the 2010 Winter Olympics in Vancouver, and the 2014 Winter Olympics in Sochi, where she won a silver medal. I included the 2014 Olympics because it frequently recalls and describes Kim's 2010 performances. I read the top 50 articles for each category sorted by relevance, in total about 100 articles, and closely analyzed 16 that exemplified the racialized and gendered consumption of Kim. I utilized Google as the search engine because of its extensive data collection and the accuracy of its page rank mechanism. In constructing my search, I employed the model proposed by media scholars. Michael Scharkow and Jens Vegelgesang, 'Measuring the Public Agenda Using Search Engine Queries', International Journal of Public Opinion Research, 23, no. 1 (2011): 7.
46. Dwight Conquergood, 'Performance Studies: Interventions and Radical Research', *TDR/ The Drama Review* 46, no. 2 (2002): 149.
47. Graham, 'The Sad, Perfect End'.
48. Philip Hersh, 'Kim Yuna is a Champion for All Time', *The Los Angeles Times*, February 27, 2010, https://www.latimes.com/archives/la-xpm-2010-feb-27-la-sp-olympics-figures27-2010feb27-story.html (accessed June 23, 2019).
49. Jeré Longman, 'Kim Seizes Lead; Then the Surprises Start', *New York Times,* February 19, 2014, https://www.nytimes.com/2014/02/20/sports/olympics/kim-yu-na-leads-figure-skating-after-short-program.html (accessed June 23, 2019); Juliet Macur, 'Kim Yu-na Wins Gold in Figure Skating', *The New York Times*, February 26, 2010, http://archive.nytimes.com/www.nytimes.com/2010/02/26/sports/olympics/26skate.html (accessed June 23, 2019).
50. Amy Bass, 'A Shocker from Figure Skating Judges?', *CNN*, February 22, 2014, https://edition.cnn.com/2014/02/21/opinion/bass-olympics-skating-judging/index.html (accessed June 23, 2019).
51. Fabos, 'Fairytale', 47.
52. Macur, 'Kim Yu-na'.
53. Graham, 'The Sad, Perfect End'.
54. Kang Seung-woo, 'Queen Yu-na Makes History', *The Korea Times*, March 29, 2009, www.koreatimes.co.kr/www/news/sports/2009/03/136_42177.html (accessed July 6, 2019).
55. Alex Abad-Santos, 'Russian Figure Skater Evgenia Medvedeva is as Talented as She is Terrifying', *Vox*, February 22, 2018, https://www.vox.com/culture/2018/2/22/17040376/evgeniamedvedeva-olympics-figure-skating (accessed January 15, 2019); Gallagher, 'Choreography Legend'; Simon Hart, 'Winter Olympics 2010: Kim Yu-na Sets Out to Prove She is Queen of the Ice in Vancouver', *The Telegraph*, February 22, 2010, https://www.telegraph.co.uk/sport/othersports/winter-olympics/7293223/Winter-Olympics-2010-

Kim-Yu-na-sets-out-to-prove-she-is-queen-of-the-ice-in-Vancou%e2%80%a6/ (accessed July 6, 2019).
56. Sweet Home, 'Yuna Kim - 2010 Vancouver Olympics SP (007 James Bond Medley)', *YouTube*, posted July 12, 2014, https://www.youtube.com/watch?v=6KV9cUupflo (accessed January 1, 2019).
57. Darnell, 'Orientalism', 1003, 1010.
58. YunaTimes, '[Yuna Kim] Vancouver 2010 Winter Olympics Figure Skating SP NBC - CTV Commentary', *YouTube*, posted November 17, 2013, https://www.youtube.com/watch?v=PH58rf7USh0 (accessed January 1, 2019).
59. Casey Quackenbush, 'How Old Do You Have to be to Compete in the Olympics?', *Time*, February 13, 2018, http://time.com/5154982/age-requirement-olympics-2018/ (accessed January 1, 2019).
60. Ibid.
61. Abigail M. Feder, '"A Radiant Smile from the Lovely Lady": Overdetermined Femininity in Ladies' Figure Skating', *TDR/The Drama Review* 38, no. 1 (1994): 71.
62. Hogan, 'Staging the Nation', 100.
63. Olympics, 'Yuna Kim - Short Program – Ladies' Figure Skating | Vancouver 2010', *YouTube*, posted February 23, 2016, https://www.youtube.com/watch?v=ecKnyyuMsmw (accessed January 1, 2019); SBS, 'Gim-yeon-a! Pigyeo Yeowang-ui Sidaega Yeollibnida! [Kim Yu-na! The Age of Figure Queen Opens!]', *YouTube*, posted March 3, 2018, https://www.youtube.com/watch?v=2DEDNW5Jq4Q (accessed January 1, 2019).
64. Hart, 'Winter Olympics'.
65. Fabos, 'Fairytale', 207.
66. Associated Press Sports Staff, 'Retired Figure Skater Brian Orser Delights in Coaching Job He Never Thought He Wanted', *Cleveland*, February 23, 2010, https://www.cleveland.com/olympics/index.ssf/2010/02/retired_figure_skater_brian_or.html (accessed January 15, 2019).
67. Juliet Macur, 'Olympic Hopes Rest with Skating Favorite Kim Yu-na', *New York Times*, February 13, 2010, https://www.nytimes.com/2010/02/14/sports/olympics/14kim.html (accessed January 12, 2019).
68. Ibid.
69. Philip Hersh, 'Globetrotting: For Orser, Hope That Kim Can Help a Good Guy Can Finish First', *Chicago Tribune*, February 25, 2010, https://newsblogs.chicagotribune.com/sports_globetrotting/2010/02/by-philip-hershvancouver-bc-maybe-its-because-brian-orser-skates-along-with-kim-yuna-has-she-does-her-programs-doing.html (accessed July 6, 2019).
70. Ibid.
71. Jack Gallagher, 'Choreographer Wilson Regrets "Transformative" Kim's Early Retirement', *The Japan Times*, March 15, 2016, https://www.japantimes.co.jp/sports/2016/03/15/figure-skating/choreographer-wilson-regrets-transformative-kims-early-retirement/#.XE0pFc9KgfF (accessed January 1, 2019).
72. Gallagher, 'Choreographer Wilson'.
73. Macur, 'Olympic Hopes'.
74. Macur, 'Kim Yu-na'.
75. Hersh, 'Globetrotting'.
76. Hart, 'Winter Olympics'.
77. Selma K. Sonntag, 'Linguistic Globalization and the Call Center Industry: Imperialism, Hegemony or Cosmopolitanism?', *Language Policy* 8, no. 1 (January 2009): 5–25.
78. Olga Trofimova, 'Johnny Weir 2010 Winter Olympics FS', *YouTube*, posted January 30, 2011, https://www.youtube.com/watch?v=oMY4J6HQs8I (accessed June 30, 2019).
79. hgn0611, '2010 OG Mao.Asada SP JPN (NBC)', *YouTube*, posted December 1, 2010, https://www.youtube.com/watch?v=Ti1yUBVW7aM (accessed January 30, 2019).
80. hgn0611, '2010 Winter Olympics – Ladies' Long Program - Asada Mao', *YouTube*, posted September 8, 2010, https://www.youtube.com/watch?v=hzlFB5_1-_Y (accessed January 30, 2019).

81. hgn0611, '2010 OG Rachael.Flatt SP USA(NBC)', *YouTube*, posted November 15, 2010, https://www.youtube.com/watch?v = NGq_rFo5Psw (accessed January 30, 2019).
82. '2014 Winter Olympic Games Sochi Yuzuru Hanyu SP', *YouTube*, posted March 10, 2018, https://www.youtube.com/watch?v=Frno_5qKkjU (accessed January 30, 2019).
83. Yamamoto, 'In/Visible', 52.
84. ForeverYunaFever, 'Yuna Kim Documentary Aired on ABC', *YouTube*, posted March 27, 2018, https://www.youtube.com/watch?v=oo7GReWVmio (accessed June 16, 2019).
85. Associated Press, 'Americans Flatt, Nagasu Sit 5th, 6th', *ESPN*, February 25, 2010, https://www.espn.com/top/story/_/id/4940453 (accessed June 16, 2019).
86. Associated Press, 'License to Thrill: Korea's Kim Yu-na Carries Nation's Expectations on Ice', *Cleveland*, February 24, 2010, https://www.cleveland.com/olympics/index.ssf/2010/02/license_to_thrill_koreas_kim_y.html (accessed July 6, 2019).
87. Ibid.; Hart, 'Winter Olympics'.
88. Peggy Phelan, *Unmarked: The Politics of Performance* (New York, NY: Routledge, 1993), 10.
89. Yamamoto, 'In/Visible', 52.
90. BsLullaby, '2010 Vancouver Olympics NBC TODAY Yuna Kim', *YouTube*, posted March 23, 2010, https://www.youtube.com/watch?v=wUMecYZ3ris (accessed January 30, 2019).
91. Clara Kim, '10 Questions with Figure Skater Kim Yu-Na', *Time*, August 19, 2011, http://content.time.com/time/world/article/0,8599,2089091,00.html (accessed June 16, 2019).
92. Ibid.
93. Hersh, 'Kim Yuna'; Flora Carr, '5 Things to Know About Yuna Kim, Lighter of the Olympic Cauldron', *Time*, February 9, 2018, https://time.com/5141402/yuna-kim-olympics-2018/ (accessed June 16, 2019).
94. Bass, 'A Shocker'.
95. Hogan, 'Staging the Nation', 117.
96. Sam Kang, 'Reflecting Upon a Golden Moment: Olympic Icon Kristi Yamaguchi Prepares for 25th Anniversary Performances', *Nichi Bei Weekly*, August 3, 2017, https://www.nichibei.org/2017/08/reflecting-upon-a-golden-olympic-icon-kristi-yamaguchi-moment/ (accessed January 15, 2019).
97. Ibid.
98. PeopleTV, 'Meet Karen Chen: Olympic-Bound Figure Skater Kristi Yamaguchi Calls the Complete Package', *YouTube*, posted February 8, 2018, https://www.youtube.com/watch?v=FMUYy6Cz8dc (accessed January 17, 2019).
99. Kestnbaum, 'What Tanya Harding Means', 53–77.

Acknowledgements

I express my sincere gratitude to the anonymous reviewers' and *The International Journal of the History of Sport* editors' generous support and constructive feedback during the revision process.

Disclosure Statement

No potential conflict of interest was reported by the author.

Reading Yani Tseng: Articulating Golf, Taiwanese Nationalism, and Gender Politics in Twenty-First-Century Taiwan

Daniel Yu-Kuei Sun

ABSTRACT
Media narratives reveal a variety of perspectives on Taiwanese golfer Yani Tseng in Taiwan during her dominant years, roughly from early 2008 to the end of 2013. Tseng, a former top-ranked woman golfer who competed in the Ladies Professional Golf Association (LPGA), was celebrated as a heroic figure of the Taiwanese nation. Yet, her gender, sexuality, and physical prowess was also questioned and scrutinized because of her transgressive presence as a strong woman athlete. Through critically analyzing media narratives and contextualizing them with both Taiwan's political history and golf history, this research illustrates the complex intersection of Taiwanese nationalism, transnational capital, US cultural hegemony, and identity politics in the era of global capitalism.

In 2008, Yani Tseng, a 19-year-old golfer, caught the national spotlight in Taiwan by winning that year's Ladies Professional Golf Association (LPGA) championship at Bulle Rock Golf Course in Havre de Grace, Maryland.[1] Tseng had started to play professional golf just a year before this tournament, and this win made her the first Taiwanese woman to win a major LPGA championship. Named the Rookie of the Year in 2008, Tseng continued to dominate women's golf in the following few years, winning two major championships in 2010, another two in 2011, and claiming the number one spot in the LPGA rankings from February 2011 to March 2013. Now dubbed 'light of Taiwan' (台灣之光) by the press, Tseng's sudden surge in women's golf soon earned her fame and a national following, in a similar way to other internationally recognized Taiwanese athletes such as baseball player Chien-Ming Wang.[2] Moreover, her unprecedented success made golf, a popular if still class-exclusive sport in Taiwan, much more widely appreciated by the general public.

This research focuses on the media narratives of Tseng in Taiwan during her dominant years, roughly from early 2008 (the start of her rise to stardom) to the end of 2013 (the moment when her golf performance started to decline sharply). The unique context of contemporary Taiwan, especially regarding its complicated issue of national identities (Taiwanese, Chinese, or both) as well as its ambivalent place in global politics, made the narratives and meanings of Tseng both intriguing and important. These media narratives illustrate the complex intersection of Taiwanese nationalism and identity politics, with a specific focus on the intersection of nation, gender and physicality.

The 'National' Question of Taiwan

Since the end of World War Two, Taiwan has been a key site for Cold War politics and a hotbed of international political tensions. After Taiwan and its surrounding isles became the only territories of the Republic of China (ROC) in 1949 as a result of the Chinese Civil War, its political status, especially regarding its complicated and troubled relationship with mainland China (People's Republic of China, PRC, established in 1949), has been one of the most significant issues on the island for more than seventy years. With the political, cultural, and economic impacts of China continuing to loom large, the Taiwanese people have struggled to establish, maintain, re-orient, and even revise their national identity through a variety of political and cultural venues. In this context, scholars of Taiwanese politics have argued that what constitutes Taiwan the nation is indeed ambiguous, even undetermined, ranging from a broader sense of Chinese nationalism on the one hand to an independent and distinctive Taiwanese nation on the other.[3]

The relationship between sport and nationalism(s) in the Taiwanese context has been profound and complicated. Indeed, sport has not only been one of the major elements of nationalistic discourse, but it has also been linked with different nationalistic ideologies in different historical periods. For example, Taiwanese youth baseball teams' dominant success in the Little League World Series (LLWS) in the 1970s and 1980s was closely associated with the ideology of an overarching *Chinese* nationalism.[4] In the mid-2000s, after the island went through the process of 'Taiwanization' which promoted a more Taiwan-centered national identity at the turn of the century, a frenzied celebration of Chien-Ming Wang – the ace pitcher of the highly decorated New York Yankees in Major League Baseball (MLB) in 2006 and 2007 – further pushed forward a renewed version of *Taiwanese* nationalism.[5] The ways Yani Tseng was understood and celebrated followed this historical trend, as her 'light of Taiwan' status signified her Taiwanese identity and a much stronger identification with the island-nation. The narratives of Tseng, however, illustrated a different picture than other 'lights of Taiwan' such as Wang because she was a female athlete. Issues of gender, sexuality, and physicality were prominent in these narratives because female athletes, especially those who displayed physical prowess, were usually at odds with heterosexual attractiveness and traditional femininity. It took a variety of strategies for the Taiwanese media to negotiate the contradictory images of Tseng: While the press wholeheartedly celebrated her golf achievement and presented her as a sporting hero who represented the Taiwanese nation, it was still necessary to 'contain' her physical prowess while portraying her as an unintimidating, cute, and attractive young woman.

Reading Sport Critically

This research follows the theoretical framework of 'reading sport critically', a critical media analysis strategy which seeks to explore cultural meanings and power relations of mediated narratives revolving around high-profile athletes. As Susan Birrell and Mary McDonald argue, mediated narratives of high-profile athletes provide meaningful patterns of our contemporary world in which power relations divide nations and societies along various, intersecting lines of power such as gender, sexuality, race, ethnicity, social class, national identity, and other categories. In a sense, the media representations of sport stars reveal the ways in which mainstream societies construct, celebrate, and police meanings and social norms. Through reading these narratives as cultural texts, this analysis interrogates the relations of power which precede the mythical constructions of a transnational sport star.[6]

This approach to a critical analysis of media narratives, however, does not mean the audiences of these mass media accounts are powerless and voiceless in the meaning-making process. Indeed, the sporting events and the meanings revolving around them are always open to contestation. The analysis thus seeks to suggest an alternative understanding of a highly celebrated athlete in Taiwan, and in doing so provides a counternarrative that is usually 'decentered, obscured, and dismissed by hegemonic forces'.[7]

The sources for this research included the major newspapers published in Taiwan, such as *United Daily News*, *United Evening News*, *China Times*, *Liberty Times*, and *Apple Daily*. The primary focus is on media narratives of Tseng published roughly from 2008 to 2013, when she occupied the top spot of the LPGA ranking during most of this period. However, specific attention is also paid to 2004, when she first became known by the general public for defeating Korean American golfer Michelle Wie in an amateur event. While the various newspapers chosen to analyze Tseng adhered to different institutional political inclinations, the ways she was portrayed presented rather similar ideological messages in terms of national and gender politics.[8]

LPGA and an Unorthodox 'Light of Taiwan'

The year 2011 was a spectacular one for Yani Tseng. After a year of great performances in 2010, she finally claimed the number one spot on the Women's World Golf Rankings in February 2011 after winning the Australian Ladies' Masters. In June 2011, Tseng won the Women's PGA Championship, one of the four LPGA major tournaments. Just a month later, she grabbed another major title, the Women's British Open. The two major titles in 2011, along with two major titles in 2010 and another back in 2008, made Tseng the youngest (at the age of 22) professional golfer, male or female, to win five major tournaments. At this young age, Tseng was already a golf figure who was constantly compared with other legendary female golfers such as Se Ri Pak, Lorena Ochoa, Annika Sörenstam, and even male golfers such as Tiger Woods.

It was not a surprise that Tseng's unprecedented achievement in golf, like New York Yankees pitcher Chien-Ming Wang's great performance in baseball several years earlier, articulated a rigorous Taiwanese nationalism which involved several key elements: the LPGA, the world's most dominant women's golf organization, with its ever-increasing transnationality; multinational corporate sponsors; and, an intersectional matrix of gender, sexuality, race, social class, and physical capability. The issue of intersectionality is especially important in my analysis not only because of the class-exclusive nature of women's golf in Taiwan, but also because of the unusual juxtaposition in Tseng's status as another 'light of Taiwan': Tseng – a 'tomboyish' young woman who was once described as a 'boy next door'[9] by Taiwanese media – was to some extent at odds with the typical standards of Taiwanese femininity. Although her accomplishment in golf was universally celebrated in Taiwan, her identity as a *female* golfer who did not completely follow the traditional gender roles, feminine qualities, and heterosexism, all further complicated the typical narrative of sporting nationalism in Taiwan. It was thus necessary for the popular media to apply various discursive strategies to negotiate between Tseng's heroine status and her subjugated, and sometimes transgressive, social positions.

On October 23, 2011, Tseng won the Sunrise LPGA Taiwan Championship at Sunrise Golf and Country Club in Taoyuan, Taiwan. This marked her seventh LPGA championship of the year. This was not only a special event for Tseng, but it was also understood as an important landmark for Taiwan's golf history because this was Taiwan's first ever LPGA tournament. Golf, a sport only accessible to a small, selective group of people in Taiwan, was developed on the island thanks to its colonial history and complex relationship with both Japan and China. Similar to baseball, golf was introduced to Taiwan by Japanese colonizers in the 1910s during the Japanese colonial period. Before World War Two, golf was a recreation for Japanese military personnel, and most Taiwanese could only serve as caddies on these exclusive golf courses.[10] After Chiang Kai-shek's Kuomintang (KMT) government fled to Taiwan in 1949, KMT's military elites strongly supported the sport and helped construct several golf courses in different parts of the island. Golf was an important activity in international military conferences, and while KMT's Taiwan was in dire need of diplomatic and military support, playing golf was strongly encouraged for high-ranking military officers.[11] Thus, the inception of golf in Taiwan was directly connected with colonial legacies and international politics, and its exclusiveness was established from the beginning.

Throughout the 1960s, 1970s, and 1980s, both male and female Taiwanese golfers achieved considerable success on Japan's golf tour and in tournaments on the Asia Golf Circuit, with some participating in US-based PGA and LPGA tours. Because of their achievements, Taiwan was hailed as the 'Golf Kingdom of Asia' in the 1970s.[12] Nevertheless, not many golf tournaments were played in this 'Golf Kingdom' at the time, and golf in Taiwan was transnational from the beginning. Aside from the annual national open, the Republic of China Open[13], Taiwanese golfers played at a variety of sites around Asia such as Hong Kong, the Philippines, Thailand, India, Malaysia, Indonesia, and Japan. Japan, with its fully established golf tours in the region for both male and female golfers, was the primary destination for Taiwanese players. Women golfers in Taiwan were especially disadvantaged when it came to tournament opportunities. The Republic of China Open did not hold its first women's tournament until 1977, and thus playing in Japan's professional tournaments seemed to be the only option for talented women well into the 1990s. Taiwan's own women's golf association was not formed until 1997, then only as a section of the Taiwan Professional Golfers' Association (TPGA). In 2001, the Taiwan Ladies Professional Golfers' Association (TLPGA) finally became an independent association.[14]

The LPGA, the US-based golf association headquartered in Daytona Beach, Florida, has increasingly been a global sports agency, aggressively recruiting foreign golfers by the turn of the twenty-first century.[15] The association first held tournaments outside of North America in 1976, but it was not until the 1990s that it started to seriously engage with the golfing world in Europe, Australia, and Asia. In 1998, Americans were outnumbered by non-Americans in tournament wins for the first time, and this trend continued thanks to the dominant performances by Se Ri Pak (South Korea), Annika Sörenstam (Sweden), Karrie Webb (Australia), and Lorena Ochoa (Mexico). Tournaments held outside of America were also increasingly common. In 2005, LPGA tournaments were held in Canada, Mexico, France, England, Japan, South Korea, and Singapore, and were further expanded to other Asian countries in the following years – 2006 in Thailand, 2008 in China, and 2010 in Malaysia.[16] Taiwan's first LPGA tournament, the Sunrise LPGA Taiwan Championship in 2011, was in keeping with these developments. It was a product of both the LPGA's increasingly transnational approach and the efforts of Taiwan's golf community to engage with the powerful transnational association.

On the global scene of women's golf, the LPGA is no doubt the most dominant organization. It was thus not a surprise that the 2011 LPGA event generated much excitement in Taiwan. When Yani Tseng's father was interviewed before the tournament, he described the event as 'one of the best days in Taiwan's history'.[17] Taiwan Sports Lottery, the only legal sports betting agency in Taiwan, held its first ever golf betting event on this tournament. On the first day of the tournament, attendance had already reached over 10,000 people, an unusual number for regular LPGA events. For the final round, fans were lining up at the gate before seven o'clock in the morning, and attendance for the day peaked at more than 28,000 people. The total attendance of the four-day tournament, 66,971, easily broke the attendance record for a golf tournament in Taiwan.[18] On the golf course at Sunrise Golf and Country Club, the national flag of Taiwan could be seen in all sizes and everywhere. After Tseng won the tournament, several of the major Taiwanese newspapers covered the story with front page headlines. A *United Evening News* article noted that:

> ... during the past few days, ordinary people were talking about golf. Taxi drivers were watching live broadcast of the tournament when driving, and golf terminology such as 'birdie' and 'bogey' were no longer foreign to us. It is hard to say if golf would become another 'national ball' like baseball, but we can be sure that the image of golf has been significantly changed. It is no longer a sport for the rich only.[19]

Taiwan's Centennial Pride: The LPGA, Nationalism, and the Changing Image(s) of Golf

Golf, of course, would still be an exclusive sport in Taiwan long after the 2011 LPGA festival because of its historical connections with business and political elites and expensive membership fees, since most golf courses in Taiwan are privately operated. However, the 2011 LPGA event, as well as Tseng's championship, was indeed highly celebrated not only by well-versed golf fans but also by 'the masses' who might not have had much knowledge of the sport. The LPGA's hegemonic status certainly played an important role. Tseng, the 'light of Taiwan' who had just become the top-ranked woman golfer in the world earlier that year, also helped boost the hype with her great performance on the course. In addition, Tseng's victory articulated another important political context of Taiwan: the centennial celebration of the Republic of China. Just ten days before the tournament started, on October 10, the National Day Celebration (also known as the 'Double Tenth Day', 雙十節) was held in front of the Presidential Palace in Taipei to commemorate the establishment of the Republic of China in 1911. The National Day Celebration is observed every year, but the centennial Double Tenth Day was celebrated with a higher level of excitement. President Ma Ying-jeou held a large-scale military parade in front of the Presidential Palace, and two extravagant fireworks shows attracted about 500,000 people in total to enjoy the national holiday outside. These expressions of nationalism were further boosted by Taiwan's first LPGA tournament and Tseng's championship two weeks later. *Apple Daily* headlined Tseng's win as 'Taiwan's Centennial Pride; Ni-Ni's Glorious Tenth Championship', since this was Tseng's tenth overall championship of the year, and the 'tenth' coincidentally matched the 'Double Tenth Day' celebration.[20] Thus, the LPGA, golf, and nationalism were strongly articulated in this event. Even though women's golf was typically not included in Taiwan's national narrative, Tseng's win and the reaffirmation of her 'light of Taiwan' status led to the glorious but usually forgotten past of golf in Taiwan, namely the 'Golf Kingdom of Asia' narrative, reemerging in popular media.[21]

Golf in Taiwan had endured a tainted image since the early 1990s. In 1989, a national scandal of illegal lobbying over constructions of several golf courses revealed the unscrupulous nexus of golf and politics. There had been complicated relationships between politicians and construction companies, and this might have led to fast-track approvals of a number of golf course construction plans. The number of golf courses in Taiwan rapidly increased in the 1990s. From 1991 to 1996, more than thirty new golf courses were opened, and many worried this would cause serious environmental issues in mountainous Taiwan.[22] Lee Teng-hui, then president of Taiwan, was known as an avid golfer and possessed several extremely expensive golf club memberships. His golf partners included other high-ranking politicians, lawmakers, and business moguls. This situation contributed to a negative image of golf as only for the rich and the powerful, and harmful to Taiwan's already vulnerable landscapes, environment, and water conservation.[23]

In this sense, the ubiquitous and nationalistic celebration of Tseng's victory in the 2011 LPGA Taiwan Championship suggested that the Taiwan-centered nationalism, in this specific historical moment, overshadowed the environmental concerns over golf. Media narratives of Tseng's championship were overwhelmingly celebratory, and several popular accounts praised the president of Sunrise Golf and Country Club, Xu Dianya (許典雅), for making this tournament happen.[24] On the other hand, the government, especially President Ma's lacklustre attitude towards golf, was heavily criticized. Several media sources recalled that in 2008 after Tseng won her first LPGA major tournament, she was invited to meet President Ma for her achievement. During the meeting, Tseng asked the President if the government was willing to sponsor a LPGA tournament in Taiwan the following year. Ma asked about the amount of money required for this plan, and Tseng's answer, approximately US$6,004,000, shocked Ma. He was quoted as replying, 'that much money! It could be enough for holding several dozens of road running events!'[25] The plan to hold this LPGA tournament in 2009, thus, did not materialize.

In retrospect, Ma's response and the government's inactivity regarding Tseng's request in 2008 were now almost universally ridiculed and deemed shortsighted because the LPGA tournament not only 'brought light to Taiwan ' but also 'heightened Taiwan's international visibility'.[26] Most media accounts argued that the privately funded golf tournament was much more effective in terms of international publicity and 'marketing Taiwan' than other government-sponsored international events which cost much more money, such as the Taipei International Flora Exposition held in 2010 and the Deaflympics held in Taipei in 2009.[27]

President Ma's comparison between the LPGA golf tournament and road running events, however, led to an important question regarding the purposes of government-sponsored sports events. Although it was true that the LPGA tournament brought elite golfers to Taiwan and boosted Taiwan's international publicity, the tournament lasted only four days and golf would still be an exclusive sport which was only accessible to the most affluent and privileged, even though the general public might understand better its rules, etiquette, and terminology. On the other hand, road running events were much cheaper and inclusive, and they did not require a top-down supervision from a powerful transnational agency (LPGA) and expensive down-payment (US$2,000,000) to be deposited.

The lack of counternarrative against golf and the LPGA in this episode suggests that for the general public, Taiwan's visibility and recognition in international societies was more important than other critical internal issues. Golf's tainted image in 1990s Taiwan was almost completely forgotten, and the desire to be seen by the world articulated the LPGA's global approach to attracting new audiences and furthering transnational sponsorship. The meanings behind Tseng's 'light of Taiwan' status thus need to be understood within the intertwining forces of neoliberal practices, global political economy, US cultural imperialism, and local nationalism. The case of Tseng also reveals that the LPGA enjoyed a hegemonic status in Taiwan as it dominated local golf consumption. Just as talented baseball players prioritized opportunities to join MLB organizations over Taiwan's own professional baseball league, young women golfers looked up to LPGA players, thereby leaving local golf organizations such as the TLPGA to receive a skimpy level of attention and media exposure.

The 'Tseng vs. Wie Rivalry': Korea as the 'Significant "Other"'

The discursive construction of a national rivalry is important in the media representations of Tseng. To situate Taiwan in the historical context of East Asian politics, China has long been Taiwan's primary 'enemy' and source of military and economic threat, but South Korea has also served as another 'significant "other"' in Taiwan's nationalistic discourses, especially in the arena of sport.[28] During the Cold War, both countries were on the front line of anti-communism, and Taiwan had long seen South Korea as a 'brotherhood nation' (兄弟之邦) because of their longtime diplomatic partnership and similar historical trajectories after World War Two. However, since the 1970s, Taiwan and South Korea had been economic rivals as both countries were among the 'Four Asian Dragons' which developed through rapid industrialization and gained ground in the regional economy of East Asia. In 1992, South Korea terminated its diplomatic relation with Taiwan after formally recognizing the People's Republic of China, and it did so in a humiliating fashion. These factors contributed to the increasing hostility against Korean people among Taiwanese in the 1990s.[29]

Anti-Korean sentiments were especially common in the 2000s.[30] For example, during the 2009 East Asian Games a controversial taekwondo decision which resulted in a loss for Taiwan and a gold medal for South Korea provoked a nation-wide hatred against Korean people. In the popular media it was reported that a restaurant owner posted a banner in front of the entrance stating 'this establishment forbids Korean people from entering'. As a result, 'business was not affected at all. Indeed, it was even better with the banner on'.[31] Similar anti-Korean sentiments also appeared during the 2010 Asian Games over another controversial taekwondo decision, the 2013 World Baseball Classic, and other international competitions. In this context, Korea's role as a key rival and 'significant "other"' has been firmly established in a variety of sports, including baseball, basketball, taekwondo, and golf.

Korean and Korean American golfers played important roles in media narratives of Tseng. Indeed, the reason that Tseng reached the national spotlight for the first time in 2004 when she was still an amateur golfer, was largely because of the golfer she beat: Michelle Wie. In the 2004 US Women's Amateur Public Links, Tseng, then just fifteen, defeated the fourteen-year-old and defending champion Korean American by one shot and won the championship. This event made Tseng a household name in Taiwan, and almost every account highlighted the loser, Wie. At the time, Wie was already a sports celebrity for being a talented fourteen-year-old amateur golfer, but it was apparent Taiwanese media further heightened Wie's status to make Tseng's victory look even better. In an article on *Min Sheng Bao*, Wie was described as the 'best contemporary golfer in the world'.[32] *United Evening News* covered this news on its front page under the headline '15! A Comeback Win in US Women's Amateur Golf Tournament; Tseng Yani defeats Michelle Wie, Making Wie Cry', emphasizing Wie's emotional reaction after the final hole.[33] An *Apple Daily* article started with Tseng's claim that 'I was not afraid of Michelle Wie at all!' and followed by describing Wie as the 'Korean-descent genius girl'.[34] In another article, Tseng was described as a 'world champion' for winning this amateur tournament, and her victory 'should have a long-lasting effect on Taiwan's golf development'.[35] These media narratives all mentioned Wie's 'Korean' identity, even though she was born in Hawaii and is an American citizen.

After Tseng turned professional, Wie continued to be a constant focus in media narratives. After Tseng won another LPGA tournament in September 2010, *Apple Daily* ran an article which detailed the two golfers' achievements side by side. In the article, Tseng and Wie were described as 'deadly enemies' since their amateur careers, and Wie's career highlights mentioned in this article included her early fame, lucrative sponsorship from Nike and Sony, and her several appearances in men's PGA tournaments for 'creating media hype'.[36] In August 2011, Wie's relatively poor performance that year was paralleled with Tseng's outstanding record. A *United Evening News* article noted that Wie 'has not won any LPGA tournament this year. Throughout her career, she had only two championships, Ochoa Invitational in 2009 and last year's Canadian Women's Open. Not one major championship trophy'. The article even mentioned that Wie 'did not give a damn' about Tseng before her rise to stardom, and now 'she can only look up to her'.[37] In all, when Wie was mentioned in comparison with Tseng, she was usually portrayed as a media darling or an attractive player who received more attention than she should, and her golf achievement was much lower than Tseng.

The 'Tseng vs. Wie' rivalry was thus transformed into the 'Taiwan-Korea' rivalry on the national level. The fact that Tseng dominated the world of women's golf and outperformed Wie and other high-profile Korean LPGA golfers symbolically signified that Taiwan beat Korea, one of its important national rivals, despite the fact that Wie is an American citizen. This phenomenon revealed that Taiwan's national desire to 'beat Korea' followed the logics of both nationalism and transnationality: Tseng's success was translated as the success of the Taiwanese nation, yet the (mis)signification of Wie's Koreanness indicated that Wie's legal status of nationality became irrelevant.

Moreover, such a rivalry followed the cultural logic of flexible citizenship and transnationality in the era of globalization. As Aihwa Ong argues, transnational subjects 'emphasize, and are regulated by, practices favouring flexibility, mobility, and repositioning in relation to markets, governments, and cultural regimes'.[38] The constructed rivalry between Tseng and Wie, from the Taiwanese perspective, demonstrated a flexible configuration of nation-based identities to serve the discourses of Taiwanese nationalism. On the other hand, in Korea, Wie was also marketed as an 'overseas Korean'.[39] Rachael Joo argues that as South Korea has increasingly embraced ideologies and policies of globalization since the 1990s, global celebrities of Korean descent such as Michelle Wie would still be understood as a citizen of 'global Korea' and be expected 'to maintain a sense of loyalty to the South Korean nation'[40] regardless of her nationality or political membership. Wie continued to be presented as an ethnic Korean who shared the Korean 'blood' and possessed 'an innate and natural connection to one another' with other Korean people.[41]

Negotiating among Gender, Physical Capability, and Nation

The intersection of gender, race, physicality, and nation was especially profound in the media narratives revolving around Tseng. As a female athlete who was only

19 years old when she won her first major tournament in 2009, Tseng was not a typical figure who could be considered a representative of the Taiwanese nation. She was too young to be treated seriously, and her gender worked against her profession. Nevertheless, the narratives and meanings revolving around Tseng did articulate an uneven relationship between women's sports and nationalism in the Taiwanese context.

As Ying Chiang argues, female athletes in post-war Taiwan have had a complex relationship with the nation. While they typically received less attention than male athletes, their success in international sporting events has closely articulated the national politics in different ways throughout the latter half of the twentieth century. Although nationalism has been traditionally associated with masculinity in the Taiwanese context, notable female athletes such as Chi Cheng (1968 Summer Olympics medallist) and Chen Yi-An (1988 Summer Olympics gold medallist) as well as the women's national basketball team in the early 1970s were heavily incorporated in the nationalistic discourses, specifically being utilized to reinforce the legitimacy of the *Chinese* nation (Republic of China) the KMT government claimed to represent.[42] However, these narratives still reinforced the hegemonic notion of femininity, constructing these women as girly and hyperfeminine figures who nevertheless fit in the patriarchal Taiwanese society despite their athletic prowess. In what follows, I argue that although Tseng articulated a different version of nationalism in the twenty-first century Taiwan, the ways she was portrayed still largely conformed to heterosexism and a traditional view of femininity in the Taiwanese context.

Although Tseng was considered a legitimate 'light of Taiwan' thanks to her unprecedented achievements in golf, her femininity, physicality, and even sexual orientation were at times under question in media narratives. Her appearance, which did not follow the typical standard of Taiwanese femininity, was usually under media interrogation. The Taiwanese media have described her appearance as 'gender neutral' or even 'manly', and her figure and weight were also focussed upon once she seemed to be too 'big' to maintain her feminine qualities.[43] For example, in June 2011, Tseng won her fourth LPGA major tournament in New York. Aside from celebrating the fact that Tseng became the youngest ever golfer to win four major championships, her somewhat visible 'love handles' became another talking point in media narratives. A reporter asked her the reason why she gained some weight, and a *United Daily News* article even consulted and quoted bariatric professionals, suggesting that Tseng should 'have a more restrained diet' and do more sit-up exercises to 'help shrink her waist figure'.[44] Tseng was also quoted as saying that she cared about her own appearance and body image. 'She likes to wear shorts because she is satisfied with the way her lower legs look', an *Apple Daily* article wrote, but whenever she plays on hilly golf courses, 'she is worried about thickening them [after all the walking]'.[45] In another *United Evening News* article which compared Tseng's appearance with that of the hyper-feminine Michelle Wie and other Korean golfers, the journalist mentioned that woman golfers from Korea would all put on make-up to attract more attention from fans. He then commented that 'Ni-Ni is a woman after all. She has thought about putting on make-up and looking really beautiful on course, but she still prioritizes her golf performance over other things'.[46]

The cultural expectation for Tseng and other Taiwanese female athletes to maintain their 'feminine qualities' can be best exemplified in an episode of Taiwan's popular variety show *Kangxi Lai Le* (康熙來了) which Tseng joined as one of the special guests in 2009. In this episode titled 'who's to say female athletes are not feminine,' Tseng and four other Taiwanese woman athletes joined host Tsai Kang-yong and hostess Little S for an hour of entertainment. In the beginning, the athletes introduced their respective sports and achievements to the audience, but the main focus, or the real reason and ultimate goal for them to be invited to the show, was to exploit the contradiction between femininity and athleticism – two elements which were not considered compatible in Taiwan. It was telling that host Tsai opened the show by asking half-jokingly, 'are they all women?'[47] For entertainment purposes, the athletes were there to be 'feminized' and 'fashionized' – the climax of this episode was the contrast between how they originally looked and how they looked after the 'grand transformation'. Appearing with a gender-neutral outfit of polo shirt, vest, and trousers, Tseng said that she would like to be transformed into a style of being 'sportingly cute'. After she further explained that she would like to look more feminine, she was asked a series of provocative questions such as 'how short can your skirt be?', 'will you show a little cleavage?', 'have you been shaving your armpit hair?', and so on. At the end of the episode, Tseng was successfully transformed into a 'French-style little cutie' by the programme staff: She donned a fashionable beret over a curly wig, wore a casual, unbuttoned blue shirt over a black tank top, and decorated her chest with an elegant necklace cowl. The grand transformation was completed by her capri pants and dress shoes, along with a successful posing/flirting demonstration, guided by hostess Little S.

The ways in which Tseng was represented in this variety show and her willingness to be 'transformed' into a more feminine being indicated that female athletes in Taiwan, especially those who displayed physical prowess, were usually at odds with heterosexual attractiveness and traditional femininity. Although Taiwanese women's participation in sport and physical activities has been on the rise in the latter part of the twentieth century, dominant gender ideology and the effects of Confucianism remain decisive factors which discourage women from pursuing sport rigorously.[48] Indeed, for Taiwanese women, their options in sports are structurally and culturally limited. They are more encouraged to pursue community- and family-based physical activities, yet organized, competitive, and more physically-demanding sporting activities are still very much considered a male preserve.[49] In all, women athletes in Taiwan are subject to a higher level of cultural restraint than men. The example of Tseng indicates that sexualization, heterosexism, and other forms of dominant gender ideology, to some extent, discredited and detracted from her superb achievement in women's golf. Even her heroic status would not make her escape these cultural forces.

It is also important to note that Tseng's superior physical capability – her ability to hit almost-300-yard drives – provoked the media to call her gender into question. An *Apple Daily* article mentioned that Tseng not only had a 'big heart' (a Chinese/Taiwanese idiom which refereed to her ability to remain composed under pressure), but she also had 'big hands and big feet, completely like a male golfer', which gave her advantage in driving distance.[50] Another *United Daily News* article quoted a golf expert as saying that he 'has never seen a female golfer [like Tseng] with that much explosiveness in the upper body'.[51] Her driving distance was also compared with golfers on the PGA tour, and it was concluded that she was as good as these male sluggers.[52] Her untypical female body, strength, and physical prowess troubled the narrow scope of female athleticism in Taiwan. Although the media, in general, praised these physical traits, the narratives reaffirmed the presumed inferiority of the female body. Tseng's physical power was thus deemed transgressive and unique, and she would not fit the typical image of Taiwanese womanhood.

In order to cope with Tseng's transgressive physicality while maintaining her status as a Taiwanese role model, I argue that the Taiwanese media applied certain discursive strategies to negotiate between her femininity and physical prowess. The media tended to emphasize the men who were considered significant to Tseng's success – her father Tseng Mao Hsin (曾茂炘), her coach Gao Bosong (高柏松), and her major sponsor during her early playing career, Xu Dianya. These figures served somewhat as Tseng's 'guardians' in media narratives thanks largely to her identity as a young woman in a still patriarchal society. Yani's father Tseng Mao Hsin has often served in a spokesperson-like role for his daughter, and Xu, an entrepreneur and the president of Sunrise Golf & Country Club, was also a regular source of comment for journalists.

The relationship between Tseng and these older men was especially revealing when she was in trouble. In early 2013, Tseng underwent a lengthy slump and dropped from the top spot of the World Rankings, a coveted status she had kept for 109 consecutive weeks. Worse, during the 2013 Kia Classic LPGA tournament, she was forced to withdraw because she missed the Pro-Am tee time the day before the official tournament, citing oversleeping as the reason for not showing up on time. This embarrassing mistake prompted Xu to openly criticize Tseng and her agents in the media, stating that 'the person whom I have nurtured was ruined'. Xu implied that Tseng's performance downturn was partly because she made 'bad friends' and frequented night clubs, thus not focussing on her golf career. Moreover, her sports agency group was also responsible for not making her steer away from these distractions.[53] In this incident, Xu apparently saw himself as a figure of authority to Tseng, so much so that Tseng's golf achievement became what he had invested in and 'nurtured' – it belonged to him. In this light, Tseng was removed from her own agency and subjectivity; her athleticism became a belonging of an older businessman, and her potential power as a star athlete and a role model for an alternative version of womanhood in Taiwan to challenge the traditional gender order in physicality and beyond was completely stripped.

In addition, journalists word choices when describing Tseng and other female golfers also revealed the institutional bias against women athletes in Taiwan's mass media industry. Media representations of women athletes in Taiwan largely follow a narrow scope of womanhood: they are commonly described in an ultra-feminine way and regarded as sex objects of heterosexual men.[54] *United Evening News* once used the word *jinchai* (金釵), a term metaphorically used to refer to concubines of a patriarch, to refer to Tseng and other Taiwanese women golfers.[55] The fact that

Tseng's Chinese name, *Yani* (雅妮), consists of a feminine character *Ni* (妮) did not help either. *Ni* literally means 'little girl', and to combine this character with others makes phrases such as *xiaonizi* (小妮子), a term meaning 'petite young lady', usually in a flirting sense. *Xiaonizi* appeared commonly in media narratives of Tseng, and her nickname 'Ni-Ni' also conveyed a sense of cuteness, docility, and intimacy.[56] Other examples of such feminization in media discourses included calling Tseng '咱ㄟ寶貝' ('our baby' in Taiwanese Hokkien), '姝' ('beautiful woman'), and '小女孩' ('little girl').[57]

Thus, through positioning Tseng under the authority of older men and practicing the media custom of feminizing sporting women, her image appeared to be less threatening to the patriarchal gender order in Taiwan. It was only under these conditions that Tseng was able to be perceived as a 'light of Taiwan'. In the end, the case of Tseng revealed that the celebratory, nationalistic discourse had its limits, and the tide of Taiwanese nationalism was unable to incorporate progressive forces of feminist politics without a radical paradigm shift in Taiwan's dominant gender ideology, especially in the intersections of sport, physicality, and femininity.

Hollow Nationalism?

By the end of 2013, Yani Tseng's dominance in women's golf appeared to come to an end. After 109 weeks of occupying the top spot in women's golf, she fell to second place on the Women's World Golf Rankings in March 2013. Later in 2013, she could not make the cut in consecutive tournaments. She continued to struggle during the following years, falling out of the top 100 since 2016. As of 2019, Tseng, now at the age of 30, still plays golf professionally in LPGA tournaments and other regional events, but since she is unable to repeat her brilliant performance several years ago, the Taiwanese media interest in her has waned significantly. Nevertheless, the media narratives of Tseng during her dominant years reveal how Taiwanese nationalism had operated and been reproduced in the era of global capitalism. Taiwanese nationalism, or the political consciousness of a distinctive *Taiwanese* nation which explicitly positions itself against Chinese nationalism, gained traction in the 1980s through a series of political and cultural reforms, and it continues to be the national consciousness among the majority of Taiwanese people despite the constant threat from mainland China. The cultural meanings of Tseng, as an articulation of sport and Taiwanese nationalism in the 2010s, can be understood as one of the latest examples of this trend.

Importantly, the narratives of Tseng also reveal other significant issues. Transnational corporations such as the LPGA have enjoyed a powerful status on the island, an example of the unchallenged American cultural hegemony in Taiwan since the Cold War era. From the constructed rivalry between Tseng and Michelle Wie, it is evident that some of these nationalistic excitements were instigated by a fluid and flexible definition of nation and nationality. Looking more closely at how the media narratives articulate Tseng's gender, sexuality, and physicality in a sense that they are deviant from traditional gender roles and conventional femininity, I contend that the popular discourses followed the long tradition of sexualizing and objectifying female athletes, while applying certain strategies to neutralize Tseng's physical prowess and masculine traits. Although Tseng's spectacular achievements in golf problematized the nationalistic and masculine discourses of a typical Taiwanese national sporting hero, the meanings of these media narratives suggest a rather hollow nationalistic excitement while reinforcing dominant gender ideology and deemed athleticism and femininity mutually exclusive. While nationalism and political issues between China and Taiwan remain the driving forces which dictate the mediated images of Taiwanese sporting stars, progressive change of gender equity and inclusiveness will not happen without a greater awareness of these issues in the sporting arena.

Notes

1. When referring to Chinese names, this article typically follow the East Asian language convention with the surname fist and the given name last, unless the person is generally referred to by the English-language media following the English language convention. For example, 'Yani Tseng' and 'Chien-Ming Wang' both follow the English name order of given name first and surname last. Since these name orders were commonly used in the English-language media, they have not been changed back to the Chinese language convention in this article.
2. Wang was a starting pitcher for the New York Yankees from 2005 to 2009. The Taiwanese media dubbed him the 'light of Taiwan' to praise his success in Major League Baseball. Soon after, this term was used broadly to celebrate other athletes, professionals, or artists from Taiwan or of Taiwanese descent.
3. See John Makeham and A-chin Hsiau, eds., *Cultural, Ethnic, and Political Nationalism in Contemporary Taiwan: Bentuhua* (New York: Palgrave Macmillan, 2005); A-chin Hsiau, *Contemporary Taiwanese Cultural Nationalism* (New York: Routledge, 2000).
4. Sumei Wang, 'Taiwanese Baseball: A Story of Entangled Colonialism, Class, Ethnicity, and Nationalism', *Journal of Sport & Social Issues* 33, no. 4 (2009): 355–72; Junwei Yu, *Playing in Isolation: A History of Baseball in Taiwan* (Lincoln: University of Nebraska Press, 2007); Junwei Yu and Alan Bairner, 'Proud to Be Chinese: Little League Baseball and National Identities in Taiwan during the 1970s', *Identities* 15, no. 2 (2008): 216–39.
5. J. Bruce Jacobs, '"Taiwanization" in Taiwan's Politics', in *Cultural, Ethnic, and Political Nationalism in Contemporary Taiwan: Bentuhua*, ed. John Makeham and A-chin Hsiau (New York: Palgrave Macmillan, 2005), 17–54.
6. Susan Birrell and Mary G. McDonald, eds., *Reading Sport: Critical Essays on Power and Representation* (Boston: Northeastern University Press, 2000); Mary G. McDonald and Susan Birrell, 'Reading Sport Critically: A Methodology for Interrogating Power', *Sociology of Sport Journal* 16, no. 4 (1999): 291.
7. Birrell and McDonald, *Reading Sport*, 11.
8. For example, *United Daily News*, *United Evening News*, and *China Times* were more inclined to the KMT party and its political allies, while *Liberty Times* and *Apple Daily* were considered more pro-DPP party and inclined to the pro-independence political orientation.
9. Shuheng Wang, '上月爲建仔打氣 今天, 自己爭氣 [After cheering for Chien a month ago, today she is making it herself]', *United Evening News*, June 9, 2008, AA1.
10. I-Pang Wang, '台灣高爾夫運動的回顧與展望 [The retrospect and prospect of Golf Development in Taiwan]', *Body Culture Journal (Taiwan)* 7 (2008): 48.
11. Xiaojuan Lei, 'Zhou Zhirou and Taiwan's Golf Development', *Journal of Golf Science (Taiwan)* 10 (2013): 1–11.
12. Jianzheng Sun, '世界高球壇 一場技術戰 [The world of golf: A game of strategy]', *United Daily News*, December 8, 1975, 3.

13. The Republic of China Open was founded in 1965, and its name was changed to 'Taiwan Open' in 2004. Its last event was held in 2006.
14. Wang, 'Retrospect and Prospect of Golf', 58.
15. K-y Kim, 'Producing Korean Women Golfers on the LPGA Tour' (PhD diss., University of Toronto, 2012), 104.
16. Ibid., 105.
17. Sen-Hong Yang, 複製曾雅妮 [Cloning Yani] (Taipei: Yushanshe Publishing, 2011), 32.
18. '台灣百年驕傲 妮妮光輝十冠 [Taiwan's centennial pride; Ni-Ni's shinning ten championships]'. *Apple Daily (Taiwan)*, October 24, 2011, http://www.appledaily.com.tw/appledaily/article/sports/20111024/33762150/.
19. '台灣之光 魅力無限 [Light of Taiwan with endless charm]', *United Evening News*, October 24, 2011, A2.
20. '台灣百年驕傲 妮妮光輝十冠'.
21. Xintian Zhao, '衝著妮來 高球熱開始發酵 [Thanks to Ni, Golf's popularity is heating up]', *Liberty Times*, October 24, 2011, http://news.ltn.com.tw/news/focus/paper/533893.
22. Wang, 'Retrospect and Prospect of Golf', 57.
23. Ya-Li Lee, 'The Research of Golf Development in Postwar of Taiwan, 1945-2006' (Master's thesis, National Taitung University, 2007), 198.
24. Meifen Lin, '許典雅辦比賽 複製曾雅妮 [Xu hosts tournament to clone Tseng Yani]', *Liberty Times*, September 26, 2011, http://news.ltn.com.tw/news/business/paper/526981.
25. Chunnan Jiang, '司馬觀點：曾雅妮替台灣爭光（江春男）[Sima Perspective: Tseng Yani is earning pride for Taiwan]', *Apple Daily (Taiwan)*, October 24, 2011, http://www.appledaily.com.tw/appledaily/article/headline/20111024/33762474/.
26. Ibid.
27. Ibid.
28. For the concept of 'significant others' within the theoretical framework of nationalism, see Anna Triandafyllidou, 'National Identity and the "Other"', *Ethnic and Racial Studies* 21, no. 4 (1998): 593–612.
29. Jiyeon Kang, Jae-On Kim, and Yan Wang, 'Salvaging National Pride: The 2010 Taekwondo Controversy and Taiwan's Quest for Global Recognition', *International Review for the Sociology of Sport* 50, no. 1 (2015): 98–114.
30. Chang-de Liu, 'The Cultural/Economic Logic of "Festival Nationalism": An Analysis of "Anti-Korea" and "Anti-China" Discourses in Taiwanese Media Reports on Sports', *Mass Communication Research (Taiwan)* 122 (2015): 79–120.
31. Ibid., 102–3.
32. '整晚都沒睡 雅妮電話報佳音 看到幾年努力成績 [Xu: Staying up all night for the good news from Yani; Years of efforts paid off for her]', *Min Sheng Bao*, June 29, 2004, B2.
33. Sijie Wang, '15歲！逆轉贏得美國業餘高球女錦賽 曾雅妮打哭魏成美 [15! A comeback win in US Women's amateur golf tournament; Tseng Yani defeats Michelle Wie, Making Wie Cry]', *United Evening News*, June 28, 2004, A1.
34. Zhongjie Liu, '美業餘高球曾雅妮奪冠 [Tseng Yani wins an amateur tournament in the U.S.]', *Apple Daily (Taiwan)*, June 29, 2004, http://www.appledaily.com.tw/appledaily/article/headline/20040629/1043111/.
35. Baoqing Lin, '華人的照顧 奪冠的後盾 曾雅妮 18歲要當職業高手 [Thanks to the care of fellow Chinese, Tseng Yani wins tournament and seeks to turn pro at the age of 18]', *Min Sheng Bao*, June 30, 2004, B5.
36. Jianzhong Li, '唯一目標 世界第1 [The only goal is number one of the world]', *Apple Daily (Taiwan)*, September 15, 2010, http://www.appledaily.com.tw/appledaily/article/sports/20100915/32813778/.
37. Shuheng Wang, '加拿大公開賽 曾魏對決 [Tseng faces off Michelle Wie at Canadian Open]', *United Evening News*, August 24, 2011, A16.
38. Aihwa Ong, *Flexible Citizenship: The Cultural Logics of Transnationality* (Durham: Duke University Press, 1999), 6.

39. Rachael Miyung Joo, *Transnational Sport: Gender, Media, and Global Korea* (Durham: Duke University Press, 2012), 149.
40. Ibid., 7.
41. Ibid.
42. Ying Chiang, 'Multiple Margins: Gender, Sport and Nationalism in Taiwan' (PhD diss., National Taiwan Sport University, 2013).
43. '曾雅妮台北以酒會友 豪邁嗑燒肉 [Tseng Yani enjoys barbeque and drinks with friends in Taipei]', *Apple Daily (Taiwan)*, April 29, 2010, http://ent.appledaily.com.tw/enews/article/entertainment/20100429/32473505/.
44. Shuheng Wang, '小腹婆 媽媽菜害她變胖 [A woman with belly fat: Mom's cooking makes her gain weight]', *United Evening News*, June 27, 2011, A5; Jianfu Zhan, Guanghan Lei, and Zengxun Zeng, '醫師勸她控制 小肚肚搶鏡 「我家沒體重器」' [Doctor advises Tseng to watch her weight; 'I don't have a weight scale at home'], *United Daily News*, June 28, 2011, A3.
45. Guowei Chen, '微笑妮妮 最滿意自家小腿 [Smiling Ni-Ni is most proud of her lower legs]', *Apple Daily (Taiwan)*, August 3, 2011, http://www.appledaily.com.tw/appledaily/article/sports/20110803/33570977/.
46. Shuheng Wang, '阿肯色斯奪冠後 … 妮妮甩稚氣化妝打扮 [After winning in Arkansas, Ni-Ni puts on make-up and gets rid of her childish look]', *United Evening News*, September 15, 2010, A16.
47. '康熙來了 2009-10-23 pt.1/5 誰說女運動員沒有女人味? [Who's to say female athletes are not feminine]' YouTube Video, 9 min., 6 sec.; from a performance televised by CTi Variety on October 23, 2009, https://youtu.be/RP_U_H4-Www.
48. Chia-Chen Yu, Yin-Hua Liaw, and Susan Barnd, 'Cultural and Social Factors Affecting Women's Physical Activity Participation in Taiwan', *Sport, Education and Society* 9, no. 3 (2004): 379–93.
49. Ibid., 388–9.
50. Guowei Chen and Weiyuan Yin, '打垮世界高爾夫球后 台灣傳奇 曾雅妮 [Defeating Golf's World Champion, Tseng Yani a Taiwanese legend]', *Apple Daily (Taiwan)*, June 10, 2008, http://www.appledaily.com.tw/appledaily/article/headline/20080610/30638091/.
51. Guanghan Lei, '老爸從小扎根 妮妮 上半身爆發力驚人 [With dad's help since childhood, Ni-Ni commands explosive upper-body power]', *United Daily News*, August 30, 2010, B4.
52. Jianzhong Li, '開球平均293碼 妮不輸男子重砲 [Ni's average driving distance of 293 is no less than male sluggers]', *Apple Daily (Taiwan)*, May 4, 2015, http://www.appledaily.com.tw/appledaily/article/sports/20150504/36529972/.
53. Ji Ye, '曾雅妮離譜賴床，恩人許典雅怒轟：別再上夜店 速換經營團隊 [Tseng Yani irresponsibly sleeps in; Xu scolds: No night clubs anymore, and get a new sports agency group soon]', *Chinatimes Weekly*, April 15, 2013, http://magazine.chinatimes.com/ctweekly/20130415005573-300106.
54. Pei-Hua Lu and Yu-Pei Chang, '性別差異政治：女性運動員的媒體再現與認同糾葛 [The politics of gender differences: Media representation and identity entanglement of female athletes]', *Chinese Journal of Communication Research (Taiwan)* 17, (2010): 139–70.
55. Xiang Wang, '單場抓5鳥 曾雅妮 獨居領先 [Five birdies lead to Yani's lone lead]', *United Evening News*, July 31, 2010, A8.
56. Chen, '微笑妮妮 最滿意自家小腿'; Xiang Wang, '射鷹抓鳥 小妮子輕鬆打 [Eagles and birdies, Little Ni is taking it easy]', *United Evening News*, July 30, 2010, A19.
57. Guowei Chen, 開幕戰 妮妮領軍4台妹作夥衝 [Ni-Ni led Taiwanese female golfers take on LPGA's opening tournament]', *Apple Daily (Taiwan)*, January 28, 2016, http://www.appledaily.com.tw/appledaily/article/sports/20160128/37036119/; Jianzhong Li, '妮用戰鬥雞 添可愛氣息 [Ni makes herself cute with her fighting rooster-themed club cover]', *Apple Daily (Taiwan)*, October 21, 2011, http://www.appledaily.com.tw/appledaily/article/headline/20111021/33754478/; '妮 咱ㄟ寶貝 奪 LPGA 台灣賽首冠 [Ni is our baby: Wins

the first championship of LPGA Taiwan]', *Apple Daily (Taiwan)*, October 24, 2011, http://www.appledaily.com.tw/appledaily/article/sports/20111024/33762144/applesearch/%E5%A6%AE%E5%92%B1%E3%84%9F%E5%AF%B6%E8%B2%9D%E5%A5%AALPGA%E5%8F%B0%E7%81%A3%E8%B3%BD%E9%A6%96%E5%86%A0.

Disclosure Statement

No potential conflict of interest was reported by the author.

China's Sports Heroes: Nationalism, Patriotism, and Gold Medal

Lu Zhouxiang and Fan Hong

ABSTRACT
Sport has been of great importance to the construction of Chinese national consciousness during the past century. This article examines how China's sport celebrities have played their part in nation building and identity construction. It points out that Chinese athletes' participation in international sporting events in the first half of the twentieth century demonstrated China's motivation to stay engaged with the world, and therefore led to their being regarded as national heroes. From the 1950s, China's status and relative strength among nations became measured by the country's success at international sporting events. The nation's appetite for gold medals resulted in the rapid development of elite sport, but has placed a heavy burden on star athletes.

In all human communities, according to Liam Ryan, 'sports and pastimes not only give pleasure and relaxation but, more importantly, provide opportunities for creativity, group identity and cohesion'.[1] Sport has been of great importance for the construction of Chinese nationalism and national consciousness during the past century. In the last 20 years, research has been conducted by historians, social scientists and political scientists to examine the relationship between sport and nationalism in China, with Andrew D. Morris's *Marrow of the Nation* and Lu Zhouxiang and Fan Hong's *Sport and Nationalism in China* the most comprehensive works of this kind.[2] The majority of these publications examine the issue from a historical perspective, highlighting the role of sport in China's identity construction, nation building and modernization in the twentieth century. Nevertheless, the complexity and the nature of sports nationalism in China needs to be explored further. This article investigates the issue from a different perspective, by exploring the lives of the country's sporting celebrities. Unlike previous research that primarily focuses on the role of Chinese star athletes in relation to the globalization, commercialization and professionalization of sport,[3] the aim here is to offer some insight into how China's top athletes have played their part in the construction and transformation of nationalism and patriotism, and how they have been turned into national heroes. This article also explains why the nation's appetite for gold medals has placed a heavy burden on celebrity athletes.

From the FECG to the Olympics

Since the 1910s, when modern sport and the Olympics were introduced to China, sport has been consistently interwoven with politics and nationalism. In the Republic of China era (1912–1949), against the background of imperialist expansion, foreign aggression and domestic unrest, and guided by a government policy based on self-strengthening, sport and physical education were promoted as a means of cultivating healthy citizens for a new China, consolidating national unity and promoting patriotism. International sporting events such as the Far Eastern Championship Games (FECG) and the Olympic Games came to be regarded as important vehicles for building up China's national image and enhancing international recognition. This gave rise to the first generation of Chinese sporting celebrities.[4]

The FECG were created by the Young Men's Christian Association (YMCA) to spread the idea of Christian morality in East Asia, build up international friendship, encourage masculinity and cultivate social morals through sport. The first FECG were held in the Philippines in 1913. Organized by the YMCA, 36 Chinese athletes participated. It was the first international sporting event Chinese athletes had ever taken part in. Chen Yan won the long jump gold medal, making him China's first international sports champion. Wei Huanzhang captured gold in the high jump and the 110-yard hurdles. Pan Wenbing won decathlon gold. The event must be credited for changing the Chinese people's worldview and mindset. By sending its national team to compete with athletes from other Asian countries, the newly established Republic confirmed its position as a modern and independent nation state.[5]

The second FECG were held in Shanghai in 1915. For China, this was another important move toward modern nationhood. Chinese athletes performed well at the Games and captured five gold medals in track and field, three gold medals in swimming, one gold medal in volleyball and one gold medal in football. The national team was crowned overall champion. Wang Zhengting,[6] Chairman of the Games, commented that 'China's success is the result of the cooperation of all the Chinese athletes. This will cultivate the concept of nation state among the Chinese people … the Games also promoted a sense of unity.'[7] The FECG enlightened the Chinese people and made many of them aware of the political significance of international sporting events to their nation. The sports arena was regarded as a violence-free battlefield where the Chinese could build up their confidence and restore dignity by defeating foreign competitors. Between 1917 and 1933, eight FECG were held in Asia. Headed by champion swimmer Yang Xiuqiong and football star Li Huitang, China's sporting heroes brought pride and honour to the people and fostered national consciousness and patriotism.[8]

The FECG were not truly international, as their scope was limited to East Asia. Since the 1910s, the Olympic Games, a real international sporting event, had caught the attention of the Chinese. In 1932, China sent its first athlete, Liu Changchun, to participate in the Los Angeles Olympics. The initiative was prompted by Japan's attempt to gain legitimacy for its invasion of northeastern China by sending a team from puppet state Manchukuo to Los Angeles.[9] On June 17, 1932, Tianjin-based *Taidong Daily*, a Japanese-backed newspaper, announced that two athletes from northeastern China – the country's best sprinter, Liu Changchun, and top middle-distance runner, Yu Xiwei – would represent Manchukuo at the Los Angeles Olympics. Upon hearing the news, Liu Changchun issued a statement to the *Dagong Daily* and declared: 'As the offspring of the Yellow Emperor of the Chinese nation, as a Chinese, I will never represent the puppet Manchukuo at the 10th Olympic Games!'[10] With the support of Zhang Xueliang, President of the Northeast University, and Hao Gengsheng, Dean of the College of Sport at the Northeast University, Liu and Yu decided to compete for the Republic of China in Los Angeles. However, Yu was not able to leave Manchuria.[11] A special ceremony was held at the dock of Shanghai Port on July 8, 1932 for the three-man national squad, which consisted of Liu Changchun, his coach Song Junfu and team leader Shen Siliang. More than 400 people attended. Hao Gensheng, Inspector for Physical Education in the Ministry of Education and Chairman of the China National Amateur Athletic Federation (CNAAF), explained that sending Liu to represent China at the Los Angeles games could 'stop the Japanese attempt to legalize the Manchurian puppet state … tell the world about Japan's crime in China' and 'raise the Republic of China's national flag at the Olympics and set an example for future generations'.[12]

After three weeks at sea, the Chinese delegation finally arrived in Los Angeles on July 29, 1932. The next day, Liu Changchun attended the opening ceremony and marched with the Chinese national flag. On July 31, 1932, he competed in the men's 100-metre preliminaries but failed to qualify for the final. The Chinese delegation then attended the World Youth Debate Convention in Los Angeles, where Song Junfu took the opportunity to deliver a speech in English condemning the Japanese invasion of China.[13]

Although Liu Changchun did not perform well at the Olympics, back in China he was regarded as a national hero who competed for the country's pride and dignity. Thereafter, people began to pay attention to the role of sport in diplomatic gains, in winning recognition from the international community and building up national confidence.[14] Four years later, China sent a large delegation to the 1936 Berlin Olympic Games. In total, 69 Chinese athletes participated. Although they failed to win a single medal, the trip was considered to have been valuable from a political perspective. The government believed that the national squad's participation in the Berlin Olympics had further cultivated the people's sense of patriotism and national unity and enhanced China's international status. As team leader Shen Siliang explained: 'The achievement of international recognition alone is worth millions to us.'[15]

After 1936, drained by the Second Sino-Japanese War (1937–1945) and the subsequent Civil War, the government's attention was drawn away from the Olympics. With limited funding and resources, the CNAAF still managed to send a team to the 1948 London Olympics, but this ill-prepared and poorly organized team failed to win a medal. Nevertheless, the athletes successfully demonstrated China's motivation to stay engaged with the world and to compete with foreign countries, and therefore were regarded as heroes of the Republic.[16]

People's Hero, China's Glory

Following the establishment of the People's Republic of China (PRC) in 1949, sport and physical education continued to be promoted by the communist regime as efficient ways to train strong bodies for the country. At the same time, policy-makers saw elite sport as a vehicle for enhancing national self-esteem, and an elite sport system was established to produce high-performance athletes. The objective was to win medals at international sporting events and help the new China to achieve international recognition and domestic unity.[17]

The elite sport system quickly bore fruit. In June 1956, weightlifter Chen Jingkai lifted 133 kg at a Sino-Soviet friendship match in Shanghai, breaking the men's 56 kg clean and jerk world record held by America's Charles Vinci. Qi Lieyun broke the men's 100 m breaststroke world record in Guangzhou in May 1957. In the same year, he won the silver medal in the men's 200 m breaststroke at the Sixth World Youth and Students Festival in Moscow. In November 1957, high jumper Zheng Fengrong broke the women's world record with a jump of 1.77 m at the National Athletic Championship in Beijing, making her the first Chinese woman to hold a sporting world record. The three athletes' successes were regarded as some of the PRC's most important achievements in socialist modernization. They were received by Premier Zhou Enlai and hailed by state media as role models for their hard work.[18] Thereafter, sporting success was portrayed as a symbol of national revival and sports champions became national icons. At the 25th World Table Tennis Championships, held in West Germany in April 1959, Rong Guotuan won the gold medal in the men's singles table tennis event, making him the first world champion in Chinese history. In April 1961, China hosted the 26th World Table Tennis Championships. The national team won three gold medals and the men's team won the overall championship. After the event, national team members were honoured as 'People's Hero' and 'China's Glory'.[19] China's conquest of Mount Everest in 1960 was seen as another major sporting victory. After the British successfully reached its summit in 1953, the Sports Ministry began to make plans to send a team to conquer the mountain.[20] The mission was launched on May 24, 1960. At an altitude of 6,000 m, the team suffered a heavy storm that meant only about ten people remained to complete the mission. One of them, Wang Fuzhou, recalled: 'It was a battle of life and death. Everyone believed that there was no way back. We must accomplish the mission, even at the cost of our lives!'[21] Finally, on the morning of May 25, 1960, Wang Fuzhou, Gong Bu and Qu Yinhua (1935–2016) reached the peak. After returning to Beijing, the heroes were received by state leaders at Beijing Workers' Stadium and honoured with the title of 'Brave Peak Conquerors' by the Sports Ministry.[22]

In 1952, the PRC sent its best athletes to participate in the Helsinki Olympics. Due to the political conflict between the PRC and the Nationalist China (ROC), known as the 'two Chinas' issue, the athletes missed most of the competitions and did not win any medals. Despite so, they were hailed by Premier Zhou Enlai for rising the PRC's national flag at the games. Due to the same political issue, the PRC did not participate in the 1956 Melbourne Olympics, and in 1958 Beijing withdrew from the IOC and several international sports federations. It was not until 1984 that athletes from mainland China returned to the Olympic arena after the 'two Chinas' issue was settled by the IOC.[23]

The Fall of Sporting Heroes

Up until the mid-1960s, sport enjoyed steady development in China. However, when the Cultural Revolution (1966–1976) began in 1966, the sport system descended into chaos. The aim of the Revolution was to get rid of anything regarded as revisionist, bourgeois or capitalist. It opposed elitism and advocated the rise of the proletariat. Therefore, elite sport was regarded as a facet of bourgeois ideology and mass sport as communist idealism. Winning medals at sports competitions came to be seen as a capitalist practice.[24]

In May 1966, Red Guards and rebels began their offensive against 'authorities' and 'experts' in the Sports Ministry and its local commissions. Officials, world champions and celebrity coaches became targets. Table tennis world champion Xu Yinsheng recalled: 'Top athletes and coaches were condemned as proponents of revisionism, chauvinism and championism, which went against the Maoist road. They [the rebels] said that the trophies and medals won by the national team were named after the bourgeoisie.'[25] The national table tennis team, which had been held up as a role model in the late 1950s and early 1960s, was attacked by the rebels. Leading team members, including Zhuang Zedong, Rong Guotuan, Fu Qifang, Xu Yinsheng, Li Furong and Zheng Minzhi, were condemned as the 'seeds of revisionism'. They were mentally and physically abused by the Red Guards and were forced to self-criticize and admit that they had been on the wrong side of the Revolution. On April 16, 1968, Fu Qifang, head coach of the national men's table tennis team, hanged himself in the Beijing Gymnasium. In May, Jiang Yongning, China's first national table tennis champion and head coach of the national table tennis team, committed suicide as he could no longer endure the physical and mental abuse inflicted on him during the struggle sessions. One month later, on June 20, 1968, famous table tennis world champion Rong Guotuan hanged himself beside Dragon Lake in Beijing.[26]

After hearing of the ongoing deaths of top athletes and coaches, and especially shocked by the death of Rong Guotuan, Premier Zhou Enlai instructed in late June 1968 that elite athletes must be protected. Subsequently, training sessions slowly began to take place again in early 1970.[27] At the same time, the elite sport system was revived to meet Beijing's need to conduct diplomacy through sports exchanges and competitions, a sea change triggered by the well-known Ping-Pong Diplomacy of 1971 which eased hostilities between China and the United States.[28]

Gold Medal Fever – The Burden of Heroes

After the Cultural Revolution ended, China launched its reform and opening-up policy to achieve the goal of modernization and to catch up with the Western capitalist world. Sport played an important part in stimulating the nation's enthusiasm and in motivating the Chinese people towards modernization. From the early 1980s, China's status and relative strength among nations came to be measured by the country's success at international sporting events. Sports arenas became places where Chinese people could witness the glory of their country, feel proud to be Chinese and experience a sense of national unity. The determination to revive China gave rise to 'gold medal fever'.[29] The Chinese women's volleyball team is the best example. The team won its first world championship in Japan in 1981. This success coincided with China's reform and opening-up and was a perfect occasion for Chinese people to regain confidence and express their patriotism. After defeating Japan at the World Cup on November 16, 1981, tens of thousands of students and other citizens gathered in Tiananmen Square in Beijing to celebrate for the whole night, shouting 'Long live China! Long live China's women's volleyball team!'[30] The following day, the victory was the top headline in almost every newspaper in China. An editorial titled 'Learn from the Women's Volleyball Team, Restore the Chinese Nation – China Wins' was published in the state-run *People's Daily* to propagate the spirit of the volleyball team and link it to modernization and national revival.[31] In total, the women's volleyball team won five world titles between 1981 and 1986. This became known as the 'Five Successive Championships', seen as bringing hope and glory to the Chinese people. Many believed that the team represented the Chinese spirit. Thereafter, the 'women's volleyball spirit' was disseminated throughout the country as ideological indoctrination, a model to be emulated by people from all walks of life.[32]

However, nationalism and patriotism could turn sporting heroes into losers overnight. Li Ning, an outstanding Chinese gymnast, is a prime example. Li won three gold medals at the 1984 Olympics, becoming known as the 'Prince of Gymnastics' by the Chinese media. The Sports Ministry honoured him as one of its 'Top Ten Athletes' in 1985, 1986 and 1987. The Communist Youth League also named him a 'Pace-setter of the New Long March' in 1984, making him a role model for the Chinese people. Li Ning decided to retire after the 1984 Olympics, due to injury. However, the national team needed him to stay on. He agreed for the sake of the team, despite knowing he might not be able to defend his world titles at the next Olympic Games. In 1988, he did compete at the Seoul Olympics, but failed to finish either the rings or the vault events. After falling in the latter event, he smiled to his team mates to encourage them.[33] Li Ning's failure and his smile led to trouble. Some people condemned him for the 'shameless smile', as they believed he should have felt sad.[34] A letter from Liaoning Province with a plastic rope enclosed read: 'Li Ning, you are the death prince of gymnastics, please hang yourself!'[35] He was condemned for letting his country and people down. After coming back from Seoul, Li didn't dare leave his home, as he feared people would humiliate him on the street.[36] In the face of this criticism and pressure, Li retired from the national team. 20 years later, he recalled: 'The Chinese people in the 1980s wanted gold medals rather than sport. The Sports Ministry wanted champions rather than athletes.'[37]

The same thing happened to the celebrated Chinese women's volleyball team. After its five straight championships, the squad was defeated by the Soviet Union and Peru and only won bronze at the 1988 Olympics. The result disappointed the Chinese enormously. Wang Chong, a journalist who worked for the *Nanguo Daily*, recalled:

The Chinese women's volleyball team used to be icons. They represented the spirit of never giving up. They were 'the light of the Chinese nation'. When they were defeated at the Olympic Games, people refused to accept this reality and kept asking, 'How can they lose?' Suddenly, people began to criticise and curse the players. Some people were so angry that they even sent funeral telegrams to the head coach.[38]

To sum up, in the 1980s, having just ended the ten-year Cultural Revolution, the Chinese people desperately needed to restore their confidence. Many believed that the nation could not afford to lose anymore, including in sport. Celebrity athletes shouldered all the burdens of the nation.[39] As Gao Min, an outstanding Chinese diver who won gold in the women's springboard event at the 1988 Seoul Olympics, commented: 'I felt like every gold medal was a heavy burden on my shoulders. Sometimes I hoped I would lose, even though I knew that I could not afford to. I wish the Chinese people could understand that Gao Min is not a god. She is an ordinary person and it is normal for her to lose.'[40]

In the late 1980s, against the background of a strong call from academia and policy-makers for thorough political and economic reforms – which eventually led to the pro-democracy demonstrations in Tiananmen Square in June 1989 – the Chinese people began to question the country's sport system and the obsession with gold medals. In April 1988, sports journalist Zhao Yu published an article, 'The Dream to Be a Strong Country', in *The Contemporary Age*, one of China's most popular literary journals. The piece harshly criticized the sports system and people's inordinate expectations for gold medals, and suggested that the government should pay more attention to mass sport rather than elite sport.[41] It received positive responses from the media, the general public and some state leaders. The state-run *Gangming Daily*, *Literature Daily* and *Wenhui Daily* praised the article as a breakthrough.[42] The *People's Daily* commented: 'Mass sport has been neglected for a long time. Sport in China has focussed on competitions and gold medals. We should not ignore this problem and should begin sports reform. Zhao Yu's criticism and warnings have inspired many. It is an expression of honesty and real patriotism.'[43] The criticism of gold medal fever stimulated a reform of China's sport system. After the establishment of the socialist market economy system in 1993, the government set out a framework for the future development of sport. It issued three decrees in June 1995: the 'Olympic Strategy', the 'National Fitness for All Programme' and the 'Development of Sport Industry and Commerce Outline'.[44] These decrees were designed to complement each other and to form new sports policy and practice. Since their implementation, mass sport and the sports industry have experienced rapid growth.[45]

Although more attention was now being given to mass sport and the sports industry, elite sport still dominated and received strong support from the government. Sporting success continued to be linked with the goal of modernization and the rise of China. After the 1996 Atlanta Olympics, President Jiang Zemin called for the promotion of Chinese athletes' 'five spirits': 'the mother country first', 'solidarity and struggle', 'professional dedication', 'scientific integrity' and 'hard work'. People from all walks of life were encouraged to study the 'five spirits' and use them to aid the great cause of modernization.[46] The national squad's success continued at the 2000 and 2004 Olympics, as did the cultivation of the 'five spirits'. In 2008, the Chinese team finished top of the gold medal table at the Beijing Olympics. Hosting the Olympic Games was also seen by most Chinese people as a means of national revival, of supporting the construction of national identity, economic prosperity and international recognition. They believed that the Beijing Olympics coincided with China's economic development and was evidence of the revival of China.[47]

However, after the Beijing Olympics an increasing number of scholars and critics urged the government to focus more on ordinary people's health and fitness instead of gold medals.[48] Criticism of the elite sport system and its fixation on gold medals was further triggered by the 2010 Guangzhou Asian Games. Chinese athletes put on a dazzling display, dominating the Games with 199 gold medals and topping the gold medal table for the eighth consecutive time.[49] During the Games, Yang Ming, a journalist from the state-run Xinhua News Agency, published an editorial entitled 'No More Challengers' to criticise China's macabre gold medal fever. He observed:

> The motto of the Asian Games is 'Friendship, Harmony and Development'. It is a festival which brings all the Asian countries together. The gold medal is not the most important thing... China's elite sport has been heavily influenced by gold medal fever. In recent years, we have over-emphasized gold medals and neglected the nature of sport. Sport belongs to the people. It should be used to improve people's health and physique.[50]

Yang's article triggered a nationwide debate on the government's sport policy. It also provoked a discussion on the relationship between sport and patriotism and stimulated a new way of thinking – to free sport from politics and have it serve the all-round development of the society. In March 2010, a news report entitled 'Officials in the Sports Ministry Criticize the Winter Olympic Champion' was published in China's leading right-wing newspaper, *South China Weekly*. According to the report, the vice-minister of the Sports Ministry, Yu Zaiqing, criticized China's Winter Olympics champion Zhou Yang because she only thanked her parents in front of the media after winning the gold medal in the women's 1,500-metre speed skating race at the 2010 Winter Olympics. Yu argued that the state had put a lot of effort and resources into cultivating and training the athletes, who should not forget the support they received from the state and should be grateful.[51] The report sparked nationwide criticism of sports patriotism. Many journalists and commentators published articles to support Zhou Yang. They criticized Yu Zaiqing and called for the abolition of blind patriotism in sport. Bai Yansong, a famous news commentator on state-run Chinese Central Television, stated:

> In the past, sporting success was closely linked to patriotism and the general public was in favour of it. But now, as we Chinese have become more confident than before, there is no need to advocate patriotism at every occasion and on every day... I want to tell Zhou Yang and other athletes: there is nothing wrong with competing for your parents and yourself. It is your right to say whatever you want![52]

Many Internet users showed their support for Zhou Yang by posting comments on blogs and forums. One stated, 'Only a machine doesn't know how to thank its parents.'[53] Another argued, 'In order to change the fate of her family, Zhou Yang trained hard and won two gold medals for China. Yu Zaiqing's criticism is the shame of the country!'[54] Some attacked Yu personally and urged him to resign.[55]

Tennis Queen Li Na

One year after this public criticism of sports patriotism, a news report on tennis player Li Na provoked another debate. Li Na was born in Wuhan in 1982. She joined China's national tennis team in 1997 and turned professional. She won 52 singles matches on the ITF tennis circuit in 2000 and captured her first world title at the 2001 Summer World University Games. By 2007 she was ranked 16th in the world, making her the best Chinese tennis player in history. After a change in the rules governing the national tennis team in 2009, Li Na quit the team and began to manage her own career as a 'freelance' player.[56] In January 2011, Li beat world number one Caroline Wozniacki in the Australian Open semi-final and became the first Asian woman to reach a Grand Slam final. On June 4, 2011, she won the French Open, making her the first Asian Grand Slam singles champion. Her success at the French Open was praised by the Chinese media as a landmark victory, and her photo appeared on the front page of almost every leading Chinese newspaper. The *People's Daily* hailed her as the 'Legend of Asia'.[57] However, this good news was soon overshadowed by a debate sparked by Li Na's speech after her victory in which she thanked her sponsor, the organizers, her support team and the fans, but did not mention China. At a press conference, Li told journalists: 'Don't always say that I won honour for the country. Actually, I am competing for myself.'[58] Two different public voices were generated by Li Na's words. Many commentators and journalists supported her. Her success was portrayed as a victory for the commercialization and professionalization of sport against the old state-sponsored sport system. Her speech was interpreted as a symbol of individualism and liberalism. Tencent, China's leading Internet portal, published an editorial entitled 'The Country Should Thank Li Na'. The editor observed:

> As a freelancer, there is no need for Li Na to thank the country. On the contrary, the country should thank Li Na. The Chinese people should change their way of thinking. We should not link everything to politics and the country… We don't like the athletes who only know how to say, 'I thank the [Communist] Party, I thank the government and I thank the Chinese people.' We love Li Na not because she represents China, but because she is real and she says whatever she wants to say, for example 'I play for money' and 'I don't like my husband's snoring'.[59]

Others criticized Li Na for not showing gratitude to her former coaches and for ignoring the support she had received from the state. They argued that, like Li Na, an increasing number of Chinese athletes were being corrupted by money. In a newspaper article entitled 'Thank the Sponsor First? How about Thank the Parents First?' the author argued:

> I can remember that during the finals, a Chinese TV reporter asked another tennis player what the major difference between the Grand Slam and other tennis tournaments was, and the answer was: 'The Grand Slam has more bonus money.' I suddenly realized that Li Na will not be the only Chinese athlete to thank the 'money' first… it will become a problem for our society if everyone in this country accepts this 'value' and blindly links money with success.[60]

The debate between the two sides continued in the following months and was intensified by Li Na's words at a press conference in the United States in March

2012. Asked by a journalist why she was so straightforward and what the difference between her and other Chinese athletes was, she replied, 'I am only a tennis player. I am not playing tennis for the country. I am just doing my job.'[61] This time, many people changed their position and criticized Li Na. One blogger addressed a letter to Li Na. 'I thought you were a straightforward person and admired you. But this time, when you said that you have nothing to do with this country, that is ugly... We cared about you and we are proud of you because you are Chinese.'[62] The debate on sports patriotism has changed many people's way of thinking. However, people remain very concerned about the continuation of the country's sporting success. Despite the growing number of remarks decrying China's pursuit of gold medals, the inordinate expectation to win gold has not faded away. The pressure on sports stars is nothing new.

Flying Man Liu Xiang

Four years after the Beijing Olympics, the 2012 London Olympics again saw the powerful effect of gold medal fever on the Chinese people. Their disproportionate reaction to the failure of former Olympic champion Liu Xiang demonstrated that Chinese sport continued to be influenced by nationalism and patriotism.

Liu Xiang was one of China's best 110-metre hurdlers and won China's first men's track and field Olympic gold at the 2004 Athens Olympics. This was regarded as a breakthrough, as it proved that the Chinese could compete in a 'truly global event' that had traditionally been dominated by African, American and European athletes.[63] After the Games, Liu became a national hero and a symbol of China's, and even Asia's, global aspirations. However, in 2008 he dramatically pulled out of the Beijing Olympics at the last minute due to a hamstring injury. This put a dampener on China's celebration of hosting the Olympics and disappointed many.[64] It also spawned a slew of criticism from the general public. People began to blame Liu, using words like 'coward' and 'cheater' to denounce him. Nicknames such as 'Escaping Liu' and 'Actor Liu' were invented to insult this former national icon.[65] Despite being brought to his knees by the injury and the criticism, Liu did not give up. He underwent surgery and trained hard to recover. He returned to competition in 2009 and won gold at the 2010 Asian Games with a new Asian record of 13.09 seconds. He returned to world-class level in 2011 by winning the Shanghai Golden Grand Prix, and later came second at the 2012 IAAF World Indoor Championships. He also won the Prefontaine Classic with an amazing time of 12.87 seconds, equalling the world record.[66]

When the 2012 Olympic Games were staged in London, Liu Xiang, now 29, became one of China's best hopes for a gold medal in track and field events. For the Chinese, this 'real gold' is far more meaningful than any of the other 'less important' gold medals for events such as table tennis, badminton, diving or weightlifting.[67] Although Liu's coach and officials from the Chinese Sports Ministry had indicated that Liu was still suffering from his old leg injury and his chances of winning were not high, their voices were ignored. Most Chinese spectators had high hopes for Liu. Internet blogs and forums were flooded with millions of posts talking about his return.⁶⁸ Despite the great expectations, the competition ended in disaster for Liu Xiang. He fell at the first hurdle in the qualifiers. He moved off to the side at first, but then turned to hop to the finish line and kissed the final hurdle on the track.⁶⁹ It was later revealed that he had ruptured his Achilles' tendon when he fell. He underwent surgery in London and returned to China five days after the race.⁷⁰

Back in China, Liu's cruel exit from the Games stunned many, and his fall dominated the front pages of newspapers and websites.⁷¹ Most reports praised him for his sportsmanship. One report argued, 'What Liu Xiang did today reflects the true Olympic spirit... Winning is not so important, participation is what matters.'⁷² A good number of bloggers and netizens showed their support for Liu by posting comments online. One said, 'I think he was under too much pressure. I just hope he recovers soon.'⁷³ Another stated, 'When we saw him hopping off the track on one leg, we all thought that he's already a great guy and he has done what he should.'⁷⁴ However, these supporters' voices were soon drowned out by complaints from the angry masses. They blamed Liu and accused him of cheating the audience: 'He pretended that he was injured. The truth is that he dared not compete. It is an international scandal!', 'The actor and his sponsors have fooled us again', 'He is a shame on the country', 'Liu wasted the taxpayers' money'. A piece of doggerel began being circulated by Internet users in China: '[He] earned money from the sponsors for eight continuous years, cheated at two Olympics. See you at the Paralympic Games!'⁷⁵ A public poll conducted by leading web portal 163.com showed that only 35 percent of voters had sympathy for him.⁷⁶ Two weeks later, Liu was interviewed on television and displayed his 20 cm-long scar to the audience.⁷⁷ In response to the criticism, he stated, 'I tried, and I don't feel regret. I know people wanted me to win. I want to say sorry to everyone.'⁷⁸ Liu Xiang was brave enough to continue his career after the Beijing Olympics. He was desperate to challenge and prove himself, but underestimated the power of gold medal fever. As one commentator concluded:

> He was turned into a 'flying man' and a 'superhero' by the patriotic fans. They hoped that he could win honour for the country at the Olympics, and the expectations were too high... both his body and his mind were brought down by the great pressure... Patriotism is a double-edged sword. It can generate power but can also cause damage. The Chinese people should calm down and rethink this.⁷⁹

Coping with Sports Patriotism

The early twentieth century saw the transformation of China from a culturally bound empire into a modern nation state. Against the background of the two world wars and imperialist expansion in Asia, and fanned by nationalism and patriotism, Chinese people believed that sport could help the country to recover its strength and win international recognition. In this period, international sporting events functioned as important vehicles for nation building and identity construction, giving birth to the first generation of Chinese sports heroes who competed for the country's honour and dignity in sports arenas. After the establishment of the PRC in 1949, both mass sport and elite sport were promoted by the government to train healthy and strong citizens. Sporting success became a symbol of achievements in socialist modernization. An elite sport system was established and produced China's first world champions. However, during the Cultural Revolution, elite sport came to be seen as a capitalist practice and sports stars were attacked by the rebels for being on the wrong side of the revolution. It was not until the early 1970s that the sport system was revived to meet Beijing's need to conduct diplomatic exchanges. From the 1980s on, in the context of reform and opening-up and the launch of the 'four modernizations', China's status and relative strength among nations began to be measured by the country's success at international sporting events. The nation's appetite for gold medals resulted in the rapid development of the elite sport system, but placed a heavy burden on star athletes. From the late 1980s, the Chinese began to question the country's sport system and the obsession with gold medals. Today, an increasing number of Chinese people have moved away from extreme sports patriotism and the obsession with gold medals. However, as long as athletes compete under their national flags, it will be impossible to free them from politics. A better solution, therefore, would be to guide sports patriotism in a positive direction that is less violent and more tolerant, humane and mature.

Notes

1. Liam Ryan, 'The GAA: 'Part of What We Are': A Centenary Assessment'. *The Furrow* 35, no. 12 (1984): 752–64, 757.
2. See: Andrew D. Morris, *Marrow of the Nation: A History of Sport and Physical Culture in Republican China* (Berkeley: University of California Press, 2004); Susan Brownell, *Beijing's Games: What the Olympics Mean to China* (New York: Rowman & Littlefield Publishers, 2008); Guoqi Xu, *Olympic Dreams: China and Sports, 1895-2008* (Cambridge: Harvard University Press, 2008); Francis L.F. Lee, 'Negotiating Sporting Nationalism: Debating Fan Behaviour in 'China vs. Japan' in the 2004 Asian Cup Final in Hong Kong', *Soccer & Society* 10, no. 2 (2009): 192–209; Lu Zhouxiang and Fan Hong, 'From Celestial Empire to Nation State: Sport and the Origins of Chinese Nationalism (1840–1927)', *The International Journal of the History of Sport* 27, no. 3 (2010): 479–504; Lu Zhouxiang, 'Sport, Nationalism and the Building of the Modern Chinese Nation State (1912–49)', *The International Journal of the History of Sport* 28, no. 7 (2011): 1030–54; Lu Zhouxiang and Fan Hong, *Sport and Nationalism in China* (London: Routledge, 2013); Liu Li and Fan Hong, 'The National Games and National Identity in the Republic of China, 1910–1948', *The International Journal of the History of Sport* 32, no. 3 (2015): 440–54; Huijie Zhang, 'Rising Nationalism and the Diminishing Role of the Christian Institutions in Chinese National Physical Education and Sport, 1919–1928', *The International Journal of the History of Sport* 34, no. 12 (2017): 1213–30; Huijie Zhang, Fan Hong, and Fuhua Huang, 'Cultural Imperialism, Nationalism, and the Modernization of Physical Education and Sport in China, 1840–1949', *The International Journal of the History of Sport* 35, no. 1 (2018): 43–60.
3. Wang Chih-ming, 'Capitalizing the Big Man: Yao Ming, Asian America, and the China Global', *Inter-Asia Cultural Studies* 5, no. 2 (2004): 263–78; Susan Brownell, 'Why 1984 Medalist Li Ning Lit the Flame at the Beijing 2008 Olympics: The Contribution of the Los Angeles Olympics to China's Market Reforms', *The International Journal of the History of Sport* 32, no. 1 (2015): 128–43; Pu Haozhou, 'Mediating the Giants: Yao Ming, NBA and the Cultural Politics of Sino-American Relations', *Asia Pacific Journal of Sport and Social Science* 5, no. 2 (2016): 87–107; Pu Haozhou, Joshua I. Newman, and Michael D. Giardina. 'Flying Solo: Globalization, Neoliberal Individualism, and the Contested Celebrity of Li Na', *Communication & Sport* 7, no. 1 (2019): 23–45.

4. Shiming Luo, *Aoyun laidao zhongguo* [Olympics arrives in China] (Beijing: Tsinghua University Press, 2005), 102–15.
5. Ibid.
6. Chinese names appearing in this article follow the East Asian convention of family name followed by given name.
7. Mingxin Tang, *Woguo canjia aoyunhui cangsang shi 1896-1948* [China and the Olympic Games 1896–1948] (Taipei: Olympic Committee Press, 1999), 214.
8. Ri Yu, 'Zhong ri yuanyun juezhu shi' [Competition between China and Japan at the Far Eastern Championship Games], *Tiyu wenshi* [Journal of the History of Sport], no. 2 (1990): 44–50.
9. Japan launched the invasion of China on September 18, 1931. After occupying northeast China, the Japanese established a puppet regime in Changchun, Manchuria in March 1932.
10. Changchun Liu, 'Wo guo shouci canjia aoyun hui shimo' [The first time that China participated in the Olympic Games], in *Wenshi ziliao xuanji* [Historical materials], ed. National Committee of the Chinese People's Political Consultative Conference (Beijing: China Book Press, 1980), 221–8.
11. Ibid.
12. Tang, *Woguo canjia aoyunhui cangsang shi 1896-1948*, 214.
13. 'Aoyun meng Qilu qihang' [Olympic dream starts from Qilu], *Baokan huicui* (Newspaper collection), no. 2 (2008), 15–16.
14. Siliang Shen, 'Di shi jie shijie yundong hui he chuci canjia de woguo' [China and the 10th Olympic Games], *Tiyu yanjiu yu tongxun* [Sports Studies and News], no. 1 (January, 1933): 7.
15. Xu, *Olympic Dreams: China and Sports*, 47.
16. Shouyi Dong, 'Aolin pike jiu shi' [Old stories about the Olympics], in *Tiyu shiliao* [Historical materials for sport], 2, ed. People's Sport Press (Beijing: People's Sport Press, 1980), 11–14.
17. Lu Zhouxiang and Fan Hong, *Sport and Nationalism in China* (London: Routledge, 2014), 80–1.
18. Ping Zheng, 'Shou po shijie jilu de Zhongguo nvxing: Zheng Fengrong' [Zheng Fengrong, the first Chinese woman to hold a sports world record], *Sohu*, November 20, 2007, http://news.sohu.com/20071120/n253370284.shtml (accessed October 24, 2018).
19. Yannong Fu, ed., *Zhongguo tiyu tongshi 1949-1979* [*The history of sport in China 1949–1979*], vol. 5 (Beijing: People's Sport Press, 2007), 179.
20. The 2nd Literature Research Centre of the Central Committee of the Communist Party of China. *Gongheguo tiyu: 110 wei jianzheng zhe fangtan* [The history of sport in China – 110 interviews] (Guiyang: Guizhou People's Press, 2008), 171.
21. Ibid., 171.
22. Yannong Fu, ed. *Zhongguo tiyu tongshi* [The history of sport in China], 1949–1979, vol. 5 (Beijing: Renmin tiyu chuban she, 2007), 177.
23. Qin Hao, ed. *Zhongguo tiyu tongshi* [The history of sport in China], 1980–1992, vol. 6 (Beijing: Renmin tiyu chuban she, 2007), 83–4.
24. Ibid., 300.
25. Eastern China Satellite TV, 'Tong Guotuan – guanjun yunluo' [Rong Guotuan – The fall of the world champion], *Eastern China Satellite TV*, April 7, 2009.
26. Ibid.
27. Shaozu Wu, ed., *Zhonghua renmin gonghe guo tiyu shi 1949-1998* [The history of sport in the People's Republic of China 1949-1998] (Beijing: China Book Press, 2002), 176.
28. Fu, *Zhongguo tiyu tongshi*, 358.
29. Hao, *Zhongguo tiyu tongshi*, 76–7.
30. Ming Li, '1981: Zhongguo nupai duoguan rang guoren yangmei tuqi' [1981: China Women's Volleyball Team Brought Glory to the Chinese Nation], *Nandu zhoukan*

(Nandu Weekly), July 18, 2008, http://news.sina.com.cn/c/2008-07-18/154215957890.shtml (accessed November 2, 2018).
31. Hao, *Zhongguo tiyu tongshi*, 77.
32. Guang Lu, 'Zhongguo guniang' [Chinese girls], in *Qiangguo meng* [The dream to be a strong country], ed. Li Bingyin and Zhou Baiyi (Wuhan: Changjiang Literature Press, 1998), 19–96.
33. 'Ticao wangzi, Li Ning' [The story of the prince of gymnastics, Li Ning], *Nanning ribao* (Nanning Daily), November 13, 1988.
34. 'Women de aolin pike: weixiao 1988' [Our Olympics: The smile in 1988], *Sina*, July 7, 2008, http://sports.sina.com.cn/o/2008-07-17/15303789341.shtml (accessed November 3, 2018).
35. 'Li Ning huigui' [The return of Li Ning], *Xinhua*, December 18, 2018, http://www.xinhuanet.com/fashion/2018-12/18/c_1123867672.htm (accessed May 30, 2019).
36. Xiaoqiao Wang and Muzi Cai, 'Li Ning: san fenzhong yu ershi nian' [Li Ning: Three minutes and twenty years], *Nanfang zhoumo* (Nanfang Weekend), August 14, 2008.
37. Ibid.
38. Ibid.
39. Xu, *Olympic Dreams: China and Sports*, 218–19.
40. China Central Television, *Women de aolin pike* (Our Olympics), China Central Television, July 2008, http://tv.cctv.com/2012/12/15/VIDA1355571182862792.shtml (accessed May 30, 2019).
41. Yu Zhao, 'Qiangguo meng' [The dream to be a strong country], in *Qiangguo meng* [The dream to be a strong country], ed. Bingyin Li and Baiyi Zhou (Beijing: Changjiang Literature Press, 1998), 97–170.
42. Nan Hu, '1988 aoyun qian you pian wenzhang re nu tiwei' [Sports ministry outraged by an article before 1988 Olympics], *Dajia gushi* (People's Stories), no. 10 (October, 2007): 38–9.
43. Wu, *Zhonghua renmin gonghe guo tiyu shi 1949-1998*, 352.
44. For the details of the three decrees, please see: Shouhe Cao, ed., *Zhongguo tiyu tongshi* [The history of sport in China], 1993-2005, vol. 7 (Beijing: Renmin tiyu chuban she, 2007), 84–135.
45. Ibid., 102.
46. Ibid., 296.
47. Yajie Li, Weihan Yang, and Zhanyi Luo, 'Aoyun huimou ningju minzu fuxing de jingshen liliang' [The Olympics, a spiritual power that contributes to national revival], *Zhongguo qingnian bao*, September 19, 2008.
48. Xiang Qing, 'Aoyun jinpai daguo de jueqi yu fansi' [Rethink the Olympic strategy], *Sina*, August 23, 2008, http://blog.sina.com.cn/s/blog_52e9bd8d0100akvp.html (accessed November 15, 2018).
49. Rod Gilmour, 'What the Asian Games and China's Dominance Tell Us About the London 2012 Olympics', *The Telegraph*, November 30, 2010.
50. Ming Yang, 'Yi ji juecheng yinfa de sikao' [Some thoughts on China's dominance at the Asian games], *Chengdu Business Daily*, November 15, 2010, https://sports.qq.com/a/20101115/002724.htm (accessed December 2, 2018).
51. 'Tiyu zongju fu juzhang po dongao guanjun: ying xian xie guojia zai xie fumu' [The vice-minister of the Sports Ministry criticizes the Winter Olympic Champion: Athletes should thank their mother country first instead of their parents], *163 News*, March 8, 2010, http://sports.163.com/10/0308/07/6183QOHL0005452P.html (accessed December 2, 2018).
52. 'Bai Yansong: guojia yinggai wei Zhou Yang jiaoao' [Bai Yansong: The country should be proud of Zhou Yang], *Chongqing Evening Post*, March 10, 2010, http://sports.sina.com.cn/o/2010-03-10/05154876991.shtml (accessed December 2, 2018).
53. 'Guojia bu qian xie, Zhou Yang you quan xian xie fumu' [No need to thank the country, Zhou Yang has the right to thank her parents first], *163 News*, March 8, 2010, http://sports.163.com/10/0308/19/619BPOD100053L8V.html (accessed December 2, 2018).

54. Ibid.
55. 'Wangyou relie huiying Yu Zaiqing pi Zhou Yang' [Netizens respond to Yu Zaiqing's criticism against Zhou Yang], *Tianya*, March 8, 2010, http://bbs.tianya.cn/post-free-1828402-1.shtml#79_66388256 (accessed August 3, 2019).
56. 'Chinese Tennis Star Li Na Criticizes National Programme', *The Telegraph*, April 15, 2009, https://www.telegraph.co.uk/sport/tennis/5157639/Chinese-tennis-star-Li-Na-criticises-national-programme.html (accessed June 2, 2019).
57. Evan Osnos, 'Li Na and the Politics of Saying Thank You', *The New Yorker*, June 7, 2011, http://www.newyorker.com/online/blogs/evanosnos/2011/06/li-na-french-open.html (accessed December 6, 2018).
58. Chong Zhu, 'Li Na bu ganxie guojia' [Li Na Refused to Thank the Country], *EEO*, June 7, 2011, http://www.eeo.com.cn/2011/0607/203126.shtml (accessed December 6, 2018).
59. 'Guojia ying ganxie Li Na' [The country should thank Li Na], *Tencent News*, January 30, 2011, http://sports.qq.com/zt2011/thankslina/ (accessed December 10, 2018).
60. 'Ganxie zanzhu shang? He bu xian ganxie fumu?' [Thank the sponsor first? How about thank the parents first?], *Chengshi Daobao* (City News), June 13, 2011, http://citynews.eastday.com/csdb/html/2011-06/13/content_42232.htm (accessed December 10, 2018).
61. 'Li Na cheng daqiu bu wei guojia yinga zhengyi' [Li Na's arguments raised debates], *Sohu*, March 13, 2012, http://sports.sohu.com/20120313/n337553084.shtml (accessed December 10, 2018).
62. 'Li Na, qing buyao ba ziji daqiu he guojia huaqing jiexian' [Li Na, please don't draw a line between you and the country], *Sina*, March 15, 2012, http://blog.sina.com.cn/u/2654046923 (accessed March 16, 2012).
63. Christopher Clarey, 'For Chinese Hurdler, an Achilles' Heel Again Lives Up to Its Name', *The New York Times*, August 7, 2012, https://cn.nytimes.com/sports/20120808/c08liuxiang/en-us/ (accessed June 2, 2019).
64. Peter Foster and Richard Spencer, 'Liu Xiang Limps out of Beijing Olympics Breaking Chinese Hearts', *The Telegraph*, August 18, 2008, https://www.telegraph.co.uk/sport/olympics/2577623/Liu-Xiang-limps-out-of-Beijing-Olympics-breaking-Chinese-hearts.html (accessed June 2, 2019).
65. 'Shunjian paoqi Liu paopao maozi, Liu Xiang beiju rangren dongrong' [The escaping Liu? No! Liu Xiang has touched our soul], *Sina*, August 7, 2012, http://blog.sina.com.cn/s/blog_48d33f2e0102e31u.html?tj=1 (accessed January 1, 2019).
66. Cheng Wen, 'Liuxiang xianxiang yu Aoyun jingshen' [Liu Xiang and the Olympic spirit], *China.com*, August 14, 2012, http://opinion.china.com.cn/opinion_87_49787.html (accessed August 2, 2019).
67. Xuedong Dai, 'Liuxiang duoguan zhendong guoji aoweihui' [Liuxiang's victory inpressed the IOC], *Nanfang ribao*, August 29, 2004.
68. 'Sun Haiping: Liu Xiang chuxian xin wenti' [Sun Haiping: Liu Xiang is facing new problems], *Sohu*, August 3, 2012, http://2012.sohu.com/20120803/n349810445.shtml (accessed January 1, 2019); Li Fei, 'Duan Shijie: Liu Xiang bixu yonggan miandui shangbing jieguo hennan yuliao dao' [Duan Shijie: Liu Xiang must face his injury, it is difficult to predict the result], *Sohu*, August 5, 2012, http://2012.sohu.com/20120805/n349865255.shtml (accessed January 1, 2019); Martin Yip, 'London 2012: Can Liu Xiang Conquer His Olympic Demons?', *BBC*, August 7, 2012, http://www.bbc.co.uk/news/world-asia-china-19045091 (accessed January 1, 2019); Zihang Xia, 'Sun Haiping: Liu Xiang jiaobu laoshang fufa muqian zhengti zhuangkuang haisuan zhengchang' [Sun Haiing: Liu Xiang is suffering a relapse of his leg injury], *163 News*, August 7, 2012, http://2012.163.com/12/0807/03/889B58PU000506A2.html (accessed January 1, 2019).
69. 'Liu Xiang Falls, but Hobbles to the End', *China Central Television*, August 8, 2012, http://english.cntv.cn/program/china24/20120808/106134.shtml (accessed March 23, 2012); 'CCTV Informed of Liu Xiang's Injury before London Race; Emotional Narration Carefully Scripted', *Caijing.com*, August 23, 2012, http://english.caijing.com.cn/2012-08-23/112077325.html (accessed January 1, 2019).

70. 'Injured Chinese hurdler Liu Xiang to have Achilles surgery in Britain', *BBC*, August 9, 2012, https://www.bbc.com/sport/olympics/19194945 (accessed January 1, 2019).
71. 'China Mourns Hurdler Liu Xiang's Olympic Exit', *BBC*, August 8, 2012, http://www.bbc.co.uk/news/world-asia-china-19174696 (accessed January 1, 2019).
72. Cheng Wen, 'Liuxiang xianxiang yu Aoyun jingshen' [Liu Xiang and the Olympic spirit], *China.com*, August 14, 2012, http://opinion.china.com.cn/opinion_87_49787.html (accessed August 2, 2019).
73. 'Support and Tears in China after Liu Xiang's Cruel Exit From London 2012', *The Independent*, August 8, 2012, http://www.independent.co.uk/sport/olympics/athletics/support-and-tears-in-china-after-liu-xiangs-cruel-exit-from-london-2012-8021829.html (accessed January 2, 2019).
74. Ibid.
75. 'Zhang Wenxiu: Liu Xiang you shang dui li quan zhidao hanlei kan ta tiaodao zhongdian' [Zhang Wenxiu: We knew that he was injured. We watched him hopping toward the finish line with tears in our eyes], *163 News*, August 15, 2012, http://2012.163.com/12/0815/07/88UB39UF000506A2.html (accessed January 2, 2019).
76. 'Liu Xiang zai 110 lan yusai shoulun shuaidao, wufa wancheng bisai, nide kanfa shi?' [Liu Xiang failed to finish the competition. What is your opinion?], *163 News*, September 6, 2012, http://vote.sports.163.com/vote2/resultVote.do?voteId=17239 (accessed January 2, 2019).
77. 'China's Liu Xiang Responds to Fall at Olympics', *China.org*, August 25, 2012, http://www.china.org.cn/video/2012-08/25/content_26333432.htm (accessed 10 January 2019).
78. Wei Liu, 'Liu Xiang shangkou chaixian shoudu huiying jiashuai' [Liu Xiang responds to the fake fall after surgery' *Yangzi Wanbao* (Yangzi evening post), August 24, 2012, https://2012.chinadaily.com.cn/2012-08/24/content_15702736.htm (accessed January 10, 2019).
79. Long Hushan, 'Liu Xiang meng sui Lundun liugei women de fansi' [We should rethink Liu Xiang's story], *Sina*, August 7, 2012, http://blog.sina.com.cn/s/blog_73924721010129wj.html (accessed January 10, 2019).

Disclosure Statement

No potential conflict of interest was reported by the authors.

Sports Celebrities and the Spectacularization of Modernity at the Far Eastern Championship Games, 1913–1934

Lou Antolihao

ABSTRACT
Based on archival documents covering the Far Eastern Championship Games (1913–1934), this paper traces the emergence of early Asian sports celebrities while contributing to the theoretical discussion on the origins of celebrity in sports. It argues that the emergence of sports celebrities in Asia during this period can be traced to the 'spectacularization of modernity'. This concept refers to the production of mass and media spectacles during the series of competitions to promote the primacy of 'modern institutions' – whether as empires, nation-states, religious groups, or any of its multiple enactors.

A glossy brochure welcomed the participants and visitors to the second Far Eastern Championship Games (FECG) held in Shanghai from May 19 to 21, 1915. The 18-page booklet is notable for featuring individual athletes at a time when similar publications often focused on the main organizers and prominent patrons. Photographs of Pio Robillos and Generoso Rabaya from the Philippines as well as of Wei Hwen-Tsang and Pan Wei Pang[1] from China show the athletes posing proudly in their athletic gear. They were some of the best athletes from the region who had left their mark at the first FECG in Manila two years earlier. Under the track stars' photos was an elaborate ten-arched decathlon trophy that they would contest as the event's top competitors. The trophy would be presented by Yuan Shi Kai, the first official President of the newly established Republic of China.[2] Months earlier, the *Boston Evening Transcript*'s report of the first 'Olympiad of the Far East' had also highlighted the records of Wei Hwen-Tsang and Pio Robillos as two of the Games' top athletes.[3] Omitted from the Shanghai brochure, however, was the celebrated victory of the Japanese Inakagata Zenji in the modified marathon event, considered as the most grueling competition at the Games. Nevertheless, the timekeeper's words, 'That kid is a warrior!' would be printed in local and international newspapers to describe Inakagata's exploits in fighting off fatigue and the tropical heat to win the event.[4] With the thousands of spectators who came to attend the second FECG, and with the event's widespread coverage by local and international newspapers, these featured athletes could well have been the first Asian sport celebrities.

A closer examination of the FECG sheds light into the role of this series of sports events in the emergence of the earliest Asian sports celebrities while contributing to the theoretical discussion on the origins of celebrityhood in sports. As the first regional sports tournament in Asia, which ran from 1913 to 1934, the FECG highlighted the significance of theatrical performance, episodic staging, and entertaining narratives in the production of sports celebrities. Moreover, the analysis pays more attention to athletics than other sports events due to the sheer number of individual competitions. These individual contests appeared to be more popular to spectators and were given more attention by administrative and print media sources, especially during the earlier editions of the FECG. By examining the popular and media accolades received by prominent athletes, it becomes evident that the emergence of sports celebrities can be traced to the 'spectacularization of modernity'. This concept refers to the production of mass and media spectacles to promote the primacy of 'modern institutions' – whether as empires, nation-states, religious groups, or any of its multiple enactors.

Following Guy Debord, spectacularization refers to the translation of modernity as a worldview into an objective and transformative force.[5] Modernity, as a panacean ideology, has to be showcased through monumental infrastructure projects, science and industrial fairs, and mass entertainment productions. Later on, sports events were also proven to be effective channels in articulating discourses of civilizational advancement and national development. Major sports events, such as the FECG, trumpeted the cultural influence of imperial powers, the political might of nation-states, or the economic progress of provinces and local administrative units. At the individual level, the organization of national and regional sports competitions served as a platform for prominent athletes to be recognized and admired. Sports events served as spectacles where celebrities were created, their reputations boosted, and records challenged by emerging stars. More importantly, they also allowed for the composition of heroic narratives that intertwined with personal stories and political rhetoric.

The Kautz Family YMCA Archives at the University of Minnesota, Minneapolis and from the Jose B. Vargas Museum and Filipiniana Research Center at the University of the Philippines, Diliman served as the main sources of archival data that were used to bring to fore some of the significant events and personalities from the FECG. The collection includes reports of YMCA secretaries, newspaper clippings from various Asian and American periodicals as well as official reports from regional and international sports governing bodies. These data sources provide a multi-faceted vantage point of the development of sports, events, and the emergence of sports celebrities that combined personal perspectives and institutional frames. Overall, sports were presented as modernizing tools and as manifestations of the modern system increasingly appropriated by Asian societies. At the individual level, sports involvement was viewed as an expression of agency and the adoption of a modern lifestyle.

Agency, Modernity, and the Origins of Celebrity

The emergence of sports celebrities in the early twentieth century has been linked to the rise of mass media. 'With the emergence of mass communications', according to Barry Smart, 'the profile of the sporting figure has been raised and extended, if not radically transformed. The sporting hero has become the sport star and, increasingly, the celebrity'.[6] In his study of the emergence of basketball celebrities in the Philippines, Antolihao argued that the emergence of sports celebrities is largely seen as a product of the 'Hollywoodization' of sports, which refers to the rise of professionalism, the invention of mass media technologies, and the growth of commercial sponsorship.[7] However, the emergence of Asian sports celebrities in the early twentieth century was influenced by more fundamental social transformations.

In his study of the cult of celebrity, Chris Rojek defined their emergence as a result of the following major interrelated historical transformations: (1) the democratization of society; (2) the decline of organized religion; and (3) the commodification of everyday life.[8] Although they were drawn from a different historical and social context, these three elements influenced the emergence of Asian sports celebrities in the early twentieth century. First, the dramatic social transformations that resulted from the Meiji restoration in Japan, the decline of the Qing Dynasty in China, and the anti-colonial struggles in the Philippines had led to varying degrees and expressions of democratization in these societies. Overall, the decline of traditional economic and political power led to the emergence of new institutions whose leadership and support drew from a broader range of actors and communities. Second, the decline of organized religion occurred not through a widespread secularization of Asian societies but was characterized by the destabilization of traditions. Political instabilities that were brought about partly by the encounters and confrontations with Western imperial powers ushered in a period of religious and spiritual upheavals in the region. Not only did imperial powers such as the United States introduce their religions to Asia but these religions themselves and the political and economic dominance of those who professed them led locals to rethink the efficacy and relevance of their own belief systems. Lastly, the commodification of everyday life resulted from the deepening influence of the world economic system. The modernization of many Asian societies was seen through the establishment of shipping and rail networks, the growth of export-oriented agriculture and manufacturing, and the increasing use of everyday technology.[9]

Furthermore, Dennis J. Frost's emphasis on how 'transnational forces' interplayed with local traditions in the social construction of the sports celebrity sheds light on the interconnecting channels of national, colonial, regional, and global elements that shaped the emergence of star athletes at the FECG.[10] This transnational force fittingly describes the role of the Young Men's Christian Association (YMCA) in promoting sports and in training top athletes in the region during the early twentieth century. Distinctly called as secretaries, its religious workers stood out even more for being part of a non-denominational organization that promoted closer ties with non-Christians and for advocating for local leadership.[11] 'While most missionary groups exercise a strong sense of paternalism', according to the Chinese historian Jun Xing, 'the YMCA's non-dogmatic and service-oriented men preached the earliest spirit of racial equality among their own ranks'.[12] The YMCA was known for actively recruiting local staff and, generally, in fostering the indigenization of its local branches. Moreover, their work in alternative education and social work brought them closer to the people, even among non-Christians. However, their involvement in physical education and sports development ultimately became the key element that distinguished the YMCA from other Christian missions. In some countries, the organization has become known more for propagating the 'religion' of sports than for spreading the Christian faith.

Sports' emphasis on personal development and the YMCA's more inclusive organizational structure reflected the wider democratization of society, which fostered a greater sense of agency among the local population especially among the young people who were increasingly exposed to cosmopolitan worldviews. The establishment of modern armed forces, the increasing availability of education, and the professionalization of state administration and commercial trade provided new opportunities for self-actualization and social recognition.[13]

The greater opportunities that were accorded to these young people represent the growing emphasis on individuality and personality 'as a new supersession of the value of class and status'.[14] Sports emerged as one of the earliest social spaces where the modern ideals of meritocracy were compellingly articulated, vigorously practiced, and earnestly defended. This sense of agency, however, was not defined by an unbridled individualism but was conditioned by the more abstract ideals of duty and loyalty. Such modern ideals were contrasted against the traditional feudal system that the new political system sought to replace.

In 1913, YMCA missionaries in China reported a successful national convention in Peking (Beijing) that was filled with an enthusiastic crowd who were 'aglow with patriotism for the Republic of China and for the coming Kingdom of God'.[15] A year later, O. Garfield Jones, an American colonial official, equated the YMCA's evangelical Christianity to the ideals of citizenship when he wrote about how sports helped develop a 'self-governing ability' among young Filipinos. 'Such progress has not been achieved in those fields where the older generation retained control', he added, 'but with the development of individual self-control, a vigorous sense of fair play, and respect for duly constituted authority ... and the recrystallization of Philippine society upon a municipal as opposed to relationship basis, the groundwork for real political progress is being laid'.[16]

The popularity of early sports celebrities, therefore, rested not merely on their exceptional athletic skills but on the fulfilment of their duties and the expression of their loyalty to the nation-state. The ultimate demonstration of this loyalty was through acts of heroism. 'Heroes', according to Graham Kelly, 'provide a means by which society celebrates its collective achievements'. They also serve as 'a vehicle to communicate, both internally and externally, the essential values, aspirations, and ambitions that bind their populations together'. In particular, sports increasingly provides an arena in which individuals can display 'heroic' levels of performance, achieve success, and gain recognition.[17] Athletic competitions served as a more rational and less violent but equally spectacular expression of heroism, which provided the same means by which societies symbolically celebrated its triumphs, mourned its defeats, and drew inspiration for its future challenges.

Heroism, Sports Events, and the Emergence of Asian Sports Celebrities

The FECG emerged as an expansion of the Carnival Games that were held as part of the festivities during the Manila Carnival in the early twentieth century. The Carnival was organized annually from 1908 to 1939 by the American colonial regime to promote its colonial legacy and showcase the economic progress of the Philippines. Apart from the agri-industrial exposition and other activities, the sports competitions became one of the crowd-drawers; soon, foreign teams were invited as part of the attraction. In 1913, the first FECG was organized mainly through the initiative of the YMCA, particularly its Manila Physical Director, Elwood Stanley Brown. It started as a triangular meet between China, Japan, and the Philippines, although its organizers laboured hard to include other Asian countries. Netherlands East Indies (Indonesia) finally sent an official delegation in 1934, the last time the FECG was held.[18] It was dissolved in that year due to the escalating political tensions that emerged from the Japanese occupation of Manchuria. Japan had insisted on the inclusion of Manchuria in the FECG, which the Chinese vehemently opposed.[19] Nonetheless, the FECG was not only the first regional sports event in Asia, it also provided opportunities for local sports celebrities to episodically engage an international audience.

In his study of the lives of English football celebrities in the 1930s, Graham Kelly argued that 'there needs to be a "terrace" before there can be a "hero"'.[20] The terrace, both as a physical space and subsequently as the symbolic representation of the spectators is an essential element to the emergence of the sport celebrity. 'The power lies with the mass, the crowd on the terrace, to confer a specific status on an individual and then celebrate it'.[21] In Japan, China, and the Philippines, the YMCA built the first sports facilities and coordinated with government administrations to construct stadiums and other major facilities for national and regional sports events. For instance, to host the second FECG in Shanghai, an athletic track and a stadium were added to the Hongkew Recreation Park in 1915. The complex became the first major sports venue in China and was also used for the fifth FECG in 1921 as well as other important events.[22] Apart from Shanghai's Hongkew Stadium, the Meiji Jingu Stadium in Tokyo, and the Rizal Memorial Stadium in Manila were primarily built to accommodate the FECG. Such venues facilitated the congregation of large numbers of spectators who came to witness the performance of their national teams and sports celebrities. The attendance at FECG events ranged from about 60,000 (1917 Tokyo) to 450,000 (1930 Tokyo). The first FECG (1913) in Manila attracted 150,000 people while the second FECG in Shanghai (1915) was graced by a crowd of 95,000 spectators.[23] When sports became a popular attraction, the stadium turned into a stage and its players into celebrities.

It was at the Hongkew Recreation Park in 1915 where Pio Robillos lost his 100-yard and 220-yard track crowns to his Filipino compatriots Genaro Saavedra and Nicolas Llaneta. Wei Hwen-Tsang was just as unfortunate, losing his 120-yard hurdles crown to fellow Chinese Huang Yuandao. Wei also lost the high jump trophy to Genaro Saavedra. Apart from these two gold medals, Saavedra also won titles in pole vault and decathlon as well as a bronze medal in long jump, turning him into an instant celebrity. He was welcomed as a hero when he returned home to Manila and was tagged by an American newspaper as the 'Thorpe of the Orient'.[24] This turn of events showed how the terrace, as Kelly has pointed out, is important in the creation of sports heroes.[25] However, the second FECG also demonstrated that a larger influence contributes to the emergence of sports celebrities – sports events. Events not only serve as occasions for sporting heroes to rise but their periodic staging also allowed for individual, team, and national stories to be narrated. The downfall of Robillos and Wei as well as the emergence of Saavedra and Huang were just two of the many stories of triumphs, defeats, and redemption that made FECG a spectacular, popular, and a much-anticipated event.

Two years later, the FECG was held in Tokyo in 1917 and served as the first international sports event hosted by Japan. A makeshift sports complex had been hastily constructed on an open space facing Tokyo Bay for the various competitions but the occasion was significant enough to be graced by the Japanese Premier and some members of the imperial family. Just as in the two previous FECGs, the host country won the overall championship including most of the track-and-field events. Only C. Cardenas of the Philippines retained a title from the 1915 Games, holding on to his long jump gold. Notably, Taku Gishiro completed a middle-distance running double while Fortunato Catalon grabbed both the 100-yard and 220-yard races earning a double in the sprint events.[26] Catalon would successfully defend his 100-yard crown four times from 1919 to 1925 and his 220-yard gold three times from 1919 to 1923, winning a total of nine gold medals and becoming the most successful athlete in the FECG history.[27]

The FECG returned to Manila in 1919 where the three original participating countries returned to contest the five-day event. The host country won 13 of the 18 athletics events. Apart from Fortunato Catalon, fellow Filipinos Alejo Alvarez and Constantino Rabaya were the only athletes to repeat as champions. Ikuta Kiyoji of Japan won the one-mile and five-mile modified marathon gold while Chu Ente of China won both the pentathlon and decathlon events. Ikuta gave Japan its fourth consecutive victory in the five-mile marathon. Chu, on the other hand, became the first athlete to capture both the pentathlon and decathlon events, a feat that broke all previous FECG records.[28] By the fourth Games, each country had established its 'competitive advantage' with China taking most of the titles in football, Japan ruling in baseball, and the Philippines dominating the basketball tournaments, winning all the titles since the first FECG in 1913.[29] Athletics, however, was much more contested but with Ikuta's win, Japan started to demonstrate its superiority in distance running.

The fifth edition of the FECG was again held in Shanghai from May 30 to June 3, 1921. Ceylon (Sri Lanka), Dutch East Indies (Indonesia), India, Malaya (Malaysia), and Siam (Thailand) were invited but all decided not to participate. The Japanese delegation included athletes from Taiwan which were then under Japanese control.[30] In athletics, the Philippines broke the FECG trend of the host country winning the overall championship by prevailing over China. Again, Fortunato, Catalon dominated the sprint events, but Antonio Alo was the only other athlete to successfully defend his title, pocketing his second consecutive gold in pole vault. Tu Juntang was the most notable Chinese athlete, winning a double in discus and pentathlon. Chu Ente, the record-breaking pentathlon and decathlon champion in the previous FECG only managed to place third in decathlon, which was won by the Philippines' Juan K. Taduran. The most outstanding athlete in the fifth FECG, however, was Okazaki Katsuo who won a gold medal in the one-mile and a silver in the 880-yard races. Okazaki won both events in the following sixth FECG and also participated in the 1924 Paris Olympics.[31] After his athletics career was over, he became a distinguished diplomat and politician, serving as Japan's Minister of Foreign Affairs from 1952 to 1954.[32]

The FECG returned to Japan in 1923 but the venue was moved to Osaka. Dutch East Indies (Indonesia), French Indochina (Cambodia, Laos, Vietnam), and Siam (Thailand) were invited but declined to send delegates. An unofficial competition for women was organized between the Japanese and Chinese in volleyball and tennis, marking the first competition between women from two opposing countries. Along with the two women's indoor baseball teams from the Philippines, which played an exhibition game in Shanghai eight years earlier, these were the few instances when women participated in the FECG. However, field calisthenics and mass demonstrations by school girls were traditionally part of the attraction of the event, and one of the notable performances was during the 1921 Shanghai FECG when '500 to 1000 students, under the direction of the YMCA Physical Director broke into small groups on the field and demonstrated various games and activities, which could be adapted to popular use'.[33]

In athletics, Japan dominated the competitions, winning 12 of the 19 events. The Chinese team did not compete well, with high jumper Yu Huaian as their sole medallist. For the Filipino team, Juan K. Taduran defended his decathlon title, turning him into a celebrated athlete in his home country.[34] Fortunato Catalon also defended his 100-yard crown in a record-breaking fashion at 9.45 seconds and earned the honour of receiving his medal from Prince Chichibu, the Emperor's second son. After watching him receive the royal handshake on the podium and with his photograph circulated in local newspapers, Catalon was besieged by Japanese followers who wanted to shake his hand. However, they were doing it not for their extreme admiration for Catalon; the crowd thought that by doing this gesture, they would be indirectly touching the hand of the revered prince.[35] Despite Taduran and Catalon's achievements, two Japanese athletes emerged as the brightest stars of the event – Okazaki Katsuo who successfully defended his one-mile and 880-yard titles and Oda Mikio who won gold medals in long jump and triple jump, as well as a bronze in high jump. Oda managed to defend his triple jump title three times from 1925 to 1930 and won the second-highest number of gold medals after Fortunato Catalon. More importantly, he managed to carry his winning ways to the Olympics where he won the triple jump gold in Amsterdam in 1928, becoming the first Asian to win an Olympic gold medal.[36]

The seventh FECG (1925) returned to Manila for the third time. The track events shifted to the international standard metric system from the imperial distances that had been previously used in the tournament. As expected from the host nation, the Philippines won 13 of the 19 events, placed top two in 16 events, and swept the medal prizes in seven events. Juan K. Taduran achieved a special distinction for winning the decathlon for the third consecutive time. Wu Topan, who grabbed the pentathlon title, was the only Chinese gold medallist. Oda Mikio retained his triple jump crown while another compatriot, Nambu Chuhei won two silvers and a bronze in the long, high, and triple jump events.[37] Nambu followed Oda's footsteps as he went on to win the gold medal in triple jump, as well as a bronze medal in long jump, at the 1932 Los Angeles Olympics seven years later.[38]

The eighth FECG was hosted by Shanghai in 1927. A demonstration volleyball match was held between two Chinese women's teams, adding to a number of occasions where women appeared in a regional sports event.[39] Japan regained the overall championship in athletics, winning the gold medal in eleven of the nineteen events. Despite being the host, China failed to win an individual medal and managed to get only two bronze medals in team relays. Among the Filipino athletes, David Nepomuceno, the first Filipino Olympian (1924 Paris Olympics) won the gold medal in the 100 metres. His compatriot, Simeon Toribio, won the high jump title; he would go on to become the Philippines' first Olympic medallist when he won bronze at the 1932 Los Angeles Olympics. After his stint in athletics, Toribio became an engineer and a politician, but his Olympics achievement cemented his legacy as one of his country's top athletes of all time.[40] Among the Japanese athletes, Oda Mikio and Nambu Chuhei continued to weave their magic while Oshima Kenkichi joined them on the podium to complete a triple-jump sweep for Japan. Later on, Oshima won bronze at the 1932 Los Angeles Olympics. Fluent in German, he became his country's flag bearer at the 1936 Berlin Olympics where he rose to prominence for his interview with Adolf Hitler.[41] He eventually became a respected journalist, educator, and a prolific author.

The FECG returned to Tokyo from May 24 to 27, 1930. India sent a delegation as a guest participant. Although the three Indian track athletes did not compete for medals, it marked the first instance when the regional sports event added another country to its roster. Japan retained its athletics title in dominant fashion, winning all but two of the contested events. China, on the other hand, continued its poor performance, winning only a bronze medal in the 400-metre relay. Oda Mikio (triple jump) and Simeon Toribio (high jump) held on to their titles, along with two other Japanese athletes. After a couple of runner-up finishes in the previous two FECGs, future Olympic medallist Nambu Chuhei finally won his first gold in long jump.[42] Another notable performer was Filipino track star Miguel White who won bronze in the 400-metre race. White reached greater heights six years later at the 1936 Berlin Olympics where he would grab another bronze medal in the same event.[43]

The tenth and last FECG was held in Manila in 1934, four years after the previous edition in Tokyo. It was agreed in an earlier meeting to adjust the schedule to a quadrennial tournament that would alternate with the Olympic Games. The games welcomed the Dutch East Indies (Indonesia), which sent a football team, marking the second occasion when a nation outside the three original countries joined in the tournaments. Official events for women were also included for the first time. Unfortunately, the deteriorating diplomatic relations between China and Japan spilled over to the tournament and eventually led to the dissolution of the FECG after the competitions were concluded.[44] Japan won a third consecutive athletics title, winning 12 of the 19 contested events. Only Yoshioka Takayoshi (200-metre) and Simeon

Toribio (high jump) managed to successfully defend their titles. Miguel White won the hurdles gold medal and a Japanese newcomer, Oe Sueo, soared in the pole vault championship.[45] Oe would eventually win a medal in the 1936 Berlin Olympics in an inspiring fashion. He tied for second place with his best friend, Nishida Shuhei but both refused to compete with each other to determine the winner. Officials ended up arbitrarily giving the silver medal to Nishida and the bronze medal to Oe. However, the teammates decided to cut their medals in half and had a jeweller splice them together into two half-silver, half-bronze 'friendship medals'. Their match became part of a documentary that was produced for the 1936 Olympics and their tale lived on to become one of the most inspiring stories in Olympic history. With a life that was underscored by heroic expressions of loyalty, Oe Sueo died fighting for Japan during the Second World War five years later.[46]

This brief discussion of the prominent competitors in the athletics events of the FECG highlights the importance of major sports events in the emergence of sports celebrities. Their stories demonstrate the importance of the venues and the occasions in staging their talents and travails. Athletic competitions provided them with loftier goals and greater motivations to further hone their skills and to aspire for higher honours. Due to the FECG, early Asian athletes were given opportunities to compete on a larger stage, far greater than their schools or communities. Wearing official playing kits and delegation uniforms also turned sports into an important badge of membership to the nation.[47] For instance, Bai Bao-Kun, a Chinese athlete who had fainted and sprawled on the ground after finishing second in a gruelling 8-mile road race during the second FECG in Shanghai, surprisingly sprung up to face the cheering crowd. When asked about how he managed to quickly stand on his feet after the exhausting run, he replied, 'When the Chinese people cheer, my strength comes back'.[48] As part of emerging modern nations, the games embodied the new sense of belonging and duty that were propagated through sports, as well as through other channels.

In addition, the FECG allowed for a greater number of spectators to witness the talents and performance of the top athletes and those from neighboring countries. It was estimated that the number of spectators who came to the FECG rose from 150,000 in 1913 to about 400,000 in 1930.[49] People came to witness their sports heroes rise, watched them prove their celebrated reputation against worthy adversaries, and cheered with excitement and joy as they triumphed under arduous and heroic circumstances. The neck and neck dash of Kuo Yu-Pin (China) and Taku Gishiro (Japan) for the 880-yard title, for instance, became one of the highlights of the 1915 Shanghai Games. Kuo won the race by a small margin to exact revenge against Taku who, a few days earlier, beat the valiant Bai Bao-Kun in the eight-mile road race.[50] The amazing display of resilience and fighting spirit turned Kuo into a hometown hero.[51] Thus, the regional sports event provided a platform for the episodic contests between top athletes, creating a narrative that people followed and anticipated. Sports celebrities, therefore, became part of the 'spectacularization of modernity' as the embodiment of power, precision, and efficiency that would define the impending future.

While this essay features the FECG alone, other national, provincial, and local sports meets also turned into important events where top athletes emerged to take on greater challenges in national and international competitions. Moreover, the discussion has focused on athletics, but other sports tournaments were also very popular. They produced well-admired sports celebrities, some even more celebrated than featured track and field stars. The team sports of football, baseball, and basketball were important events in the FECG as the three participating nations tried to show their 'competitive advantage' and demonstrate their regional superiority.[52] Baseball became a hotly contested event between the Japanese and the Filipinos, the sport becoming the national pastime in the former when the American colonial regime in the Philippines contributed to its widespread popularity. The FECG baseball tournaments nurtured the emergence of a number of notable players including Ono Machimaro and Shimada Zensuke, both inductees into the Japan Baseball Hall of Fame.[53]

Football, on the other hand, was clearly China's turf as it bagged nine of the ten FECG championships from 1915 to 1934. China was represented by the South China Athletic Association, a club based in Hongkong. Among its top players were Cheung Tong Fuk, Tong Lee Wai, Suen Kam Shun, and Cheong Fung King, the last two of whom represented China at the 1936 Berlin Olympics, with Fung returning for the 1948 London Games.[54] However, the region's most popular footballer during this period was Spanish-Filipino Paulino Alcantara who represented both Spain and the Philippines in international competitions. He was born in the Philippines but moved to Spain with his parents as a young boy. Alcantara was the first FC Barcelona star and still holds the record as the club's youngest scorer when, as a 15-year-old rookie, he recorded a hat trick against Catalan SC in 1912. In 1916, he returned to the Philippines and led the country's football team to the 1917 FECG in Tokyo where they defeated the host team 15-2. Alcantara retired from football in 1927 to become a doctor but returned to coach the Spanish national team in 1951. During the Spanish Civil War, he became a revolutionary fighter and leader who fought against the regime of Francisco Franco.[55]

If baseball was Japan's game and football China's turf at the FECG, basketball clearly belongs to the Philippines as the country won nine of the ten tournament titles. Among a list of notable players were Jacinto Ciria Cruz and Luis Salvador. Ciria Cruz represented the Philippines in the 1936 Berlin Olympics where his team played well and was only beaten by the US, which eventually took the title. He joined the Philippine Army after he retired from competitive basketball and became one of the many Asian athletes who perished during the Second World War.[56] Luis Salvador, however, was arguably the real celebrity among the FECG athletes. He scored 116 points in a game against China during the 1923 FECG in Osaka, which remains a world record for the highest score in international competition. As a celebrity, however, Salvador was more well-known as an immensely popular movie actor and media personality in the Philippines.[57]

The Limits of Celebrity

Given the short-lived popularity of most prominent FECG athletes, do these luminaries embody the conventional definition of celebrity? The definition of the term tends to emphasize the key role of 'mass media technologies'. Media scholar, P. David Marshall, explained how 'celebrities embody and express what can be called a mediatized identity: they are personas that are both produced and promulgated through forms of exhibition that are highly dependent on particular media'.[58] This definition, however, has a limited application to Asian sports personalities in the early twentieth century. Audiovisual reproduction (cinema) and broadcast (television) were not the primary media through which these athletes reached out to their audience. Although newspapers served as important channels in disseminating information about major sports events, their impact was not as instantaneous and widespread as the more advanced media technologies that are available today. Modern celebrities rely on print, radio, television, and Internet to connect with a much larger audience than those the early twentieth-century Asian personalities could reach. The first significant radio broadcast of an international sports event was that of the 1936 Olympics, which happen two years after the FECG was abolished. Moreover, radio was introduced in the Philippines in 1922, in Japan in 1925, and in China in 1926. The technology was still in its infancy and there are no records of a "widespread" broadcast of the FECG, especially something that would influence the emergence of sports celebrities.[59]

Apart from the role of media technologies, 'cultural intermediaries' are also crucial in the production of contemporary celebrities. Sociologist Chris Rojek used the term to refer to the coteries of agents, assistants, and experts who are tasked 'to concoct the public presentation of celebrity personalities that will result in an enduring appeal for the audience of fans'.[60] In sports, they came with the processes of professionalization and 'Hollywoodization' which saw the evolution of a multi-faceted sporting cultural industry that increasingly resembles showbusiness.[61] However, this is a post-World War Two phenomenon and sports competitions before then, with the exception of the professionalization of baseball in Japan and the Philippines in the 1930s, were largely amateur affairs, with team staff often limited to coaches and delegation officials, and where athletes themselves were mostly responsible for the upkeep of their gear and for most of their needs.

Given that our conception of celebrity is based on the crucial elements of mass media technologies and cultural intermediaries, the appeal of a celebrity, therefore, has to be continually nurtured. Often, their fame is fleeting, and celebrities are continually replaced by new emerging stars.[62] Indeed, the distinction that early Asian sports celebrities enjoyed were also short-lived. Their athletic careers were brief as they often stopped competing after completing their college degrees or simply moved on to more sustainable sources of livelihood. Apart from Fortunato Catalon and Oda Mikio, few others managed to win titles in consecutive FECG editions. Those who managed to raise their game and win medals at the Olympic Games turned into heroes for bringing greater honour to their countries. Their names were etched in record books, and historical accounts cemented the legacies of these athletes. Cheong Fung King, Nambu Chuhei, and Simeon Toribio are examples of those who attained success at the sporting world's greatest stage. A few also distinguished themselves as professional sportsmen, particularly in baseball after professional leagues were established in Japan and the Philippines. Ono Machimaro and Shimada Zensuke were famous players who later on became pioneer inductees into the Japan Baseball Hall of Fame in 1959.

Moreover, an illustrious athletic record can be used as a foundation for a successful career in other professions. Simeon Toribio and Okazaki Katsuo became well-known politicians. Regino Ylanan, who won three gold medals in athletics at the first FECG, and Paulino Alcantara became medical doctors. Oshima Kenkichi became a respected journalist, educator, and a prolific author. In addition, Luis Salvador – the real celebrity among this group of Asian athletes – became a famous movie actor and television personality. Finally, a few will be remembered forever as 'real' heroes who made the ultimate sacrifice of giving their lives to their nation during the tumultuous years that followed the dissolution of the FECG: Oe Sueo, Miguel White, and Jacinto Ciria Cruz all perished as soldiers during the WWII.

Compared to contemporary superstars, the early Asian sports celebrities did not rely much on technological and professional intermediaries. In fact, they themselves were the intermediaries. Their emergence and influence were part of larger social transformations sweeping through the Asian region in the early twentieth century. These early sports celebrities provided the linkages to the overlapping geographies, clashing ideologies, and the other many other forms of competitions, which emerged with the modernization of Asian societies. Athletes clashed, often not merely for sporting glory but as symbolic and spectacular contests to display the pre-eminence of modernity as it is appropriated by religious groups such as the YMCA, imperial powers such as the US or Japan, emerging nation-states such as China, and the Philippines, or by booming metropolitans such as Manila, Shanghai, and Tokyo. The YMCA and its secretaries, Elwood Brown in Manila as the prime mover and with the crucial involvement of John Gray in Shanghai and Franklin Brown in Tokyo, organized the first FECG in 1913 to underscore the organization's 'modernity' as the leading religious and social development institution in Asia. The American colonial officials, particularly Governor-General William Cameron Forbes, likewise supported Elwood Brown's initiative to demonstrate the United States' 'modernity' as an emerging political, economic, and cultural global superpower. Moreover, Japan displayed 'modernity' by showing its hesitance to participate in the FECG, highlighting its commitment to the larger Olympic Games. China participated in the regional sports event to display the 'modernity' of its newly established republican government, which emerged after the downfall of its 'traditional' imperial dynasty. Meanwhile, the Philippines banked on the Filipinization of its colonial administration and eventually, with the inauguration of a Commonwealth government in 1935 to showcase its 'modernity' – as a nation that is worthy of independence.[63] Manila, Shanghai, Tokyo, and Osaka all showcased their 'modernity' through their colossal stadiums, new transport infrastructure, and other advanced facilities.

Beyond these institutions, the FECG also became a stage for newly elected politicians and professionally trained bureaucrats to demonstrate their 'modern' knowledge and progressive outlook for their nations. Manuel Quezon (future Philippine President), as well as Wang Zhengting and Wu Tingfang (future Chinese government ministers) all served as top officials in the FEAA (Far Eastern Athletic Association), the FECG's governing body. Educators, sports administrators, local government officials, business leaders, and many other individual players tapped into the spectacular appeal of the FECG to display their own 'modern' characters and achievements. Finally, the athletes and the few sports celebrities who played in this major regional sports event basked in the limelight as they cherished the fruits of their advanced skills and individual progress. Overall, the FECG became a venue and a medium of the spectacularization of modernity where the various achievements of different institutions and individuals were marvellously displayed for the spectators to witness and embrace as captivating spectacles – foreign but familiar, near yet far. A spectacle that simultaneously includes and excludes them.

Notes

1. Japanese and Chinese names are rendered in their usual order, the family name preceding the given name. On the one hand, Filipino and American names are written with the given name preceding the surname.
2. 'Preliminary Announcement', *Far Eastern Championship Games*, May 1915. International Division/Foreign Work Administrative and Program Records, Kautz Family YMCA Archives, University of Minnesota.
3. 'Olympiad of the Far East', *Boston Evening Transcript*, April 22, 1913, 14. Kautz Family YMCA Archives, University of Minnesota.
4. Elwood S. Brown, Annual Reports, YMCA of Manila, 1913, 7–10. Kautz Family YMCA Archives, University of Minnesota.
5. Guy Debord, *Society of the Spectacle* (Detroit: Black and Red, 1983).
6. Barry Smart, *The Sport Star: Modern Sport and the Cultural Economy of Sporting Celebrity* (London: Sage 2005): 14–15.
7. Lou Antolihao, *Playing with the Big Boys: Basketball, American Imperialism, and Subaltern Discourse in the Philippines* (Lincoln: University of Nebraska Press, 2015): 93–120.
8. Chris Rojek, *Celebrity* (London: Reaktion Books, 2001).
9. In the field of sports history, the modernization of Asia was addressed by several literatures that deal with varying sporting traditions and geographical contexts. Among the notable are Stefan Huebner, *Pan-Asian Sports and the Emergence of Modern Asia, 1913–1974* (Singapore: National University of Singapore Press, 2016); Lou Antolihao, *Playing with the Big Boys*, 2015; Dennis J. Frost, *Seeing Stars: Sports Celebrity, Identity, and Body Culture in Modern Japan* (Cambridge: Harvard University Asia Center, 2010); and Andrew D. Morris, *Marrow of the Nation: A History of Sport and Physical Culture in Republican China* (Berkeley: University of California Press, 2004).
10. Frost, *Seeing Stars*, 13.
11. The YMCA missionaries arrived in Japan in 1889, in China in 1895, and in the Philippines in 1898, although it only attained wider influence during the early twentieth century. See Antolihao, *Playing with the Big Boys*, 2015.
12. Jun Xing, 'The American Social Gospel and the Chinese YMCA', *Journal of American East-Asian Relations* 5, no. 3–4 (1996): 227–304.
13. Antolihao, *Playing with the Big Boys*, 33–92.
14. P. David Marshall, 'The Genealogy of Celebrity: Introduction' in *A Companion to Celebrity*, eds. P. David Marshall and Sean Redmond (Oxford: Wiley and Sons, 2016): 16.
15. Eugene E. Barnett, Annual Report for the Year ending September 30, 1913, 2. Kautz Family YMCA Archives, University of Minnesota.
16. O. Garfield Jones, 'Athletics Helping the Filipino', *Outlook*, August 1914, 591.
17. Graham Kelly, *Terrace Heroes: The Life and Times of the 1930s Professional Footballer* (London: Routledge, 2005), 1.
18. Lou Antolihao, 'The Far Eastern Games and the Formation of Asian Identity in the Asia-Pacific During the Early Twentieth Century' in *Asian Communication and Media Studies: Sports, Globalization, Communication*, ed. Ding Junjie and Luo Qing (Beijing: Asia Media

19. Grant K. Goodman, 'Athletics as Politics: Japan, The Philippines, and the Far Eastern Olympics of 1934', *Pilipinas*, 20 (1993): 55–66.
20. Kelly, *Terrace Heroes*, 1.
21. Ibid.
22. Designed by a British architect and modeled after a park in Glasgow, the Hongkew Recreation Park was opened in 1909. It contained football pitches, tennis courts, a swimming pool, and a golf course. Initially, the park was designated for the exclusive use of the Westerners in Shanghai but was eventually opened to the Chinese two years later. See Lu Zhouxiang, 'From Hongkew Recreation Ground to Bird's Nest: The Past, Present, and Future of Sports Venues in China', *International Journal of the History of Sport*, 30, no. 4, (2013): 422–42.
23. Huebner, *Pan-Asian Sports*, 80.
24. 'A Second Thorpe', *Lincoln Star*, October 23, 1915, 28. Jim Thorpe was a celebrated Native-American athlete who won the Pentathlon and Decathlon at the 1912 Olympics. Apart from being a track champion, Thorpe was a versatile athlete and also played professional football, baseball, and basketball. For a view of Saavedra's exploits from Chinese sources, see Jonathan Kolatch, *Sports, Politics and Ideology in China* (New York: Jonathan David Publishers, 1972): 56. Kautz, Family YMCA Archives, University of Minnesota.
25. Kelly, *Terrace Heroes*, 1.
26. 'Far Eastern Olympiad, Japan Wins Championship', *Singapore Free Press and Mercantile Advertiser*, June 13, 1917, 7.
27. Celia Bocobo-Olivar, *History of Physical Education in the Philippines* (Quezon City: University of the Philippines Press, 1972): 63–64.
28. Regino R. Ylanan and Carmen Wilson Ylanan, *The History and Development of Physical Education and Sports in the Philippines* (Manila: Self-Published, 1965): 163.
29. Antolihao, *Playing with the Big Boys*, 90–2.
30. Morris, *Marrow of the Nation*, 96–7.
31. Ylanan and Ylanan, *History and Development of Physical Education and Sports in the Philippines*, 164–5. See also, *Athletics Weekly*, 'Far East Championships', http://www.gbrathletics.com/ic/fec.htm (accessed February 9, 2019).
32. Katsuo Okasaki, 'Japan's Foreign Relations', *The Annals of the American Academy of Political and Social Science*, 308, no. 1 (1956): 166.
33. Kolatch, *Sports, Politics and Ideology in China*, 60.
34. Ylanan and Ylanan, *History and Development of Physical Education and Sports in the Philippines*, 166.
35. 'Filipino Sprinter Makes 100 Yards in Record Time', *Independent*, August 22, 1923.
36. Ken Nakamura, *Interview with Mikio Oda, First Japanese Olympic Gold Medalist*, International Amateur Athletic Federation, April 26, 2010. https://www.iaaf.org/news/news/interview-with-mikio-oda-first-japanese-olymp (accessed August 21, 2019).
37. 'Jeux d'Extreme Orient', *Offizielles Organ des Internationalen Olympischen Ausschus*, n.d., 12. Kautz Family YMCA Archives, University of Minnesota. See also, Ylanan and Ylanan, *History and Development of Physical Education and Sports in the Philippines*, 166.
38. Sports-reference.com. Chuhei Nambu, https://www.sports-reference.com/olympics/athletes/na/chuhei-nanbu-1.html (accessed February 9, 2019).
39. Morris, *Marrow of the Nation*, 90–1.
40. Jorge Afable, ed. *Philippine Sports Greats* (Mandaluyong City: MAN Publishers, 1972): 55–66.
41. Tetsuo Nakamura, 'Japan: The future in the Past', in *The Nazi Olympics: Sport, Politics, and Appeasement in the 1930s*, ed. Arnd Kruger and William Murray (Urbana-Champaign: University of Illinois Press, 2003), 127–44.

(Research Center, 2007): 214–30. Also see Stefan Huebner, *Pan-Asian Sports and the Emergence of Modern Asia, 1913–1974* (Singapore: National University of Singapore Press, 2016): 17–101; Antolihao, *Playing with the Big Boys*, 2015.)

42. Franklin H. Brown, 'The Ninth Far Eastern Games', *Official Bulletin of the International Olympic Committee*, n.d., 14–7. Kautz Family YMCA Archives, University of Minnesota. Also see, Ylanan and Ylanan, *History and Development of Physical Education and Sports in the Philippines*, 168.
43. John Grasso, Bill Mallon, and Jeroen Heijmans, *Historical Dictionary of the Olympic Movement* (Lanham, MD: Rowman and Littlefield, 2015): 473.
44. Goodman, *Athletics as Politics*, 55–66.
45. Ylanan and Ylanan, *History and Development of Physical Education and Sports in the Philippines*, 169.
46. Phil Cosineau, *The Olympic Odyssey: Rekindling the True Spirit of the Great Games* (Wheaton, IL: Quest Books, 2003).
47. Eric Hobsbawm, 'Mass-Producing Traditions: Europe, 1870–1914', in *The Invention of Tradition*, ed. Eric Hobsbawm and Terence Ranger (Cambridge: Cambridge University Press, 1983), 263–307.
48. Charles A. Siler, 'Physical Education in China', *Chinese Student Christian Journal* VI (October 1919): 27.
49. Kolatch, *Sports, Politics, and Ideology in China*, 51–66. See also, Lou Antolihao, 'Far Eastern Games and the Formation of Asian Identity', 214–30.
50. Siler, *Physical Education in China*, 27.
51. Ibid., 28.
52. Antolihao, *Playing with the Big Boys*, 89–92.
53. Joseph A. Reeves, *Taking a Game: A History of Baseball in Asia* (Lincoln: University of Nebraska Press, 2002): 56.
54. Karen Stokkermans, *Football at the Far Eastern Championship Games*, http://www.rsssf.com/tablesf/ fareastgames.html (accessed February 10, 2019).
55. Nestor P. Burgos, 'Paulino Alcantara: RP Legend in World Football', *Philippine Daily Inquirer*, July 11, 2010, 9.
56. Afable, *Philippine Sports Greats*, 1–12.
57. Christian Bacobo and Beth Celis, *Legends and Heroes of Philippine Basketball* (Manila: Self-published, 2004).
58. Marshall, *The Genealogy of Celebrity*, 17.
59. Michael Serazio, 'Just How Much is Sports Fandom Like Religion", *Atlantic*, January 29, 2013. https://www.theatlantic.com/entertainment/archive/2013/01/just-how-much-is-sports-fandom-like-religion/272631/ (accessed February 12, 2019).
60. Rojek, *Celebrity*, 11.
61. Antolihao, *Playing with the Big Boys*, 93–120.
62. Daniel J. Boorstin, *The Image or What Happened to the American Dream* (London: Penguin Books, 1963): 75.
63. Huebner, *Pan-Asian Sports*, 17–101. See also Antolihao, *Playing with the Big Boys*, 33–92.

Disclosure Statement

No potential conflict of interest was reported by the author.

Index

agency 109, 125, 132, 155, 157
Aickinn, Phil 43
A-League 8, 17–19, 26–8
American Orientalism 9, 63–4
Apple Daily article 93, 99, 123, 126, 129, 131
Asian athletes 2, 4, 6, 163, 165
Asian Football Confederation 6, 17, 22
Asian immigrants 35–6, 61
Asian woman–white man relationship 112
athletics 53, 155, 159–61, 163, 165
Auckland 36, 42
Australia 8, 16–19, 22, 24, 27–8, 39, 90, 125

Bairner, Alan 91
Battle of the Brians 111–12
Beijing Olympics 76, 144–5, 147–8
Beijing-Zhangjiakou winter Olympics and Paralympics 2
Belgium 8, 10, 88–9, 93–4, 99
Berlin Olympics 73, 140, 161–3
bronze medal 50, 158, 161–2

Canadian media 109
Chin, Tiffany 7, 9–10, 50–1, 53, 57–8, 65–6, 115
China Doll 9, 58, 106
Chinese athletes 6, 139–40, 144–7, 162
Chinese Taipei Football Association (CTFA) 94, 97–8
Chin-feng Tong 92
Chin Spin 58
citizenship 9–10, 33–5, 42, 44–5, 74, 83, 90, 106, 157
Cold War 4, 72–3, 76, 81–3, 91, 122, 128, 133
controversies 43, 78–9, 83, 93, 97
conventional masculinity 110
critical media analysis strategy 123
cultural intermediaries 164

Donkin, Will 100
double anxiety 91

elite sport system 10, 92, 141–2, 144–5, 148–9
emotional susceptibility 108
ethnicity 2–3, 5, 7–8, 61–2, 74, 78–9, 83, 94, 98, 100, 107

Far Eastern Championship Games (FECG) 11, 139, 154–6, 158–66
female athletes 105–6, 116, 122, 129–31
female golfers 39–41, 123–4, 132
female skaters 50–1, 53, 57–8, 60, 62–3, 65–6, 110
feminine qualities 124, 130–1
femininity 55–6, 106, 130–4
fetishization 112
fetishized racial hierarchies 110
FIFA World Cup 2
figure skaters 7–10, 51, 62, 105–6, 110, 114–15
figure skating 51, 53–7, 59, 65, 105–7, 114–15
flexible citizenship 4, 45, 72, 77–8, 105, 129
Football Federation Australia (FFA) 6, 17–21
football players 78, 94–5, 97–8, 100
football savior 93
Forbes, William Cameron 165
Fortier, Anne-Marie 61
friendship medals 162
Frost, Dennis J. 156

gender hierarchies 110
Gillard, Julia 20
girlification 110
globalization 2, 4, 9, 33–4, 44–5, 89–90, 129, 138
global migration 33, 36–7
global sport celebrities 3–4
glocalization 4, 104–5, 114
gold medal fever 11, 142–5, 147–8
gold medals 6, 11, 104, 111, 138–9, 141, 143–5, 147, 149, 158–61, 165
Gong Bu 141

Hall, Stuart 52
Hao Gengsheng 140
Harding, Tonya 53
Harrison, Anthony 53
Henie, Sonja 55
heroism 158
hollow nationalism 133
hollywoodization 156, 164
Hongkew Recreation Park 158
hybridity 73–5

INDEX

identities 2–4, 7, 10, 34–5, 37, 39, 42–3, 45, 72–7, 80–1, 83, 90–1
inter-Asia subjectivities 83–4
international competitions 128, 163
international sporting events 4–5, 10, 130, 139, 141, 143, 148–9
invisible hybridity 72, 74–6, 81, 84
Ito, Midori 53–4

Japanese athletes 160–1
Japaneseness 27
Japan Professional Football League 78
Jong Tae-se 5, 8–9, 71–2, 76–7, 79–83, 95

Keng-sun Chen 94–5
Kerrigan, Nancy 106
K-league 18, 72, 78, 82
Kim, Yuna 104, 109
Ko, Lydia 9, 34–5, 37–45
Korean athletes 71–2, 75
Korean citizenship 39–40, 105
Korean golfers 38–9, 41, 130
Koreanness 7, 9, 40, 42, 45, 105, 113–14, 129
Korean New Zealanders 36–7
Korean War 81
Krause, Elizabeth 53

Ladies Professional Golf Association (LPGA) 37, 39, 42, 44, 121, 123–7, 130, 133
light of Taiwan 121–4, 126, 130, 133
Lin, Jeremy 93
Li Na 4, 6–7, 11, 17, 146–7
Li Ning 143
Liu Xiang 6, 11, 147–8
Los Angeles Olympics 139–40, 161
Los Angeles Times 57–9, 107–8

marquee players 25, 27
marquees 21–2, 28
mass sport 142, 144, 148
McGarry, Karen 54
media narratives 9, 51, 57, 122–3, 129–30, 133–4; of Tseng 121, 123, 128, 133
migration 9, 18–19, 33–4, 37–8, 44–5, 75, 88–9
Mikio, Oda 160–1, 164
modernity 11, 63, 83, 154–5, 165–6; spectacularization of 11, 154–5, 162, 166
modern sport celebrities 11
multiculturalism 4, 9, 17, 42, 60–1, 77
multi-faceted construction 5
mythical savior 93–4, 96

national identity 9–10, 17, 33–5, 39–40, 42, 44–5, 72, 76, 78–9, 90–2, 99, 106, 122–3
nationalism 11, 71, 79, 88–92, 122, 126, 129–30, 134, 138–9, 143, 147–8

National Security Law 82–3
New Zealand 8–9, 33–9, 42–4
New Zealand immigration policies 35
'Noble Prince of Football' 96
North Korea 5, 8–9, 71–6, 78–84

orientalism 10, 60, 63, 105–6, 115
Orser, Brian 108–10, 112–13

Pacchigi 82
patriotism 81, 138–40, 143, 145, 147–8, 157
Philippines 8, 11, 124, 139, 154–6, 158–61, 163–5
postcolonial East Asia 5, 71–2, 76–7, 81, 83
PyeongChang winter Olympics 2

'Queen Yuna' 107

race 2–3, 5–8, 34–5, 51, 53, 61–3, 65–6, 123–4, 129, 160, 162
regionality 2, 5–6, 8
regional sports event 158, 161–2, 165
Rojek, Chris 156
Ryan, Liam 138

Samsung Bluewings 78, 82
Savior Cometh 93
Shinae Ahn 43
Shinji Ono 17, 19, 21–2, 24, 26–8
Shuhei, Nishida 162
skating 54, 64–5, 107–8, 114–15
skating magazine 107
sleeping giants 18
Smart, Barry 156
South Korea 8–9, 22, 33, 36–7, 39–40, 42, 72–6, 78–84, 90, 125, 128–9
South Koreans' inflow, New Zealand 35
sporting events 52, 80, 123
sporting success 141, 144–5, 148
sportive expressionism 90
sport migrants 89, 94
sports events 4, 155, 158–9
sports heroes 138
sports patriotism 145–8
sport stars 2, 41, 112, 123, 147, 149, 156
Sueo, Oe 162
Sunrise LPGA Taiwan Championship 124–5
sympathetic hierarchies 110

Taiwan 5–6, 8, 10–11, 88–100, 121–9, 131–4, 159; gender politics in 121; sport nationalism in 91
Taiwanese golfers 10, 124
Taiwanese Messi 100
Taiwanese nationalism 11, 91, 93, 100, 121–2, 124, 129, 133

Taiwan-Korea rivalry 5, 129
Taiwan's Centennial Pride 126
Thailand 124–5, 159–60
Tokyo summer Olympics and Paralympics 2
Tomas, Debi 53
Toribio, Simeon 161–2
tournament 28, 121, 124–7, 160–1
transnational corporations 3, 39, 133
transnational ethnic identity 7
transnational ethnicity 7–8, 10
transnational forces 156
transnational sport celebrity 72, 83
Tseng 10–11, 121–34

United Daily News 123

Wanderers 17, 19–22, 24–8
Wang Chong 143
Wang Fuzhou 141
Western Sydney 16–17, 20–1, 23–4, 27–8

whiteness 9, 51–5, 65
White Princess skater 54, 56
Wie, Michelle 7, 9, 11, 40, 43, 128–9, 133
Winter Olympics 50–2, 112–14, 145
winter sports 52–3
women athletes 131–2
women's figure skating 53–4, 56, 59–60, 63–5
World Cup 19, 21–2, 72, 79–80, 82, 92, 95, 105, 143

Xavier Chen 5, 10–11, 89–100
Xu Yinsheng 142

Yani Tseng 121, 123, 125, 133
Ying Chiang 5, 10, 88, 91, 130
Yoshioka Takayoshi 161
Young Men's Christian Association (YMCA) 139, 156–8, 165
Yuzuru Hanyu 113

zainichi Koreans 9–10, 71–84
Zhang Xueliang 140